TANPINAR'S 'FIVE CITIES'

TANPINAR'S 'FIVE CITIES'

AHMET HAMDI TANPINAR

Translated from the Turkish by
Ruth Christie

ANTHEM PRESS

Anthem Press
An imprint of Wimbledon Publishing Company
www.anthempress.com

This edition first published in UK and USA 2018
by ANTHEM PRESS
75–76 Blackfriars Road, London SE1 8HA, UK
or PO Box 9779, London SW19 7ZG, UK
and
244 Madison Ave #116, New York, NY 10016, USA

Original title: Beş Şehir
Copyright © Ahmet Hamdi Tanpınar 2018
Originally published by Dergah Publications
English translation copyright © Ruth Christie 2018

British Library Cataloguing-in-Publication Data
A catalogue record for this book is available from the British Library.

Library of Congress Cataloging-in-Publication Data
Names: Tanpınar, Ahmet Hamdi, author.
Title: Tanpınar's "Five cities" = Beş şehir (Five cities) /
Ahmet Hamdi Tanpınar.
Other titles: Beş şehir. English | Five cities | Beş şehir
Description: London; New York, NY: Anthem Press, 2018. |
Translation of: Beş şehir. | Includes bibliographical references.
Identifiers: LCCN 2018039948 |
ISBN 9781783088485 (paperback : alk. paper) |
ISBN 1783088486 (paperback : alk. paper)
Subjects: LCSH: Turkey–Description and travel.
Classification: LCC DR428.T313 2018 | DDC 956.1/025–dc23
LC record available at https://lccn.loc.gov/2018039948

ISBN-13: 978-1-78308-848-5 (Pbk)
ISBN-10: 1-78308-848-6 (Pbk)

This title is also available as an e-book.

Contents

Foreword

The real subject of *Beş Şehir* ('Five Cities') is the craving we foster for the new, and our nostalgic regret for what is lost, in our lives. At first sight, the two emotions might seem to be at odds with one another but can be reconciled in one word: love. The cities chosen by love as its framework have all arrived in my own life by chance. In consequence, it is by following their history that we may reach a more authentic understanding of our own people, our own lives and the culture which is the spiritual façade of our country.

Like previous generations, during the long and arduous journey on which all our hopes are pinned, our generation has looked back from the difficult curves of the road at this valuable legacy which we now define as 'changes in civilization'. For 150 years, we have come down precipices, looking back at the way we left behind and ahead to the promising prospect in the distance that makes light of our problems.

The real drama of the Turkish community will continue for even longer, an experience of living through a climate of criticism, a mass of denials and agreements, hopes and dreams, with occasional periods of realistic assessment, until our lives are revitalized by work which is, in every sense, truly creative.

We all know the road we must follow. But the longer the road, the busier we are made by this everyday world we are leaving. Now we become aware of a gradually increasing void in our identity which, a little later, becomes a heavy burden that we are more than ready to discard. Even when our willpower is at its strongest, there is all the same a painful ache within us which sometimes speaks to us like a pang of conscience.

Such an inner turmoil is not at all strange if you consider that the process known as the work of history sows the seed and creates the real meaning and identity not only of states and communities but also of personalities. The past is always present. To live the authentic life, we must take that into account and come to terms with every moment.

So, 'Five Cities' is a discussion born of the need for understanding. Perhaps it might have been clearer, more useful even, to bring this complex conversation down to fundamental matters – in short, to introduce and answer questions like 'What were we?' and 'What are we and where are we going?' But during my life, I came upon these issues only by chance. They appeared while I was roaming among the Selçuk remains that fill Anatolia, or while I was feeling humbled and small under the dome of Süleymaniye, or consoling my loneliness in Bursa's landscape, or listening to the music of Dede Efendi and İtri filling our rooms, nostalgic water music mingled with nomad voices.

I'll never forget how one morning on Uludağ, a veil fell from my eyes the very moment I was listening to a shepherd's pipe and watching his flock of sheep and lambs surround his music as they summoned each other to his call. I knew that Turkish poetry and music was a story of exile, but I had never realized how closely linked they were to this aspect of our lives. It was a truly touching and beautiful scene, and, for a few minutes, I contemplated it as a work of art. If one day the emotional history of an Anatolian is written and our lives are closely examined from that angle, we will see that much we now think of as fashionable has come from the original fabric of life itself.

In a word, similar events and their influence on my spiritual being have been important to me. Essentially, this book has evolved from random fragments of experience. In its second edition, even with all the changes and additions I thought necessary, I have tried to retain the traces of those first chance events.

Readers who compare the two editions will undoubtedly notice that among the additions is further material on the Selçuk era. Our historians seem to maintain that the difference between Selçuk and Ottoman lies in a change of dynasty. But we believe there was a greater difference extending from social relations to include lifestyles, manners, people and entertainments: two separate worlds, the Selçuk and the Ottoman, a continuum more or less, one from the other, but, in a larger sense, two separate philosophies of life. We think of our Renaissance as a synthesis of the Mediterranean culture and the wider European geography absorbed by the Ottomans. Today, we have discovered the Selçuks just as Europe rediscovered the Gothic and Roman arts at the beginning of last century. To see them clearly, we had to emerge from the Ottoman Empire. A split in the Ottoman psyche, very serious differences in taste, and economic problems have resulted inevitably in the present neglected condition of Selçuk monuments.

The reader will find several similar daring suggestions in 'Five Cities'.

Like all thoughtful people, I, too, am dissatisfied with our changing lives.

'I am an old Westerner,' as a foreign novelist I've always admired said in nearly the same circumstances. But I wanted to approach real life as a man with a heart, a live, feeling person, not like an engineer dealing with lifeless material. I can't do it otherwise. Only the things we love change along with us, and because they change, they always live with us as a richness in our lives.

Ankara, 25 September 1960

1
Ankara

I

I have always imagined Ankara as a legendary warrior, perhaps from memories of the years of the National Struggle for Independence,[1] or perhaps from the strong impression made by the citadel rising erect like an old-time chevalier clad in steel armour. Its site may have something to do with it. What strikes us already from a distance is the natural fortification overlooking a pass between two flat hills. The perception hardly changes if you look from the surrounding heights that dominate the city. In short, from wherever you choose to look, whether from the slopes of Çankaya, the Çiftlik route, the roads to the Reservoir, from Etlik or the vineyards of Keçiören, you will always see the fort dominating the horizon with the same calm repose under a light incisive as glass, and gathering all the land forms about it. Sometimes it rises like a warship baring its great bosom to the wind, or sometimes it sails fast and powerful in the sea of time and events; sometimes the inner fortress becomes the ultimate refuge of all hopes, or, like an eagle's nest, it reaches impossible heights.

The appearance of the city is borne out by its history. Ankara's inner fortress has always protected central Anatolia, and on its slopes, the knotty problems of history have always been played out and resolved. Whether in the time of the Hittites, the Phrygians, the Lydians, the Romans and Byzantines or the Selçuk and Ottoman Turks, this has always been the case. The Roman eagle chose the fortress for its flight eastwards. The fiercest, bloodiest phases of the Byzantine-Arabic struggle took place here. In the Selçuk period, the last Byzantine assault in Anatolia was crushed in 1197. After this battle, in which Kılıç Arslan and Melik Danişmend were joint victors, the Byzantine eagle would never again fly in Anatolia. It was in Ankara that Bayezid the Thunderbolt[2] encountered the bitter poison of his destiny in the fierce face of Tamurlane.[3] In short, most of the events that influenced the fate of the Anatolian continent developed around Ankara. The most important of these, and the most recent, is undoubtedly the War of Independence. This war was not only the struggle in which the Turkish nation won its right to life, but, in fact, the guns that boomed at Dumlupınar on the morning of 26 August proclaimed to all the nations of the East, which were living in a state of economic and political servitude, that a new era had begun. Henceforth, whenever a chain of slavery was broken, it was Ankara's name that would be remembered, every struggle for freedom would somehow become a prayer dedicated to the souls of those who died fighting at Sakarya,[4] İnönü, Afyon, Kütahya and Bursa.

There is a well-known photograph of Atatürk that has even passed into school textbooks. The hero of Anafarta and Dumlupınar,[5] alone on the morning of his final battle, a cigarette in his mouth, is slowly climbing a hill, deep in thought. In my imagination, the image of the Ankara fortress is always superimposed on the image of the great man gradually approaching the brightest hour of his life. How can I explain this surprising phenomenon? Why does this particular man combine with that fortress in my imagination? Why not with any hill in the land? I can never explain it. These correspondences come from the most secret recesses of the human psyche. One thing I know. One day, on contemplating the photograph, the idea of Ankara's fortress came before my eyes and from then on I could never separate the two images.

Right from my first arrival in Ankara in the autumn of 1928, the Ankara fortress became almost an *idée fixe*. Idly wandering the narrow streets during certain hours of the day, I observed the old Anatolian houses. I imagined a life within them, very different from my own. So when I read the beginning of Yakup Kadri's[6] *Ankara* which I loved and admired for its truth and accuracy, I was intensely moved. But I still believe, though I know how impossible it is, that beyond the harsh realism there is some point of agreement between us.

Today's old Ankara neighbourhoods that descend from Samanpazarı to the former Ministry of Foreign Affairs, the roads leading to the market and fortress and the Cebeci district have always made the same impression on me. I was not unaware of the poverty of these wretched homes built of sun-dried bricks, but I imagined they had some quality lacking in myself. I walked among them shivering with an endless desire, like an attack of fever, to be embraced and enveloped by what I imagined was the soul hidden beneath their poverty. The truth is that in Anatolian poverty there is something like the malaria that has been the scourge of the land, destroying people for centuries. All who have experienced the shudder of malaria know no other flavour like it.

I have often imagined living in one of the houses by the fortress or in Cebeci. But I led such a sociable life, first in the Ankara Lycée, then in the Gazi Institute, that I could never give it up. Besides, at that time, most of the Ankara officials were living in official residences or even in ministerial quarters. In fact, the city, while continuing its congested life as it had in the days of the National Struggle, was also being rebuilt. There were building sites everywhere. It was a period when a new city was emerging, with its areas of minor civil servants and villas of various styles, none uniform and all looking as if they had been copied from the pages of architectural magazines. In one street alone, it was possible to see houses that recalled those of the Riviera, Switzerland, Sweden, Bavaria and the Istanbul houses and villas from the Abdülhamid era. Newly built embassies increased the variety. The Soviet Embassy was one of the boldest experiments of the 1920s when modern architecture was in search of an identity. It was rather like a huge steamboat. The Iranian embassy tried for an Eastern style that evoked old Sassanid palaces. Several of my friends and I liked the classic building of the Belgian Embassy, quiet and simple. In the midst of these experiences Turkish architecture was attempting to find a style of its own. The Turkish Fraternity building, the Ethnographical Museum and the Gazi Institute of Education continued the experiment already begun with the New Istanbul Post Office and the Fourth Vakıf Han. When Professor Eğli, whom I later became friends with at the Fine Arts Academy, built the School for Music Teachers at Cebeci, he was the first to succeed in combining these diverse experiments in foreign styles by using the possibilities of modern materials.

The reality of Ankara and its new building projects were somehow related to Mustafa Kemal's life. It was like a newspaper; no one knew where it was printed, in fact you never laid hands on it, but everyone was reading it except yourself and reporting its contents to you. In the city where everyone met up several times a day, the same opinion was relayed to you within an hour by 20 people. There was only one edition. At every street corner there was the same story of heroic decisions and epic fights. Even if people did not speak of what they had lived through, you could still imagine the lives they led at the time. But the magic which had made it all seem so great and attractive had now vanished. Those who, five years ago, had made history had now emerged from its blaze and were living in the ordinary light of day. Only Mustafa Kemal continued his legendary life.

II

Ankara has a long history of amazing combinations. Centuries of invasion, of successive fires and raids, have left very few remains from the city's past, but this history is always present in a strange disorder. There are very few places where Turkish culture rubs shoulders so vividly with older civilizations. In the citadel and in the neighbourhoods scattered around its slopes lie Turkish saints, side by loving side with Roman and Byzantine tombstones. The ancient stones, carved in accordance with unknown creeds long forgotten, are softened by the sympathetic greenery that grows from our ancestors' graves; here a capital or an architrave in Ionian style springs from a brick wall; over there, on the steps of a Moslem tomb, appears an ancient stone that celebrates a Roman consul's arrival in the city; and a little further on, on a sarcophagus, laughing bacchantes sport in the basin of a fountain. For centuries, Graeco-Roman lions have faithfully kept watch over the tomb of Şerafeddin the Ahî,[7] whose mosque with the peerless *mihrâb*[8] is truly named 'Home of the Lions'. There, too, one can see the serpent, symbol of the Hittite goddess of earth and fertility, gliding among fruit with a powerful agility and the wooden columns of the mosque, painted so naively, supporting Byzantine and Roman capitals. In the fortress, the stone terrace of the Alâeddin Mosque, whose mihrâb is one of the wonders of Turkish woodwork, has for centuries overlooked the plain like a falcon, from between a row of columns arranged there completely by chance; unquestionably, these columns were in existence long before the mosque.

The most significant combination is the contrasting opposites of the Hacı Bayram Mosque and the ruined Roman temple alongside, which is like an ode in marble planted in the earth to honour Emperor Augustus. No work could summarize life on this earth so completely. What secret chance led Hacı Bayram[9] to choose his retreat in the Roman eagle's marble nest? During his hours of meditation and prayer in his narrow cell under the mosque, I wonder if he wasn't disturbed by this stone world that stood beside him reflecting the sun's dazzling rays like a kind of secret temptation on the earth where he knelt, or by these beautifully sculpted marbles that celebrated victories completely different from his own, or by those severe and noble Roman faces. How wonderful it would be to know the thoughts and feelings aroused in the saint by the proud silence of his neighbours.

Rome, intoxicated by material pleasures in its glory and majesty, continued to win victories, founded institutions and passed laws. Its era was marked by forts, bridges, roads, aqueducts, places of worship, baths, arenas, statues and many different kinds of monuments, bestowed on earth and stone, as well as garlands to adorn the victor's brow. Centuries passed while the proud warrior tried to soothe his exhausted nerves with voluptuous entertainments and bloodthirsty games, the world conqueror's map torn to shreds like a tiger skin left in the hands of an inexperienced hunter. The city of Ankara, with more than half of the empire's estates, passed into the possession of a completely different people. Over ground covered with monuments from an ancient culture, a new order blossomed; the worship of another God began in little humble places of worship, and Ankara's fortress began to echo with songs of nostalgia and longing of a different kind. And one day a pure-hearted boy, reared in the land of the new masters, settled like a migrating bird next to the monument which symbolized Rome's victory and which was later to become a Byzantine basilica. He revealed to men a truth very different from the truths that had ensured the survival of an ancient empire – this was the truth of spiritual pleasures, of the happiness of the hereafter, the truth of a soul perfecting itself through love, of a longing like a flood of light, of a contemplation which finds union with God deep within itself. In the joy of arriving at this truth, Hacı Bayram cried,

If you want to know yourself
Look for the soul within the soul
Give up your soul and find it
Know yourself, your very self!

But Hacı Bayram is not only a saint imbued with God; he also played a constructive role in building the Turkish community. The religious order he founded was an order of craftsmen and farmers. He was at the centre of the vast peasant movement begun in Anatolia by Baba Ilyas[10] of Khorasan and the Ahî organization. Already the movement had spread so far in his lifetime that Murad II, nervous of the spiritual dominion that was growing around him, had the sheikh brought from Ankara to Edirne and only agreed to let him return when he was reassured of his good intentions. Actually there was no need for alarm. Hacı Bayram was concerned with the empire's internal reign.

As I gazed at the Ankara plains, how often I have thought of the fields that, till the end of his life, Hacı Bayram sowed and reaped with his disciples. I wondered where they were. Probably near the mosque which was his own resting place. The whole plain was alive with the collective efforts of the community. Tradition has it that Hacı Bayram met up there with Akşemseddin, the spiritual and saintly symbol associated with the conquest of Istanbul. Akşemseddin was a young scholar in search of a mentor. He had studied the science of the time, theology and medicine, syntax and music, but having never satisfied his soul's thirst, he had turned to mysticism or the way of the sufi. He abandoned the *medrese*[11] at Osmancık where he taught and set off to visit Sheikh Zeyneddin Hâfi. One night at Aleppo, he dreamt that one end of a chain was round his neck while Hacı Bayram was holding the other. Understanding that his destiny was with Hacı Bayram, he retraced his steps.

When he reached Ankara, he saw Hacı Bayram and his disciples reaping the harvest. He approached, but the saint ignored him. Undaunted, he joined in the labour and worked with the disciples until it was time to eat. Hacı Bayram distributed the food with his own hand but poured no vetch soup or yoghurt into Akşemseddin's bowl. He emptied the leftovers for the dogs. Instead of becoming angry, Akşemseddin satisfied his hunger, along with the dogs, from the dogs' dish by the sheikh's door. On observing his humility and submission, Hacı Bayram accepted him as one of his disciples. When Hacı Bayram died, it was Akşemseddin who became his successor, and was even acknowledged as sheikh by the more orthodox arm of the order.

Akşemseddin, who had assisted the Conqueror (Fatih) in the capture of Istanbul and whose dignity and gravity had led him to retire to his village, advised the sultan by letter, addressing him from his moral position as an equal and opening vast horizons before him:

'If the sultan desires our presence we will come immediately and together we will conquer the lands of Arabia.' It is only in fifteenth-century Turkey that we find someone like Akşemseddin sitting at table with the dogs of his sheikh.

A poem by Hacı Bayram shows the unity of man and creation. One couplet particularly draws an almost perfect outline of fifteenth-century Turkey:

> Suddenly I was in that town and realised how it
>   was made.
> I too was made, midst earth and stones.

III

No great monument survived in Ankara from the Selçuk era or from the time of the Ahî whose art had continued in the same style. In Ankara, there were none of the buildings with imposing doorways whose stone carvings astonished us when we saw them in Konya, Sivas, Niğde, Kayseri and Aksaray, nor minarets of glazed bricks taking flight like colourful birds in the morning light.

The Alâeddin Mosque with its splendid minber still stands, but without any of the buildings that once surrounded it. It goes back to the time of Aslan II's son Mesud and, as we learn from an inscription, was restored in the reigns of Orhan Gazi and Murad II, resulting in a confusing number of styles.

But the Selçuks were great builders and we would have expected to find a number of other monuments also in existence: kitchens, mosques, religious schools and tombs. In fact, the real Selçuk story took place in Konya, Kayseri and Sivas. Ankara was never under the control of the great feudal families who appeared in Anatolia at the time of the invasions, like the

Artukid, Saltukid, Mengüçid and Danişmendid dynasties. The only Selçuk ruler in Ankara was the aforementioned Sultan Muhiddin Mesud. Moreover, the inner fortress did not over-look the main caravan routes.

For a short time, Ankara was Alâeddin Keykubad's city.[12] This sultan, uncontrollably energetic, conformed to the normal custom of his time with his ambitious acts as soon as he came to the throne. When his father, Gıyaseddin Keyhüsrev I, died in the battle fought on the frontiers of the Iznik Empire, he had made a move to seize the throne from Izzeddin Keykâvus,[13] his elder brother and fellow exile. But when he lost the struggle, he took refuge in the Ankara fort-ress. For a long time, the city supported the prince's cause, but when all hope of victory was lost, negotiations began and he submitted on condition that his life would be spared. During the prolonged siege, Izzeddin had a number of residences built to house himself and his retinue. He even had a medrese constructed beyond the city walls.

When Izzedin, a leader as great as Alâeddin, died of tuber-culosis in Sivas, Alâeddin was released from the Malatya fort-ress where he had been held under house arrest. When he succeeded to the throne, he exorcised the humiliation of his submission by destroying the medrese which reminded him of the days he had spent in fear of death. Perhaps the mosque which bears his name was built by him to commemorate the siege or it is possible that he only had it restored.

After Alâeddin Keykubad's death, Ankara witnessed one of Selçuk history's great dramas. His son Gıyaseddin Keyhüsrev II was a weak man. His vizier, Sadeddin Köpek, a cruel and ambitious man, taking advantage of the sultan's weak frailty, got rid of his rivals one by one, in particular, Taceddin Pervane, the Emir of the Emirs. In accordance with a *fatwa*[14] issued by the Konya *ulema*,[15] Sadeddin Köpek had him stoned to death in Ankara on the pretext that he had once lived with a singer as his unmarried wife. Taceddin Pervane had originally collaborated with Sadeddin Köpek to eliminate some of his emirs. But when he saw the merciless vizier's brutal behaviour and realized his own turn would come, he withdrew to Ankara, to his own estate. To remove his last rival, Sadeddin descended on Ankara, *fatwa* in hand, having achieved a lightning journey from Konya in a record two days, and (according to İbn Bibî[16]) ordered the city rabble to bury the commander to the waist and kill him. It is strange that the same vizier, in order to take possession of the throne of Gıyaseddin Keyhüsrev I, himself a patricide, spread the rumour that he himself was the illegitimate son of Gıyaseddin Keyhüsrev by a beautiful woman from Konya named Şehnaz. Indeed, İbn Bibî refers to the affair as a fact. Even in the bloody annals of the time when death was frequent, the murder of Pervane was an event of unique violence. From its humiliating character, we cannot help thinking that political envy was intensified by great personal rancour and hatred.

The Ahî buildings, planned like the Selçuk mosques, are beautiful only in their pillars and the carving on the *mihrâb* and the *minber*. Built on the slopes of the inner fortress, in their present state they add little to the city's beauty. Whether subject to the Mongols or independent, there was an Ahî sovereignty in Ankara that lasted for half a century. Even if not ruled by the bourgeoisie, it was a sovereignty of artisans and the market, a rare situation in oriental history.

The Ottoman era begins with a caravanserai and a covered market created by the great Mahmud Paşa, Mehmed II's vizier. They resulted from the new theory of proportion which began at the same time as the new empire. But unlike the Selçuks, the Ottomans were never builders at heart.

After its restoration, Ankara's covered bazaar suddenly came to light with all its ten domes as an architectural complex of great simplicity. The Hittite works, revealed by recent excavations and displayed there with their astonishing plasticity so close to contemporary art forms, have always reminded me of watchers with eyes just opened from a subterranean sleep of centuries. Life once lived is neither forgotten nor completely lost, nor, whatever we do, does it entirely relate to the patterns of today or even yesterday.

IV

It is impossible to speak of a Turkish city without mentioning Evliya Çelebi.[17] Two of our ancestors dominate the map of our native country. One is Sinan[18] the architect. Sixteenth-century Turkey can always be found in his works, and there are very few major cities that don't have a share of this genius of the Ottoman Empire. When I hear his name I immediately see, like a string of beautifully cut jewels, an endless line of buildings, large and small, that stretch from Hungary to the Mediterranean and the Gulf of Basra. The other is Evliya Çelebi, the supreme mirror of his country, sometimes adding minor details but always remaining true to the main outlines, reflecting the whole of seventeenth-century Turkey. His Ankara is not very like the city of travellers of his time or of later visitors. He wove around it a fantasy adventure. When Evliya came to Ankara, he did not hesitate to describe his own vision of the city, its fortress and castle, the governor's palace, the general's; he enumerated the sources of profit, the fruits of the orchards, the schools and religious colleges, the mosques and their customs; but it is a Turkish saint the name of whose resting place is even forgotten today who is his principal subject. Erdede Sultan was upset with Evliya who had forgotten him but had instead begun a hymn of praise for Hacı Bayram. Not only did Erdede Sultan appear to Evliya in a dream, but next morning, by means of a mysterious messenger, showed him his final resting place. Evliya Çelebi writes that he walked the streets of Ankara hand in hand with this messenger from the other world, who suddenly disappointed his too-great curiosity by vanishing; his hands were mere bones, his voice was deep and hoarse as though it came from under the earth. According to Evliya, it seems that Erdede Sultan played a very important part in the history of the sufis, and this time I searched hard for him in Ankara. But although I learned much I didn't know, I never found him. From an inhabitant of Ankara who was also interested in these matters I heard of the existence of an old tomb thought to belong to a local saint known as Kuşbaba. The tomb lay under the new school built near the modern covered market and might be that of Erdede Sultan. How far can we believe in Evliya Çelebi's dreams when he begins his travels with a dream so charming and humorous that we doubt its truth? I cannot tell. I read Evliya Çelebi not to criticize but to believe. And I always end up the winner. After reading his narrative, I have often returned in the morning from walking the lanes of old Ankara which Evliya Çelebi may have followed too, conversing on many subjects with the messenger from the other world. I have had a strange pleasure imagining that my present hour had merged with the city's past.

V

I have climbed to the fortress. Before me stretches the Ankara plain with its surprising changes. My friend and I count the surrounding mountains one by one, the little hills and the little villages that cast a bright green shadow in the middle of the steppe; and suddenly here and there in the heat the illusion of a bowl of cold water. A keen bright light sings in my ear like a trumpet blast. In the harsh wind, the flat shape of the hill where we stand – Evliya Çelebi would have compared it to an almond as he does for the town of Pest in Hungary – is exactly like the bulwark of a ship in which I am ready to sail time's seas. This wind and miraculous vessel, where will they carry us? Climbing up here with all we have seen, what centuries of civilizations will we not visit? But Ankara does not lend itself easily to this kind of historical daydream. Here it is a single event, a single era, a single man, that governs the imagination. The city has surrendered to him so completely it has become him. The Hittite lion, the Roman pillar, the stone from the Byzantine basilica, the battles waged by Tamurlane and Bayezid the Thunderbolt are all around you and take you back to the difficult days and therapeutic pain of 20 years ago, and to the serious events that followed naturally.

Ankara, it might be said, emerged from the National Struggle for Independence by setting fire to all its past.

I look at the plain; battles took place in plains like this and in mountains like these whose violet-shadowed slopes mould the horizon. As the Commander of the Western Front was writing the telegram which would announce the İnönü victory to the nation and to history, the landscape before him was a continuation, with very few changes, of the scene I now see. It was from a hill like this, or from one nearby, or a little further off, that the victorious commander watched the enemy flee and Bozöyük burning. It was in a place like this that he dictated to those around him the famous communiqué which brought good tidings for centuries to come:

After 6.30, the situation observed from Metristepe: an enemy detachment probably rearguard standing firm since morning in the north of Gündüzbey withdraws in disorder under an attack by a group from the right wing and is closely pursued. No contact or action in the Hamidiye direction. Bözüyük burning. The enemy having covered the area with thousands of their dead has surrendered the battlefield to our arms.

Commander of the Western Wing

İsmet

Here for the first time we find well-written lines that bring a panoramic vista of life before us with clear and simple eloquence; a battlefield, a fire, the dead and wounded, confusion, on the horizon soldiers fleeing and in pursuit.

What dream did the young commander-in-chief İsmet Paşa[19] see – if he slept at all – on the night of 26 August 1922, the eve of the battle of İnönü? And Commander Mustafa Kemal, on the same night at Dumlupınar? Did the vision of the future they were preparing for their nation appear to them that night? My thoughts reverted to another great night, the night of 26 August 1071, when Alparslan at Manzikert with his strong arm and powerful genius opened to us the gates of our beloved homeland. What power, what revelation came to him before he gave the signal for battle? I wonder if he foresaw that he was about to found a new Rome which would spread to three continents, that he was giving the nation, whose destiny he held in the palm of his hands, a new history and geography, and that he was giving birth to a new structure which would take root and flourish like a plane tree. Did they not wander about him like the still-unopened roses of dawn, the brilliant offspring as yet unknown, commanders of future victories, the poets of poems still unsung, the architects of masterpieces still unbuilt, the composers of melodies still unheard? Did he not have a vision of the future Sultan Han and the *İnce Minareli Mosque*, Konya's mosque with the slender minaret? Without a presentiment of all these happy events in his innermost being, how could he ever have achieved his great work? How was he able, in 10 years, to transport an ideal that this land had never known or tasted, from Manzikert to the shores of the Mediterranean? As for Fatih's[20] sleepless night before the conquest of Constantinople, what else was that but an impatience arising from carrying a destiny pregnant with the genius of Bâkî[21] and Nedim, Neşatî and Nailî, Sinan and Barbarossa, Kasım, Itrî and Dede, Seyyid Nuh and Tab'î Mustafa and others like them? How did all these works come to be born if not through divine suffering? By what miracle did new fruit flourish on the old tree of life?

The constructive and creative suffering that sent Mustafa Kemal and his comrades travelling abroad on the Anatolian roads, wrestling with a thousand and one hardships, would prolong for centuries to come the work begun by the victory at Manzikert and the conquest of Constantinople. Just as we owe Sinan, Nedim, Yunus[22] and İtrî to dreams of victory, so are we indebted to the nameless martyrs and their deeds that would bring them honour for centuries to come. They paid a heavy price of flesh and blood for the sleepless nights spent in İnönü, the Sakarya and Dumlupınar and for the burden of those battles.

At this evening hour, Ankara's fortress has taught me once again that a nation, however long its history, revolves round certain crucial events and is bound to certain sacred dreams and to the survival of a belief which is itself the very essence of creative impulse.

Notes

1 The National Struggle for Independence – The successful struggle (1919–1922) waged by the nationalists, led by Mustafa Kemal Atatürk, to liberate Turkey from the forces of the Allies at the beginning of World War I. It resulted in a political revolution, the end of the sultanate and the birth of Turkey as a new republican and secular state.

2 Bayezid I (The Thunderbolt) (1360–1403) – Fourth Ottoman sultan, known for his successful campaigns in the Balkans. But the defeat of his siege of Constantinople in 1399 meant the disruption of Anatolia and allowed Constantinople to survive as a Byzantine capital for a further 50 years. He was finally defeated by Tamurlane in the battle of Ankara (1402) and imprisoned, surviving in legend, literature and music as a tragic figure.

3 Tamurlane (1336–1405) – The great conqueror whose campaign took him from China to Iran, culminating in his confrontation with the Ottomans at Ankara in a major battle.

4 Sakarya – Tanpınar names several battles fought during the War of Independence. Sakarya, fought between the Greek and Kemalist forces, lasted for 22 days in August and September 1921.

5 Dumlupınar – In Central Anatolia. The name of the battle won by Atatürk in 1922.

6 Yakup Kadri Karaosmanoğlu (1889–1974) – A Turkish novelist. His novel, 'Ankara'.

7 Ahî – In medieval Anatolia, a fraternity or guild of artisans, known for their hospitality to strangers. They played an important part in Selçuk and early Ottoman times in maintaining political order in Anatolia.

8 Mihrâb – A niche in the wall before the door of a mosque. It indicates the direction of Mecca.

9 Hacı Bayram (1352–1430) – Born near Ankara. He founded a religious order, a community based on manual work and the cultivation of the fields around Ankara. The Hacı Bayram Mosque, in the heart of old Ankara, was built in the beginning of the fifteenth century, close to the Temple of Augustus which had become a church in the sixth century.

10 Baba İlyas of Khorasan – A dervish and one of the instigators of the great peasant revolt against the Selçuks in the mid-thirteenth century, a religious-political movement which included several shamanist elements.

11 Medrese – A college of learning for the religious. Eventually all were closed down in 1924.

12 Alâeddin Keykubad (1220–1237) – His reign was the most brilliant of the Selçuk dynasty for its territorial expansion, commercial activity and building programmes. He was an excellent athlete, draughtsman, carpenter and calligrapher, a wise statesman and a strong leader. He captured Alanya, turned it into a naval base and opened the way for the Selçuks to the Mediterranean.

13 İzzedin Keykavus I – He prevented his younger brother from seizing the throne and imprisoned him in Malatya. His reign expanded the Anatolian Empire to the shores of the Black Sea.

14 Fatwa – In the Islamic faith, a fatwa is a religious opinion concerning Islamic law.

15 Ulema – Doctors of Moslem theology.

16 İbn Bibî – A chronicler of the thirteenth century.

17 Evliya Çelebi (1611–1682) – Writer and traveller. His *Seyahatname*, or 'Book of Travels', although sometimes too fantasist, is the best source of knowledge of the seventeenth-century Ottoman Empire.

18 Sinan – The great architect and designer of Ottoman buildings. His constructions include 84 mosques, 52 oratories, 57 medrese colleges, 17 hospices, 20 caravanserai, 35 palaces and 48 public baths.

19 İsmet Pasha (1029–1072) – A great military leader of the Selçuks, defeating the Byzantines at the battle of Manzikert in 1071, thus beginning the conquest of Asia Minor by the Turks.

20 Fatih – Mehmet II (the Conqueror), who captured Constantinople in 1453.

21 Bâkî – 'The sultan of poets', the greatest representative of sixteenth-century Ottoman lyric poetry. Tanpınar proceeds to name the geniuses of Ottoman culture, including poets, historians, calligraphers and composers.

22 Yunus Emre (??–1320) – A thirteenth-century humanist poet, revered in Turkey as one of their greatest poets. He was the first to write, not in Persian, but in the Turkish of the people, a language so clear and pure that it is still accessible today.

2
Erzurum

I

I've been to Erzurum three times, each time by a different route. On the first of these journeys, I was still more or less a child. At the end of the Balkan War and at the beginning of the brief painful year between two disastrous conflicts, we were returning from an eastern province where my father held an official post. I'll never forget that journey of 11 days, perhaps more, when we spent nights under canvas, listening to the sounds of the infinite natural world, the mills and streams and the insect noises endlessly nibbling away at the great mulberry leaf of our surroundings. We shivered as the shepherds called to one another and their howling watchdogs started up fearfully at the phantoms raised by night, or growled at the animals stirring in the darkness. I was amazed in the mornings to find I couldn't feel my hands move; they were frozen stiff in the bitter cold. My imagination is still alight with the magic memory of my great grandmother who read me stories and verses about Kerem[1] and Yunus and tried to teach me the names of the stars.

A precipice between thuja trees and my father leaning over to see the stream below; a green plain caught between the channels of the Botan River, drenched here and there in sunlight and arranged in the windows of a grocer's shop, which I almost bypassed, little oil lamps that created a hint of Bitlis City; an old broken-down bridge over the river Murat where we met a reserve battalion going home exhausted after unimaginable sufferings in the Balkan Wars; and finally a night when we slept at the foot of Mount Yildiz and a day when we saw Mount Süphan from a distance – in my childish imagination, these images and mountains made a strange impression.

After the mountains, Aşık Kerem joined our caravan like a ghostly fellow traveller. And because of my grandma's many reminiscences this journey seemed a little like one made in his name. Apart from Yemen and Mecca, places she knew in her young days, all the geographical knowledge of this woman who came from Trebizond originated in the legend of Aşık Kerem. It was a knowledge more like religion than science. She regarded all streams and mountains as eternal living creatures. Poetry, religion, the yearning for one's country, the experiences of life, the remnants of belief like the successive lives that flit through our dreams, elevated mountains and streams to the rank of sacred and saintly beings. Sometimes she would summon me to her camel to tell me the name or the story, if there was one, of some eternal figure we would pass in the distance, or would soon approach, and she would recite lines from Yunus and Aşık Kerem. Before the journey she would ask the soldier in charge of the pack animals on which side of the road Mount Süphan lay and what night we would camp at the foot of Mount Yıldız. So we were both prepared.

The mountains in this corner of the land, if only by their names, were like a celestial dream. A dream of people living close to the stars, who had grazed their herds in the upland meadows for centuries, spent days in winter hunting wolves and lost their way as they chased the doe-eyed deer of fairy story. That is why the traveller who encounters these mountains for the first time and hears their names – flashes of light mirrored in a piece of water – can't help being overwhelmed by a terror of eternity, if only for a moment, and, moved by the power of their solitude, submits to a sense of destiny.

At the foot of Mount Yıldız surrounded by the innumerable sounds and murmurs the night had unloaded on our tent, I dreamt of the proud mountain peak I had almost glimpsed through the mists, as though I was looking upon the countenance of a primeval God. And I thought that if I listened more closely I would hear its conversation with the stars. Perhaps every night the mountain would stretch out its hands and alone direct all these great fluctuations we know as fate and the cosmos, like the old man I used to see as I passed every morning on my way to primary school in Sinop three years before, eagerly winding the great hanging clock of the mosque. It wound up the clock of the stars, adjusting the course of Venus, the morning and evening star, the Great Bear and Little Bear, the Weeping Women and all the others. I shared the melancholy loneliness of the great empty spaces and longed for the jewelled clusters that stretched into the dense darkness soft as velvet. It appointed the moment of sunrise and the waters the moon would cross in her enchanted boat; with a gleaming point it registered the birth of children in the notebook of the sky, gently closing the eyes of a star and erasing the names of the dead.

Lying that night on the lower slopes of Mount Yıldız, my childish fancy was under an influence whose roots I guessed were deep but to this very day still unknown. In the darkness of the tent I thought that all things were swimming in magic chemistry, washed and cleaned and made greater by the gleaming stars. In the evening we saw the roughly clad shepherds from Bingöl taking their flocks up the mountain, and when we met them again the next morning, their long shaggy cloaks of animal hair seemed to me to be woven from starlight, and the flocks of sheep filled my heart with a shiver of fear, like the amazing wild-looking ram in the map of the cosmos that I had seen among my father's books. So it was with these feelings that I entered Erzurum some days later, like the shepherds from Bingöl and Cizre who brought their sheep to the city in early autumn after they had spent all summer cropping the mountain pastures.

The Erzurum of that time was very different from the ruined city of Erzurum I saw 10 years later in 1923. It was impossible to imagine any connection between the city I saw

10 years later and the relaxed and comfortable Erzurum which had been nourished by easy commerce with Iran, with its 54 mosques and 38 colleges, with its guilds, its important notables, its storehouses full of goods and its inns which so many passed through in a year, its shops and crowds of people variously dressed who filled the marketplace, the leather workers, silversmiths and coppersmiths.

Later I learned that tens of thousands of craftsmen worked in various quarters of the market and that goods made by the leather workers went to the eastern provinces, even as far as Tabriz. Even now I remember like a fairy tale the visit my parents made to the merchants of black amber. There they sat in their little, dimly lit workshops, several men trained in a delicate, precise art, talking and bargaining where they sat, polishing the pieces of amber in their hands on their baggy trousers with the worn-away nap, and a strong smell of leather, the sound of hammer blows cushioned in the soft hide and various other noises . . .

II

This time, Erzurum was a very different place. I had come not from the nourishing solitude of the mountains in Eastern Anatolia, sanctified by time like an old wine, but from leaving behind four years of a world war and the Turkish War of Independence. In fact, this time, too, we had travelled through magnificent natural scenes, but whereas on my first journey I had found everything new and wonderful, now their magic paled before a number of bad and painful experiences. Both the beauty, more amazing at every corner, of the Zigana Mountains and the splendour of Mount Kop failed to attract me. I was more influenced by the bloody game played out there some years before rather than by the stage scenery. Just as a spectator in the theatre may be distracted by the decor of an empty stage but never notices all these details when the spoken word begins, so in the face of such human misery I felt indifferent and alien to the beauty of nature.

After Gümüşhane, the feeling gradually increased and in Erzurum became quite oppressive. The city that I was seeing for the second time was no longer the old Erzurum, the economic centre of eastern provinces, rose of the uplands, its beauty praised in most of the folk songs of the region. War, emigration, massacres, typhus and every kind of disaster had reversed and crushed all.

Nowhere was the pain experienced by a country in the World War I so clearly felt as here. It was the triumph of death that the old painters had once portrayed. For four years, wolves in the mountains feasted on human flesh, death was everywhere on the prowl, hunting voraciously. Its ill-omened scythe never stopped but mowed down everything in its path like clockwork. Yet, although the population numbers fell from sixty to eight thousand, Erzurum became a pioneer in the War of Independence, winning a victory against Armenia, and had gradually begun to gather together its surviving fellow citizens.

Alongside the triumph of death, gradually the song of life rose again, like those strange springtimes which begin as soon as the ice melts in a garden ravaged by a deadly winter.

Once again in the devastated city the young began to marry, children were born, the father lit the stove in houses half-reduced to rubble, in the dusky evenings the children who had escaped death sang folk songs; in the squares before the town gates whose names betokened places that no longer existed, the sound of drum and pipe could be heard and the game of javelin and the dances of Eastern Anatolia reappeared.

In short, the eagle's nest scattered by the storm was rebuilt, and the survivors sang hymns to the sun. Everywhere was a sense of rejoicing that was almost morbid, of a liveliness that had not yet found its level and was very different from what I had seen 10 years ago in that wonderful summer. This was life reigning triumphant despite everything, pursuing its course, abandoning those who couldn't let themselves go with the flow, to a cruel loneliness.

But there was no longer a four-gated city. Very little remained except the soul of a frontier city whose integrity and pride had been for centuries in the life of its community. Was this the first defeat that Erzurum had known? The 1828 defeat,[2] and the 1876[3] disaster and several previous uprisings had certainly shaken her. In the first, a population of 132,000 had dropped to 100,000. In the second, the city was shaken to its roots. But this defeat was very different. This time death fell on the city as though it wanted to leave no one but itself behind. Then it departed, leaving a few broken-down roads, a few so-called gates surrounding what was now a ruin, a little skeleton city on the edge of an endless cemetery, death's own true domain.

Almost everyone had a story that only they could tell. Almost everyone wept for their dead or waited for one they loved but whose fate was unknown.

They told of an old man who for years had never left his window. He was waiting for his grandson to return from the Caucasus. In the neighbourhoods, every knock at the door was still an excitement. And strange to tell, although five years had passed men were still returning one by one. As the Siberian ice melted and the Indian jungles opened to allow a poor, confused man to come back, surprised to be alive, his story of the hell he had escaped spread through the city like a new Odyssey whose superhuman greatness came from the sufferings he had undergone. Every day in any little village coffee house, tales could be heard of Kamçatka's icy cold, Ceylon's burning heat or the snakes of Madagascar.

One of my friends told me, 'Before I came here, I spent a night in an inn of Aşkale, where I met a poor one-armed fellow with a burned face, a prisoner of war just returning, who told me that he left the city on the evening of the day he arrived in it, because he couldn't find his wife or his mother or the son he'd left there or even the location of his house.'

'So where are you going now?' I asked.

He thought for a while. His face fell. Finally he said, 'Why do you ask where I'm going? I told you where I've come from, isn't that enough?'

He was right. I'd learned where he came from.

Death didn't give up easily those he had followed so closely. Sooner or later he appeared before them and invited them to his table. If nothing else he could remind them of his presence.

At every gathering, stories are recalled of old men abandoned on the road, of mothers who set off singing lullabies, wrapping their squashed bits and pieces under the feet of the babe at the breast, of dying horses, their head on their master's body, the annihilated market, the ruins of a city, the wrecked house, a whole life erased like a river whose water is suddenly cut off, wounds that bleed endlessly.

Erzurum remembered its lively past now buried in a heap of dust and mud: the caravans that came and went through the four gates; the hum of the market; its workers; its scholars with their shining faces and solid morality that was mirrored in the life of the city; the beautiful voices of the muezzins; the weddings which, every year, kept life up to date; the artisan gatherings; the handsome fellows who organized festivals and tuned up the life of the people like a musician playing his instrument; the traditional young men tossing the javelin; their dances; the old, rich landowners who sometimes entertained a whole regiment for days on end and whose carriages rode back and forth through their lands; in short, Erzurum remembered its whole life.

Still, in the days when wounds were still raw and bleeding, it was hard to understand what exactly had been destroyed and lost. The entire community had suffered such definitive events and experienced such irreversible calamities that the city resembled a man rescued from an accident and inevitable death. Like the story of the man who lost his leg and began to search for the most trivial things but his mind couldn't concentrate on the real situation and kept wandering off in search of details.

What was actually lost was a complete way of life, a whole world. In 1855, Erzurum, a city with a population of more than 100,000, had established its growth on its economic stability. Iran provided more than half of the exports and imports by means of the caravan routes that linked Trebizond and Tabriz, a route that for centuries had made Erzurum a truly oriental medieval city, with its notables and senators, its scholars and holy men and its artisan guilds. Every year, along this route passed 3,000 camels and perhaps twice that number of mules. They all passed through Erzurum and, whether coming or going from Tabriz and Trebizond, they bought their provisions from Erzurum, shod their animals, and in short stocked up with all they required, saddles and pack-saddles, horse's bits, muzzles and horseshoes.

But unfortunately a return to the former life was impossible. And even without the disaster of the Great War the Erzurum market would die away, its tradesmen would disperse, the city would shrink and turn into a village until it found a new mode of work which would enable it to flourish again. But this change would be very gradual, like a glass lamp that fell to the ground and broke, spilling all its oil until the light was extinguished. Or more probably it could find a new kind of life through other means of production. Let me say at once that Erzurum is well suited for such a future development. Three coal mines in the neighbourhood, partly worked in the past, reedbeds very suitable for a modern paper factory, petroleum from Tercan (if there is as much as they promised) and finally the Tortum waterfalls, the important source of a life which would, step by step, revive the country if it developed its electrification project to create a new Anatolia. These were major possibilities for the birth of a new energetic Erzurum, very different from its predecessor.

In 1914, two events occurred, the Great War and modern times. When the through road opened, a citizen of Erzurum, Hasan the baker, said to Cevat Dursunoğlu, 'In the old days caravans came here and bought rations for all and filled the city with money. Now a truck with a load of twenty mules sets off from Trebizond in the morning and arrives here in the evening. The driver buys a litre bottle of rakı in the supermarket, smashes the bottle on the wall, drinks it, then goes on his way.'

So that is what ended the story of the old Erzurum, the city of eastern commerce and luxuries that poured in from all directions. With a single blow the Great War had destroyed and dispersed a whole framework of life that in other circumstances and better conditions might have been transformed in a few years.

In the old Erzurum, the caravan route and the life of trade had nourished 31 arts: tanners, saddlers, makers of pack saddles, cobblers, sandal makers, makers of galoshes, furriers, makers of sheepskin cloaks, shoemakers, silk manufacturers, carriage builders, felt makers, tentmakers, weavers, ropemakers, metalworkers, coppersmiths, armourers, cutlers, goldsmiths, dice makers, carpenters, spoon makers, makers of combs, cabinetmakers, painters, builders, masons, soap makers, chandlers and makers of cigarette holders. When Evliya Çelebi came to Erzurum with Mehmet Pasha, the finance minister, and there acted as secretary of the customs, he wrote of the city gates that foreign merchants were living by the Georgian gate:

'Here is the custom-house in which I am a humble clerk. All around are the houses of merchants from Arabia, Persia, India, Sind, Khatay and Hoten. After the custom houses of Istanbul and Izmir, Erzurum customs office is the busiest. They treat the merchants justly.' These few lines are sufficient to give us a picture of Erzurum in our world of yesterday. It was one of the great cities of commerce and at the crossroads of eastern trade routes.

The Erzurum customs house also passes into history at the end of the seventeenth century by another route. When Fazı Ahmed Pasha, returning from the war with Austria, appeared in the great nomadic tent erected in the palace grounds of Edirne for this occasion and gave a detailed account to Mehmed IV of the battle of Uyvar (the battle Evliya Çelebi was so enthusiastic about in the seventh volume of his *Seyahatname*), Müverrih Raşid[4] spoke of a heroic figure named Abbas of Erzurum who accompanied him. Let's hear the story from Raşid:

There was in particular a brave warrior from Erzurum, named Abbas, alongside your humble servant. During the battle of Uyvar he boldly climbed the tower of the citadel and when several of the infidels fired on him, he never moved from his position. Seeing a brave janissary climbing up beside him, other fighters of Islam came in great numbers to the rescue and attacked the enemy, shouting together and praising the Lord, so that the infidels began to give up, thus allowing the fortress to be captured. Ahmed Pasha having spoken, the gracious sultan left his tent for his personal apartment and summoned the aforesaid Abbas, to whom he put a number of questions, after which he placed two crowns on his head chosen from his own effects, and presented him by imperial decree with a pension of 75 aspers on the revenue from the Erzurum customs; as well as a present of four rolls of material and the wherewithal to have four pairs of shalvar made, and showered him with other benefits. He also gave a pension of fifty aspers on the revenue from the Erzurum customs to the brother of the aforesaid Abbas and ordered that a pension from the army's bank should be awarded to the janissary who had climbed the aforesaid ramparts with him.

That was the way of the empire. Erzurum and Uyvar, Baghdad and Crete, Trebizond and Belgrade, Athens and Algeria, all lived side by side in a glorious confusion. This surprising unity which led Evliya Çelebi to move from humour in every line to the dignity of his Seyahatname and the inevitable changes and contrasts it brought about in daily life produced both pride and pain in the community.

Abbas of Erzurum is the only person whose name we know among the dead who returned from the Uyvar victory. When Yahya Kemal[5] mentioned his story to Cevat Dursunoğlu he suggested that the name Abbas of Uyvar should be given to one of the streets of Erzurum. A good idea. We wish the people of Erzurum might name one of the streets at the Georgian gate after Evliya Çelebi. So those two men who received a salary and pension from the Erzurum customs house are united in the memory of the city in which they had both lived.

III

Where there was wealth and work a social order was automatically born. The old Erzurum was contained within a regular framework. Landowners were at the head. In the old days these gentlemen had taken over the duties of guardians of the castles and participated in civil and military administration. They were now a real landed aristocracy similar to that in Rumeli and in the provinces of the Danube that belonged to us.

Here, as in all traditional societies, the women were highly protected and were even more fanatical than the men in their concern for equality of age and social class in their marriages. Married women who were the daughters of landowners were addressed as 'pasha'; if from the artisan class or if they were foreigners or the daughters of concubines they were addressed as 'hanım' or 'lady'. Sometimes these marriages took place beyond the provincial frontiers and the daughters of Georgian landowners came to Erzurum as 'pashas'.

In Erzurum there was a tradition of Moslem science which made the city one of the foremost intellectual centres of the east. In its schools it had educated Abdullah el-Kalı, a great Arabic linguist who made his name in Cordova long before the arrival of the Ottomans.

Recently, a class of learned doctors of Moslem theology had come from three or four important families, like the Solakzade, Kadizade, Müftizade or Gözübüyük.

After the *ulema* came the guild, which was the real backbone of the city, headed by Dabaklar, a personality who could, even when necessary, oppose government decisions. Neither the Tanzimat reforms[6] nor Abdülhamid's central administration had destroyed the authority which originally derived from the 'ahî' and which constituted the soul of the city. Formerly, the Dabaklar sheikh had always had power in the Anatolian cities, whose structure had depended on the artisan guilds. The maintenance of important and necessary skills, like the art of shoemaking and saddling, and reliance on their principal source of wealth, their animals, bound their skills mainly to the way of life of a tribal village.

Behind the Dabaklar sheikh lay the market which, from time to time, revealed its power to oppose even Istanbul in the two rebellions of the seventeenth and eighteenth centuries. But it was not the succession of such groups that was really important but the underlying vital structure that actually added strength to the life of the city. The rights of villagers and farmers were protected by the landowners, and as Erzurum was a frontier province, the relationship between landowner and villager was more of a paternal nature than elsewhere. At least this was Mehmet Arif's idea,[7] author of *Başımıza Gelenler* ('What Happened to Us'). The market was so deeply rooted that any form of domination in the city was unimaginable. So in the old Erzurum a new equilibrium had been established, despite misunderstandings which can occur in any human situation, and continued in every walk of life that led its own peaceful and independent existence, right until the Second Constitutional Government and even after.

Nevertheless, in spite of the apparent mutual understanding, a split began to appear in the mosques and preachers. Young men and the open-minded had recently gathered in the Caferiye Mosque to hear the preaching of Müftizade Edip Hoca, whom I will discuss later. The Pervizoğlu Mosque where Abdülkadir Hoca preached was frequented by bigots, while the Lala Paşa mosque, where the imperial edicts were proclaimed, was more crowded with people of various kinds. Here were preachers from the Solakzade family.

On public holidays, the people, including even the poorest, would put on their best clothes and make summer excursions to the Gorge, where city folk, particularly the wealthy, would pitch their tents and take part in javelin throwing and wrestling. Wearing baggy trousers called *zigva*, a Persian shawl, a woollen cloak or a belt for weaponry called a *gazeki*, an overcoat called a *harti* and round their heads a printed scarf from Kandilli, members of the guilds would enjoy themselves, according to a tradition 10 centuries old.

In winter, they would gather round the tellers of folk tales and the poets reading in the Coffeehouse of Mirrors (at the Tabriz gate) all before my time, stories about Aşık Kerem and Battal Gazi,[8] playing the saz, responding to one another in poetry competitions as in the time of Kerem, praising the beautiful country of their birth, singing of the ways they travelled and their feeling of homesickness.

It was the guilds that created Erzurum's real life, and what was admirable was their understanding of class, their lack of envy of anyone above them and their openness to anyone below. The wife of an artisan never wore the same clothes as the wife of an illustrious man, nor did she ever dress in silk or any silver- or gold-decorated materials. They were a group of fellow countrymen, whose creativity and hard work had endowed them with a strong personality and a deep self-respect. Even in a young person, thirteen years of age, just entering an apprenticeship, self-confidence may begin early, and we can observe how the idea of responsibility in a life that depends on manual labour can elevate a human being.

The pleasures of music were similar. At the dances, known to all the people of Erzurum as *Bar*, at javelin throwing and at weddings, the drums and pipes that brought us all the way from Manzikert[9] to Vienna, were always played. In the people's coffee houses the saz music of the wandering minstrel could be heard, and in the casinos frequented by the notables and in the public reading rooms – of course, after the Tanzimat reforms – there were little orchestras. One of the latter was a group with harmonium and dulcimer led by Blind Vahan. There were also famous reciters of the Koran, including Kitapçizade, Hâfız Hâmid the orator from the Lala Paşa mosque, Ebulhindili Hamdi Bey and Gözübüyükzade.

Into this very orderly life came the seasons with a particular ritual for each. Order mattered above all. Therefore, everything had its messengers and forerunners. Children realized that summer had arrived when the tentmakers came to their homes. Then tents piled up in the garden, among the delighted screams of children who realized how much fun they would have in the open air of the Gorge and the hot springs, while skilful old masters repaired them and patched torn places and brought them to a suitable state to resist wind and rain.

The furrier was the joyful harbinger of winter. Even before the peak of Mount Kop turned white and the slopes of Palandöken loured, the experienced ones, warned by the colour of the flocks of birds flying southward from the pastures, summoned the furrier. Then fur cloaks and useable skins of fox and wolves were heaped in the middle of spacious halls and elderly bespectacled furriers with huge needles sewed them together and patched them up. It was the period of hot stoves and long conversations, of teacups gleaming like a little dawn on silver teatrays, the beginning of Erzurum's second life.

The city closed its gates and lived in its own world: once every two or three weeks postmen with their curled moustaches, long-legged boots and their black felt capes brought on their sledges newspapers and news that led to lengthy arguments as well as strange stories of wolves and snowstorms; tales were told based on memories of the past, gossip was exchanged and allusions to friends and marriage partners subtly dropped in masterly elegant sentences. Perhaps because of the friendly conversations nourished by these intimate winter months, almost everyone from Erzurum was a bit of a wit or a satirist. But, as in everything, a few from each generation emerged as exceptional individuals. They were masters of the art of conversation.

Who doesn't remember Zakir Bey, mayor at this time, and his reply to the American commission which had come to Erzurum after the armistice years to inquire about the Armenian affair?

'Look here, sir,' he said to the interpreter, 'these gentlemen have a lot to say. Let me tell the General in a very few words who were the majority in Erzurum!' And he took the member of the commission to the window of the house where they were living, and said, 'See, the whole city is surrounded by a stony paving and in the middle of it there's a spot, a twentieth of the whole, surrounded by a wall. The bigger section is

the Moslem cemetery, the smaller one is the Armenian cemetery: for sure they haven't devoured their own dead!'

It is evident in a thousand ways that the Turks in Erzurum
had always been in a crushing majority. Zakir Bey's ready
talent for answers had found the shortest and the most indis-
putable of these. I had heard of one of these masters of conversation and the many stories that circulated about him, and
one I knew personally. Kaleli Burhan Bey died long before
1923, but his sharp wit and irony, his repartee, were still a living
memory. Edip Hoca was still alive. This amazing man is truly
worth remembering and reminds me of the sixteenth-century
poet İshak Çelebi,[10] when 300 years later he recited that
famous line in praise of Damascus: 'I named the evening I left
Damascus The Holy Night.' I met Edip Hoca in Cevat's house
and came to like him very much, a perceptive man who had
always seemed to me like an incarnation of our ancient culture. With his strong athletic frame he always appeared in the
foreground, everything else became background. In Erzurum,
despite all its shabby antiquity, he was perhaps the most lively
character.

In the Erzurum of 1923, Edip Hoca was like a souvenir
of the past who had come with one of those eastern armies
from the sixteenth or seventeenth centuries and had decided
to remain there, or else like one of the train of gifts from the
Sultan which had set out laden with prayers and holy recitations
from Üsküdar to Damascus, and from there to Mecca, and had
accidentally turned aside to Erzurum. With his high spirits,
frankness, witty replies in argument, his emotional balance and
greatness of heart, Edip Hoca was a whole world in himself.

One day he was visiting a friend and asked to see a tea glass.
He took a liking to a very beautiful set of glasses: 'Hakkı,'
he said, 'put these aside. I'll take one and try it this evening.'
But the next day he brought it back. 'Why didn't you like
these pretty glasses?' his friend asked and he replied sharply,
'Hakkı, the glasses are beautiful but they don't suit me. In
the morning I poured out tea and put one in front of me
and looked at it: then I compared myself; we were out of

proportion ... Dear Hakkı, try and find me one just a little bigger.'

This little story reveals the kind of man he was and what kind of perfect world he came from. In his youth he had entered politics. He had even for a time been an active member of the Party of Union and Progress,[11] and in the early years of the constitutional government of 1908, he was one of the commission of advisors sent to Albania. He often told the story of an adventure on that expedition.

One day when he was a guest in the house of an Albanian gentleman, they saw the chief of one of the mountain tribes approaching the mansion with all his entourage and realized he was a distant relative of the Albanian. According to Albanian custom and law he must be entertained as one of the guests. The owner of the house who knew his relation very well, explained the rule to Edip Hoca. 'We have to go along with it – there's no other way – or rather, you must submit to it, or we'll all be done for.' He also warned him to be very careful. Edip Hoca unwillingly agreed. At night the beds were prepared. The new guest placed between himself and Edip Hoca, first his weapons, his guns full of bullets, his cartridges and last of all a packet of the finest make of tobacco. When he got into bed he said, 'Roll a cigarette, I'd like to talk to you.' Edip Hoca, who was about to forget in the land of sleep the inconvenient presence of his sleeping companion who resembled a brigand of the old school, rolled his cigarette and waited. It was a very simple matter. He was in love with his brother's daughter and had decided to marry her. But some had declared it was forbidden by religion, and knowing that Edip Hoca had come from Istanbul he wanted to ask his advice. That had even been the reason for his journey, he said.

Edip Hoca naturally replied, 'How is it possible? Your brother's daughter is like your own daughter. Religion forbids it.' But the lovesick Albanian had no intention of changing his mind. He wasn't asking his opinion; he just wanted him to agree to a new kind of religious permission. The argument grew. At last the lovesick guest realized he couldn't convince his opponent, and cursing the hodja for his obstinacy in resisting his innocent desire, he took to his revolver. Edip Hoca looked at the man, his revolver and the door. It was a long way to the door. Besides, the man's followers lay in the hall behind it. So he began, 'Listen, don't be in such a hurry! Tell me – is the girl's father older or younger than you, his brother?' And when our Albanian friend answered, 'He's older than me,' Edip Hoca went on, 'Then it's a different matter. Why didn't you say so at the beginning? If he were younger it would certainly be forbidden. You couldn't marry her. It would be like marrying your son's daughter. But if he's older . . . then it's lawful. You can do what you like!'

This last turnabout delighted the guest. 'Bravo! What they told me is true, you're a great scholar. Light up and have a smoke!' And this was how Edip Hoca spent the night, till dawn, smoking tobacco and listening to his lovesick friend.

Long afterwards, I thought about this story. His surrender in the face of physical force might be seen as cynical, and we might also find in the little anecdote one of the causes of the downfall of the Ottoman Empire. So often we have recited İzzet Molla's couplet[12] outside its context:

It is not cruelty that destroys the world
But flattery of the powerful.

Those who think that certain values can only be preserved in favourable circumstances can forgive Edip Hoca. He was not a man to lay claim to heroism. He could accept responsibility for his ideas only in a regulated system. The drama of Ottoman history arises from a certain period when it was considered normal, if not to exclude characters like Edip Hoca from governing, at least to wish for his exclusion.

One of the Erzurum characters I heard stories about was Ahmet Muhtar, deputy in Erzurum in '93. I often heard about his life from Cevat Dursunoğlu, his grandson on his mother's side. Every week he would be angered by the *Envar-I Şarkiye* newspaper for praising a provincial governor he disliked and he would say to his servant Ömer Ağa, 'Take the tongs, grab that paper, open up the stove and throw it inside, then go and wash your hands.' The incident reveals a temperament whose violence could hardly be controlled by customary good manners.

But what I liked best in Erzurum was precisely this temperament.

IV

I entered Erzurum one rainy day, passing through the endless cemetery that Zakir Bey had described. Under a shower scattered by a sharp wind, its long time-worn stones turning to red – that lovely soft stone to be seen in every piece of stonework in Erzurum – rose around me like ghosts. The coincidence was enough to upset the young poet from Istanbul who had come to teach literature in the high school.

Almost the next day, I had the luck to meet Cevat Dursunoğlu. This man's family origins were rooted in the city. His study of philosophy in Germany, his life in the army which lasted for four years and his role at the beginning of the National Struggle set him apart from other men I knew. He was a collector. His knowledge of the city was great. He had tales to tell. He loved to talk and made an art of conversation. Thanks to him I had already entered the city and its affairs in less than a week.

However, a feeling of uneasiness planted in my heart at this first meeting never entirely left me. At the end of the summer, I saw its most terrifying countenance revive in me with the great earthquake. A strange and unhappy event prevented me from going to Istanbul. One afternoon when we were in school, we leapt from our seats at the sound of a loud rumble. Everything was shaking. We could hardly reach the door. In the windless air the city was smothered in dust and before we could reach the door a second and third tremor followed with an indescribable roar, and this time we could hear people screaming. Slight tremors like facial quivers filled the short intervals between. The roads were full of people and our first thought was that the city had collapsed. But no lives were lost, though from the evening onwards bad news of accidents began to reach us. In several places the earth had cracked open and entire villages were swallowed up. Almost daily we learned of new losses. From that night the city changed its appearance and came to resemble a very old barracks for migrant armies.

This particular earthquake lasted a month. It created such great continuous havoc and destruction that people were unwilling to enter their homes again even though the tremors were slight. But the arrival of Atatürk in Erzurum at the time put an end to their fear. Two places were prepared for his visit, one in the provincial hotel and one in the fortified army quarters. But almost everyone advised him to stay under canvas as a precaution. Atatürk insisted on sleeping in the hotel.

The first time I saw Atatürk was in Erzurum, and my one and only conversation with him was in the Erzurum high school. The man met by all the citizens of Erzurum two days before at the Kars gateway dropped the persona of the 'usual official presence' as soon as he reached the school and came and mingled with us.

He was calm, dignified, attentive and took an interest in everything. He had assigned that day to meeting the staff of the Erzurum high school and its students, and anyone else he might meet there. He would keep his word whatever happened. He could not stay to dine but agreed to drink afternoon tea. He was expected to leave in half an hour. He stayed with us for three and a half hours.

He had a very relaxed way of listening to what was said to him. At the same time he could put a strange distance between himself and the other, which did not come from his rank or from his actions, but from Mustafa Kemal himself.

Atatürk was a man who could make his presence felt in every situation. In his looks, gestures, hand movements, in his body language and in the lines of his face, there was total dynamism. It surrounded him with a kind of silent tremor. A few moments of conversation could reveal how this modest relaxed man, this pedagogue, could pass in a moment from one extreme to another, interrupting the most relaxed and amusing chat to make an important decision, a decision of genius, and then return to the same point where he left off. At its best we might call it dynamism ready for action, quick and agile as a warship under steam.

In the Erzurum high school, while I answered the questions he put to me in the whitewashed staffroom with its single broken canopy, my mind was certainly fully occupied with him. Ever since the time of Anafarta to the victory of Dumlupinar, until the declaration of the Republic, our lives were drawn into the orbit of his destiny and willpower.

Undoubtedly some of these thoughts were on my mind the day I spoke with him; Heine or Gautier tells the story of a young poet's visit to Goethe. The poor young man was so overcome by the thought of suddenly appearing before the god of Weimar that he forgot all the phrases of love and admiration he had been preparing for days on his journey and could only talk of the beauty of the plums he'd seen along the way. If I hadn't been faced with explicit questions that required instant answers, I would have been in the same boat as the young poet.

First he asked who I was, what work I'd done, how long I'd been in Erzurum, where I'd studied, who my teachers were. Then he suddenly turned to the closing down of the medrese colleges and wanted to know my opinion of their influence on the people. Taking a deep breath, I found my voice and replied that the medrese were just surviving. They had no particular function in the life of the people. In my opinion, their abolition would not result in any strong reaction.

Atatürk raised an eyebrow and repeated, as though thinking aloud, 'Yes, they were just surviving, just surviving,' then, 'but you never know – don't be too sure!'

He would certainly have continued but Rauf Bey, Rize's deputy, entered and recalled him to protocol. I wonder if Atatürk was in the habit of repeating certain phrases over and over?

Doctor Tarık Temel, who took the last X-ray of Atatürk before he died, asked him to take a seat to take the X-ray.

When Atatürk sat in his usual way the doctor said, 'No, my dear sir, I wanted you to sit like riding a horse.' 'Like riding a horse … riding a horse …' he muttered, taking up the position most suitable for the filming. I wonder what the hero of Anafarta and Dumlupınar was thinking about when he repeated these simple words.

I saw Atatürk several times, in Konya, Ankara and Istanbul. And thanks to the courtesy he showed that day I kissed his hand on several occasions. But I never had the opportunity to speak to him again.

The story *Erzurumlu Tahsin* ('Tahsin of Erzurum') from *Abdullah Efendinin Rüyaları* ('The Dreams of Abdullah Efendi')[13] is, in some ways, the story of the Erzurum earthquake. The appearance of the city at that time was the same as I have described in my story. Moreover, in this story I have invented nothing. Even my first meeting with Tahsin Efendi happened exactly as I have described it. I met him, as in the story, on the second or third night of the quake, and he had the effect on me of a kind of genius of the troubled earth. He spoke with me exactly as I have described. Long before I thought of writing the story, that strange man united in my imagination with the idea of nature as disordered and hostile.

But there is a point in the story that I have forgotten to relate. In the days following our first encounter I saw Tahsin Efendi once more. At that time I had it in mind to complete the 'Epic of the Deer', sections of which I had known from my childhood and which everyone in Erzurum knew and loved. One day, I heard that a saz poet who knew the epic was possibly arriving from Hasankale, and I was directed to a popular coffee house opposite the market place in a hollow beside a bridge. The next night, I went with my dear friend Fuad − now departed − in a blizzard which drove us into corners and reduced us to atoms, spinning us around where we stood. But the poet had gone to Erzincan and was not coming back. Instead, by the 5-candlepower light of an oil lamp, a hodja who read the Turkish like a memorial service was reciting the tale of Battal Gazi. His old, worn

book and the sooty lamp stood on a little wooden chair full
of drips from the candle on the coffee house bench, and
the man was reading the story, swaying interminably on his
knees before this reading desk. With his broken spectacles –
I am still amazed at how he kept them balanced on his big
nose – his beard of dirty yellow cut to a sharp greying point,
his thin face and wretched garments, rather than a human
being he seemed to be the sum of several incomprehensible
principles which had begun as social laws and which had
entered the biological order through time. A heterogeneous
crowd had gathered around him, listening to him with an
unusual attention, a gleam in their faces and particularly in
their eyes. In the half-light of the coffee house, the first thing
that struck one was this attention. It was difficult to imagine
anything more pitiful and at the same time so beautiful. On
these neglected faces eaten away by war and burdened with
heredity were expressions like some in the cruel frescoes
of Goya which later I grew to know and like; expressions
which shifted to caricature and satire. If you looked carefully at their faces you could tell that these men whose eyes
gleamed with fever and misery, revealed in the feeble lamp-
light, had discovered their greatest need to feed on dreams
and wonders. And these wonders sprang from the little
wooden seat, like a tree that spreads and covers all about it.

Then Tahsin Efendi did what we hadn't thought of doing.
Suddenly the door opened and he entered with wind and
blizzard, half-naked, his chest and below the waist covered
with a sack; then as the hodja stammered through the tale of
Battal Gazi, he placed a handful of money he had collected
from some other coffee house and departed.

V

The year I went to Erzurum the tentmaker still brought children the good news that now, at the end of spring, it was time
to leave for the Boğaz (the Gorge), and Ilica, and the upland
pastures; or knocking loudly on doors he announced the

arrival of winter months and wild snowstorms. But the city that was preparing for the two seasons, so different from one another in those parts, was no longer the city of old. Strange to tell, no traces remained as proof of such a city; a series of deaths and migrations had replaced lives of vitality and animation.

It was certainly possible to find the former city in its stories but very hard to recover the warmth of life from a few scattered memories. The city's great architectural works were of no help here. Most of them had long ago cut off their links with the life which buzzed around them. Only the *Çifte Minare* ('The Twin Minarets'), used in Erzurum in the time of Murad IV as a factory for cannons, remained as a work of architecture. Undoubtedly, 'The Twin Minarets' is a masterpiece, along with its siblings in Sivas and elsewhere. In its style, the sculpting of the stonework, the monumental appearance, is one of the finest works of its kind. First seen, at whatever hour of the day, appearing at one end of Erzurum, dominating half of the city with its minarets and splendid gateway, it is impossible not to admire it. The minaret of the Yakutiye medrese is similar as it gleams in the light like a jewel just dug up from the earth, never failing to fascinate the imagination.

From the point of view of structure, the interior of the Yakutiye is the most interesting architecural work in Eastern Anatolia. Ulu Cami, made on a simpler plan, reminds us of North African mosques with their five-arched interiors. From outside it is plain like them. An early gothic arch confronts us in Ulu Cami with an architectural feature worth noting. But those buildings are geographically so remote from our culture that it is impossible to make any connection between them and life as we know it. Architecture is not an art, like music or poetry or painting, that puts us in immediate con-tact with life. The sense of difference lies in its abstract qual-ities which soothe our sensuality without recalling anything in particular. These works belong to their own historical era. Between the construction of Erzurum's works of architecture and the ever-changing soft outlines of Bursa, İznik, Edirne and Istanbul, with their buildings that resembled great birds ready to take off from every hill they clung to, or living statues rising from the earth, a whole era of purification and synthesis had elapsed.

By comparison, there are leaders like Alparslan and Kılıç Arslan, whom we recognize as empire builders from their strong harsh faces, and princes like Murad II,[14] who left the top of his tombstone slightly open to allow a little daylight to filter through to his bones, or Selim the Grim[15] who murdered his brothers, then wept for them: 'Our wretchedness must touch their hearts.' In the first instance, there is a simple grandeur and power; in the second, a taste for life at the height of its maturity, rich with a wealth of associations and meanings.

The foundations were laid in the era when the first invading forces swept into Anatolia from the east, in successive raids whose victorious forces subdued the new country city by city. The early Selçuk works that were the result hold a very special place in our civilization.

In the chaotic period when everything turned into a confusion of customs, common law, religious beliefs and legends, when the birth of a civilization with very particular laws embraced all life like a fever, the mosques, religious schools and inns of Ahlat, Erzurum, Sivas, Kayseri and Konya all sounded the first notes of a newly formed composition, creating the major theme of a symphony that included the various elements of a new world. In the middle of the cities, they had entered in the wake of their armies, they erected certain shapes and forms, colourful minarets and graceful gateways, all brought from our ancestral home; like our swords and our language, life around them began to change; a new soul, a new order, had taken possession of the land and held it in the powerful embrace of a lion's paw.

My excitement as I wandered about Ulu Cami prevented me from even noticing the strong smell of leather which filled the building, used at the time as a military storehouse. I thought of the heads that had touched the stones I was walking on, of their destiny and of the greatness of the project for which they wore themselves out.

One of destiny's strangest aspects is that we do not know where today's decision may lead us. Bâkî's father was a poor muezzin in Fatih mosque; did he know that his son would master the Turkish language and become the immortal sovereign of words? Did Nedim's[16] mother know that her son would laugh like a spring breeze in the Turkish climate and that wherever he passed, the song of the nightingale would never cease, that every word he uttered would blush like a flourishing Judas tree in a corner of eternity? The young warriors fighting on the plains of Manzikert certainly never dreamt that the curves of their swords in the air and the horizon that resounded with their horses' hoofbeats all bore within them the seeds of Sinan, Hayreddin, İtrî and Dede. Destiny had sent them to this plain to perfect a side of the human spirit, to realize one of creation's dreams. They were under orders from the creative soul; they obeyed her.

Ottoman architecture in Erzurum is represented by the Lala Pasha Mosque. But the mosque does not overlook the city from Lala Pasha's burial place. It can only be seen from close by and is more like a small-scale clay model for a bigger statue. In short, to find the vitality and spirituality that almost penetrates the skin of the onlooker when he sees Süleymaniye and the Yeni Cami, one must be prepared for effort and exhaustion and, indeed, to desire it. It was only on my third visit to Erzurum that I was able to appreciate the beauty that was like a little diamond. One evening as I was passing, those wonderful proportions, one of the miracles of the sixteenth century, suddenly caught my attention.

And it is not possible to mention here all the arts of Erzurum, that ancient centre. But I cannot ignore the source of calligraphy in Erzurum that began with the inscriptions of the religious schools and mausoleums of the Saltuk era and continued for centuries. Thanks to the Erzurum Halkevi which has now made available a small collection of calligraphy, we know the names of some of the masters. The oldest calligrapher whose name has come down to us from the Ottoman period is Dervish Ali, who lived about the year 1080. Yusuf

Fehmi, Tahtacızade and his son-in-law Ası Efendi, Topçuoğlu Ahmed Efendi, Nâmık Efendizade and Asım Bey are all from more recent times. There were also gilders and bookbinders like Kadızade Mehmed Şerif and Kâmil Efendi, his student.

VI

During my stay in Erzurum, I experienced its music – which we might describe as local – as a personal adventure. But it was only when I came upon it again years later that I was able to understand what a burden of pain it carried. Of course, we cannot hope to find the intensity of mature art in those popular melodies, compared, for example, with the works of Tellâlzade or Tabî Mustafa Efendi, Sadullah Ağa, Seyyid Nuh or, above all, of Dede Efendi,[17] a genius who explored every aspect of the nation's sensibilities. But it is precisely for that reason that they belong to their creators who have given us the earth, the climate, the life, the people, their destiny and their sorrows. Once they have taken root in our memories, they inevitably penetrate our being like a miraculous vegetable growth. They emanate fevers that seize a man. Certainly these airs, rather than classical works, are linked to tradition. The nomadic fast *semaî*[18] that passes through various composers, changes all the time, while it is impossible to imagine the *hoyrat* or the *mayce* changing. This goblet, fashioned through centuries, will give its own particular flavour to whatever is poured into it and will always remain the same. And so its bouquet can be considered a sort of 'style' natural to its locality alone.

We cannot claim that all these songs and tunes belong to Erzurum. Some originated there. In some there is a curious flavour, often a result of a proximity to Azerbaijan and the Caucasus, a morbid sensitivity that is always found in cross-cultures. Some common tunes come from the Bingöl region and bear traces of the airs played by the shepherds' pipes as they take their sheep to graze. They begin with notes like the call of shepherds to one another from the lonely mountains.

Others, like the Yemen folk song that I will mention later, are in the dialect of Harput. Some have come from Istanbul and have reached Erzurum by the caravan route through Zigana and Kop, or by way of Samsun, Sivas and Erzincan, collecting en route a number of characteristics. The music of some is local, but the words are from elsewhere. Where the music comes from other parts but the measure has changed or is more emphatic, it has become localized, the property of the pastures and mountains. But they all reflect Erzurum like an enchanted mirror and give us a sudden taste of exile and nostalgia. Among them we can number 'The Song of the Alpine Meadows' as one of the best:

> Summer's come, I want to climb to the high pastures
> To be victim to your earth and rocks,
> Cruel destiny has added poison to my food
> Where, my master, can I find a way to the meadows?

What hopeless state of exile gave rise to this strange, powerful cry of distress? Stifled in some airless dungeon did the soul suddenly find a space and air of freedom? Where did it find a meadow, fresh milk, a herd of sheep, the fragrance of wild flowers, wave after wave of mountain winds? An exile's longing for home has rarely flown such a generous flag. As the voice rises and swoops like an eagle, it draws our soul with it. What poor man found himself in Sivas or Suşehir, having lost his dear ones on the way, and attained these heights through the power of memory alone?

Now let us sing 'The Song of the Yemen'.

> The band plays, do you think for a wedding?
> The snow-white flag, do you think it's the bride?
> The one gone to the Yemen, do you think he'll
>   come back?

> Come back, my friend, come back, I can't bear it,
> Sleep came unaware, I can't wake up,

I can't believe my friend is dead . . .
I sent my friend to the land of Yemen.

Two pistols slung from his waist
Should a young bride be separated like this?

(Chorus)

It's night, candles shine before me,
Separation is the world's way,
I dream of him by night, by day,

(Chorus)

The sheep is here, her lamb has no name.
The milkpans in a row, but have no milk.
Without my friend this place has no flavour.

(Chorus)

The three lines at the beginning are also in the 'Song of the Warriors' (*Ey Gaziler*). But the chorus is of local origin. 'The Song of the Yemen' and similar folk songs tell the inside story of Anatolia.

While the Bulgarian revolutionary members were trying to disrupt the unity of the country by carrying petitions in their pockets to present to Abdülaziz the sultan, and by ambushes laid in the Balkan mountains, the Anatolian women were weeping for their men who would never return, snatched from their homes as 'reserve soldiers'. But, for some reason, our sorrows are condemned to secrecy. They live only in some folksongs heard by chance. Perhaps they will be lost again when today's generation are gone. The Yemen represents the smallest part of the sufferings undergone by Anatolia. And there are even more painful things: the grief of those who remained behind while the poor fellows who left their own region, hoping to add a few coppers to what they scraped from the unprofitable earth, were swallowed up in the streets of Istanbul. Cries of 'Come back, my man, come back!' tell real stories of this land's inhabitants and expose the true face of the poverty and conditions in which they lived. A couplet from one of them may strike the imagination of a good storyteller and become the epic of a whole life:

I built a nest of mud and straw,
But I had no nestling to help fly away.

Of all the folk songs my favourite was *Billur Piyale* ('The Crystal Wineglass'):

At the tender hour tall as the cypress
Come with your swaying walk to the jasmine garden,
No one has ever seen, my dear one,
A beauty like you in the rose garden.
Honour me, lovely fountain, with your presence!
Oh night of solitude, be good to me,
You have a place in my heart, what need of ceremony?
You are a rose, don't tangle with thistles,
Like the nightingale I'll call from every thorny thicket,
'Don't come here, don't perch on the thistle.'
However much I warn, it's useless.
Welcome, my princess!
Wineglass of crystal, have you come for me?

From beginning to end, this little poem consists of a thousand delicate touches of taste, of fineness and purity. A crystal wineglass indeed. It has a frosted quality that improves its flavour and a tendency to crack, perhaps because it was made in the final throes of a great tradition. It has the style and air of a miniature copy that might have come from the hand of Bahzad.[19] The lovely quality of the little crystal glass is its melody from which springs a whole view of life and time, thought and pleasure. You may come on this folksong also in Central Anatolia and guess it was sung in the time of the travelling guilds. But I am certain that in Erzurum I'll never again hear the voice of Hâfiz Faruk, interpreting the local flavour which makes the song even stronger.

'The Crystal Wineglass' introduces us to the music of the middle classes which may be defined as the 'classical music of the provinces'. But before passing on to works that bore clearer characteristics of this kind of music, I want to mention two songs. One is *Sarı Gelin* ('The Golden-Haired Bride') which has the same dance-rhythm as 'The Crystal Wineglass'. I have always admired its lively energy as it begins with the notes of the Erzurum march. The other is a piece we know as 'Song of the Stars'. In it the human voice rises and falls with the gleaming stars, with the feeling of destiny that imbues everything in this region and with a fear reminiscent of old frightening superstitions. Towards its conclusion, colours of all kinds surround you like the light of a magical dawn, and you watch the dream of life through a crystal prism. There is no great sorrow in this song, although the planet Venus appears with the features of a harsh god and with bitter words. Rather, it is more like a half-prayer, half–folk song, like the strange things a child mutters when he sees the moon from his window. That is why, perhaps, we are carried to the heart of the mystery.

The best example of Erzurum's provincial classic songs is the curious melody composed by the late Hacı Hâfiz Hâmid. From a poem originating from Kami, an Erzurum poet, there suddenly sprang a symmetrical flourish of golden notes. We should also note several songs which came from mixed Eastern Anatolian sources, like the faultless 'Water Song' composed by İbrahim Hakkı,[20] one of Erzurum's great citizens. In his 'Book of the Talents', he describes Erzurum as 'my perfect and honourable city'.

Water bewildered in the valley
Fights with every rock
When it meets the sea
It's like an agile tiger.

When it reaches its basin
it eagerly attacks
sometimes it sings the songs of Rum
sometimes it plays the dances of the Franks

These verses are reminiscent of those old seals from a mystic world inscribed with quartz or agate and strong as the following five-line poem:

> The curtain suddenly opens
> In an unexpected place
> A remedy cures the ill
> The Lord – see what he does
> Whatever he does is good.

Faruk Kabli, whose early death we so much regret, was the last heir of the two musical traditions which continued in Erzurum till recently. This fine man lived so close to music that his gentle countenance grew to resemble a melody that had just taken flight in the Hüseyn[21] mode. Now, when occasionally I come across a folk song on the radio from his repertoire, I remember with a special yearning the days in the summer of 1924 when I first heard it. One of his songs was a hymn of the Celveti[22] brotherhood composed by İsmail Hakkı of Bursa, an unforgettable piece, both for its melody and its lyric.

Adjutant Major Ali Rıza Bey, who lived in Erzurum before the years of the Great War, would have been indebted to Faruk Kaleli for his future fame, if his repertoire had been completely transferred to recordings and films. This exuberant character, whose voice was so powerful when he sang at the hot springs of Hasankale that it almost lifted the dome from its roof, deserves to have a place in the history of religious poetry. The song, written on variations by the poet Faiz, includes the line

> Safety, repose, a meal, are enough

and the incantation that begins with

> Oh heart, if you want to drink from the glass of communion
> Drink this drink, oh drink, drink from this glass.

is one of the unforgettable pieces.

When I think, after so many years, of the times spent listening to these songs, I finally understand the place of music in the life of a community:

The one eternal remainder under the vault of heaven
is a lovely melody

For the cup of music holds what is poured into it till the end of time.

VII

My third visit to Erzurum took place during the last years of World War II. The journey in a sleeping car is certainly a very comfortable affair. But in a strange way it sets us apart from our environment: it almost destroys the meaning of travelling in the old sense of the word. You arrive like a projectile at your destination only with what you have brought with you, having had no chance to make contact with anything else. You get in the train at some station, either glad or sad, and get down yawning at another. Between your books and your daily concerns you might just catch a glimpse of a few landscapes. The real travel experience now is undoubtedly to be found in the third-class compartment. Just as real life is to be sought among the people, it is there, in the broadest sense, that real contact exists.

In the middle of people who enter the train, descend, come and go, weep and suffer, is the one who may have come near the feeling of the han and the caravan, and touched on the significance of the old way of travelling. These 'hans' and caravans, they created the magic of journeys of the past, to join a caravan, to pass the night in a han, to get to know other travellers for a night and separate next morning, to know one has added something to one's life. The old tales from 'One Thousand and One Nights' to 'Gil Blas' are full of such meetings which made travelling so rich an experience.

Travelling today, apart from the exceptional opportunities afforded by the last war, represents just a journalist's quest, either good or bad, in one place.

On my third visit, I discovered that Erzurum had stabilized and improved. Its wounds had stopped bleeding. Time, the great healer, had passed over it. Human life required the draught of forgetfulness as much as food. On the threshold of its new life, Erzurum remembered the old as memories from another world. There were tremendous differences between the modern newly built cement buildings and the old city now reduced to dust, crumbling away bit by bit under the fierce summer sun. But what gave me food for thought and made me really happy were areas where production was strong. The city was still waiting for the time when economic life would be restored, but in the meantime, the rich life-giving earth had rebuilt the villages. It was impossible not to be aware of this in the upland villages, in Cinis where we went that first night, in the garments of the keen-eyed Daphan peasants whom we met strolling through the Erzurum marketplace with their long hair and beards, their black heavy coats, their gigantic stature.

We were unable to find the gentlemen who drove to Aşkale in times past or their carriages with rubber wheels. Like the rose gardens cultivated with loving hard work, they too were lost. Now, their children lived according to the same rules of work as the peasants, even if they never reached the same degree of comfort. But they all made their living from the land, joined in the daily tasks, saddled up horses to the carriages, loaded the sacks, gave thought to times of water for the mill and when to plant potatoes and complained of the lack of harvesters and of the credit system installed by the agricultural bank. But what I found most important was the way the earth responded to those who worked with her.

The descendants of the former gentry of Cinis, returning to the land of their fathers after years of exile, began work with only a sack of bulgur for food and a pair of oxen which they had obtained from Kars. But the earth smiled on them.

Ten years later, both crops and herds were restored to the village. I would like to mention Mutahhar Bey's share in the success when he distributed abandoned property to the landless village peasants. I was his guest in Cinis. You could hardly find a more likeable man. He lived for farming and hardly knew the meaning of tiredness. After 14 years of struggle to establish Cinis, he suffered a raid in which he again lost his harvest and animals, and everything he possessed, even carpets and clothes. The village I saw at that time had five houses that owned radios and was actually just 10 years old. Apart from the set of silver cups in which Naci Bey presented us with sweet drinks, there was nothing left to inherit except the wealth of the past, which remained only in the memories of the old. But the village was happy and at peace.

Two thousand animals were grazing on the slopes of Germeşevi where we ate a midday meal. I noticed about 15 oxen chewing the cud as they clustered around a little spring; they were like dignified Olympian gods standing dreamily in their perfect silence. Every now and then a tremor shook their big bodies, and extending their muscular necks, they chased off a fly with a swerve of the head, then their wet dark chins moved back to their proper place; the same daydream hung in liquid threads from their jaws.

The village was restored, had regained its traditions and its folksongs. That same evening until midnight, we saw the old world come to life before our very eyes as we left Gemeşevi by the light of oil lamps. Anatolia, unsubdued by its experiences, learned a lesson instead. My four days as a guest were as useful to me as a complete library.

I must mention two inhabitants of Cinis; one is a young girl of 12 or 13, sitting regally at her threshing sledge like Semiramis in her carriage drawn by lions. Her chestnut hair among the golden gleam of straw that shone about her as it flew by and caressed her face, seemed darker. Her dark little face was like an antique medallion newly dug from the earth. Her pure regular profile was swimming in an air created by her awareness of her beauty and dignity. She stood upright on her sledge and looked at no one, her torn garments clinging to her shapely body in the wind, revealing the curves and promise of womanly beauty to come a few years later. The next day, we met her again on the road, no smaller although she had descended from her sledge. She passed close to us and went off on the little path through the melon fields with the same dignity.

The second character was the old farmer we spoke with over Mutahharr's garden wall. He was a tall, robust old man, 80 years old, with a shaggy beard and thick eyebrows. He was still as healthy as an earth god. Leaning on his walking stick, he spoke to us with courtesy and dignity. The respect he showed Mutahharr, with whom he worked as a partner, included us as his friends, but it was impossible not to sense his awareness that his ties with the earth brought him nearer to God. He was not just a human being but more like an aged plane tree. Occasionally, he would pick up a handful of straw and rub it between his palms and, as though praying, blow on it. I watched all his movements; he seemed to be praying to the nourishing forces of nature. The day of our departure we saw him again working in the same place with his son and grandchildren. We thought he resembled a happy Biblical patriarch in the bosom of his family. Those two people of Cinis struck me as triumphant, divine results of the purification of a man through close contact with the soil.

I left Cinis full of the thoughts provoked in me by those two people, one waiting on the threshold of death, the other just entering the door of life. In a world full of the skeleton clatter of the war years, in the midst of a sweeping conflagration, they seemed to teach me a lesson in real humanity, in a new world how happy people are when they work! When the impetus of creation takes over, how beautifully smoothly this death machine operates! Then, when a man's whole existence changes with happiness, everything is delightful and life-enhancing; there is nothing more satisfying than earning his bread by the sweat of his brow! He who works transfers to the universe the harmony that reigns in his being. Harmony must be a rule of life. Though everything changes, we find the balance we seek. We have great problems today, but none will be solved by bloodshed. Human souls will continue to suffer until they arrive at their own truths.

On the little train that travelled daily between Erzincan and Erzurum – it just shows how 20 years have passed that I think of its existence – my mind was preoccupied with thoughts of all the men and women, peasants and townsmen who entered the train for different reasons, a soldier on leave, a child in search of a cure, a workman, a wedding guest. We stood and watched the fertile plain. Every now and then a pelican rose from beside Karasu and, making a wide curve in the air, glided away across the plain.

I can't get rid of the images of the old man and the young girl from Cinis. I ask myself, 'If you don't find any support to lean on in life what use is strength or any kind of a lever? This point of support, it can only be the aspiration of a human being for goodness and beauty? We must try for a world which will make these qualities a supreme ideal in life. Turkey is in the best position to succeed in this. We are still at the start of a journey. We have a vast free country and our nation has great potential. We must encourage a great well-planned industrial life to develop. The Republic has achieved much in 20 years and if you think of the circumstances it could not have been done better. A handful of literate men, the remainder of the seven battlefronts, began to work. Now there are plenty of both learned men and technicians any-where in the land. Now that we see reality more clearly and at closer quarters we can overcome life's difficulties. We must plan for this vision.'

In the middle of these thoughts we arrived at İlica. That evening I was unable to think either of Murad IV or of Mustafa Paşa, the zurna player, whom Evliya Çelebi talks about as having taken possession of the hot springs so full of histor-ical memories long before us. Even the thought of an Evliya Çelebi character newly emerging from the bath, swaddled in towels, holding a huge cup of coffee and joking with friends around him, failed to captivate me.

A mass of people boarded the train. All their faces bore traces of the open air and hot spring water. The faces of chldren were fresh as fruits. The train slowly approached the city. Like a great bird swooping on its prey, the upland night seized everything in its embrace. In spite of the great crowd of people about me I became deeply depressed, a very small mummified figure lost in countless perceptions, and descended into deep dark waters and was swept away with them.

VIII

Erzurum surveys the history of Turkey from a height of 1,945 metres. And this height must always be kept in mind when we contemplate the city's story. It is one of the first great centres conquered by our forefathers when they entered their new country through the gap opened up by their victory at Manzikert.

At the second turning point of our history, it is again in Erzurum that the earliest foundation of the National Struggle was laid. It was from this eagle's nest that the first wish to live a life of freedom and independence, despite everything, took wing. Atatürk began his work in Erzurum and like previous conquerors marched from there to the Anatolian interior. From there, we once more reconquered our country in the name of our nation's historical rights.

Between the two events comes the history of two empires and within them a mass of events both bitter and sweet, also a communal soul, a national pride, a certain view of life, a sensibility and an understanding of the arts; in other words, it is we, with our faces of yesterday and today, who are here. Which is why, as I wandered round the Erzurum fortress, I seemed to see so much more than what was directly before me. I was looking at the country from its roof.

It was a very beautiful day. At first we strolled freely round the mosques, stopping to talk with friends on the way and visiting every shop that was open. I imagined I was back 20 years ago at school in Erzurum, teaching literature.

Eventually we climbed up to the fortress. From the old Selçuk Tower, also called the 'flat' minaret because its top flew off, we began to watch the epic town whose women and children had run to shelter in the trenches in February 1916 to ensure the army's withdrawal. Before us, a peerless panorama rippled with crops that were just beginning to turn yellow. In the east and south-east directions where the bare mountains ended, the steppe began, with its little villages, wooded streams and endless space. More distant were the mountains that perhaps revealed the secret of the bitter melancholy in our people's soul, the source of Anatolia's poetry and its sense of yearning. There we passed a great part of the day. Then where the city met the plain, we entered the building near the municipal garden that was the new primary school. I found it hard to understand the use of cement when Erzurum stone still stood there. Cement offers many solutions, but sometimes they are incompatible with the architecture and especially with the local colour. Erzurum stone, like that of Ankara, has many uses. It is a material that adds a monumental grandeur wherever it appears.

The primary school is attractive and comfortable and unlike any building I saw 20 years ago. We drank tea on the terrace overhanging the steppe stretching below, a peerless sunset before us. In a cloudless level sky, the sun was about to sink between the mountains of Balkaya and Kop that now seemed to be part of the plain, wider and flattened. The sky was not flushed with red nor did the colour of the sunlight change; there was no sign of sunset except a slight trace of gold. Any change was on the plain.

At first, the lower slopes of the mountains were divided from the steppe by a streak like silver armour. Then where the light fell, it turned to metal, covering the whole plain like water pouring from a burst reservoir, erasing the colour of the crops and earth. Before our eyes a lake of pure light appeared. The plain gleamed as though completely turned to crystal, and the mountains swam and floated on a polished surface. As the sun was nearly sinking, little clouds of dust flew up here and there from the plain and began to move like golden sails on this lake. It was not a sunset that we saw but music from a legend, composed of several tones of a single colour. But the sun was sinking so calmly and peacefully that our attention was attracted more by our ears than our vision. We all experienced something very deep and mysterious, like hearing a prayer uttered by nature in its own tongue. Then over this crystal mirror, darker rivers of light began to overflow, and, finally, just as the sun was about to disappear between the two mountains, a final ray of light reached us. Earth shivered deep within. The plain gradually passed through the colours of pure silver to melted gold, then to the darkness of the evening hours.

We left Erzurum that night. At the hour we set out to catch the train on 3 July 1919, the city was celebrating its victory of 30 August.

Notes

1 Kerem – Aşık Kerem – the hero of a popular sixteenth-century love story, 'Kerem and Aslı'. Some believe he was not legendary but was one of the wandering poet-musicians, an 'aşık', who wrote more than 100 poems.

2 1828 defeat – The battle lost by the Turks against the Russians in and around Erzurum, the Turkish bastion against inroads from the east.

3 1876 – In conflict with the Ottoman Empire, Russian forces advanced towards Erzurum.

4 Mehmet Raşid Efendi – Official chronicler of the Ottoman court. He wrote the history of the empire from 1660 to 1722.

5 Yahya Kemal Beyatlı (1884–1958) – The greatest Turkish classical poet of the twentieth century, to whom Tanpınar dedicated this book.

6 The Tanzimat reforms of 1839 – These reforms pronounced that the old ways had failed to fit the empire for the modern age and issued new legal, financial and military measures of administrative change.

7 Mehmed Arif (1845–1897) – A high-ranking Ottoman bureaucrat whose book 'What Happened to Us' gives a convincing account of the Russian-Turkish war of 1877. It was not published until 1903.

8 Battal Gazi – Legendary hero who fought the Byzantines in the first half of the eighth century. The epic of his heroic deeds circulated especially in Eastern Anatolia.

9 Manzikert – The battle of Manzikert between the Byzantine emperor and the forces of Alp Arslan in 1071 is considered to be a major turning point in Turkish history and opened the way into Anatolia for the Selçuks.

10 İshak Çelebi (1493–1537) – Ottoman poet. He also wrote a history of Selim I's victories and a treatise on the sciences.

11 CUP – In 1894, a number of underground factions united against Abdülhamid under the name 'Committee of Union and Progress', popularly known as 'The Young Turks'.

12 İzzet Molla – Ottoman poet of the nineteenth century, frequently exiled for his political faux pas. He died in Sivas from a poisoned cup of coffee.

13 'Abdullah Efendinin Rüyaları' – Stories of Erzurum and its characters by Ahmet Hamdi Tanpınar.

14 Murad II (1402–1451) – The sixth Ottoman sultan who, after two difficult reigns, rebuilt the empire, pushing his forces to the borders of Hungary.

15 Selim I (The Grim) (1470–1520) – Succeeded Bayezid II. His reign extended Ottoman power east and south.

16 Nedim (1681–1730) – Ahmed III became his patron and Nedim became the voice of the 'Tulip Age'. He tried to free divan poetry from some of its conventions by using the language of his own time. His poetry was lyrical, upbeat and concerned with his contemporary environment.

17 İsmail Dede Efendi (1778–1848) – The best known of the Ottoman composers named by Tanpınar from the eighteenth and nineteenth centuries.

18 semaî – A rhythmic pattern of three beats used by minstrels in folk music.

19 Bahzad – A Persian miniaturist. His work was so highly valued that many copies were made.

20 İbrahim Hakkı (1703–1780) – Poet, mystic and man of science. His *Marifatname* ('The Book of Talents') deals with mathematics, geography, astronomy and medicine.

21 Hüseyni – A simple melody.

22 Celveti – One of the mystic and ascetic religious orders. Two of its principal centres were the Hudaî centre of Üsküdar near Istanbul and the İsmail Hakkı centre in Bursa.

3
Konya

I

Konya is a true child of the steppe with which it shares a mysterious secret beauty. The steppe enjoys giving the impression of a mirage, and from whatever direction you approach Konya, the mirage is always there throughout the chequered landscape, always remaining on the horizon like a dream, like a play of light. This dream, with its cool shadows and fountains, smiles at your thirst from a distance, then at every curve of the road it is erased and lost, only to reappear grown wide and spacious until you eventually find yourself in the city of the Selçuk sultans.

Hidden from the outside world, Konya jealously guards its secrets within. Happy to live robust in spirit and independent, it resembles an inhabitant of central Anatolia rich in inner qualities but with no external show. To track it down, you must know the right time and season. Only then will you experience the secret murmur of the waters of Çarbağ that flow from its springs, the melancholy of the popular airs and the physical exhaustion that comes from taking part in the dances, and feel the dream of greatness in the Selçuk monuments behind their richly wrought gates, like women of the old days who lurk inside their embroidered veiled garments. Konya either seizes you like a fever, carrying you off to its own world, or you remain immune to it, a stranger always. To savour the vines of Meram,[1] you must be steeped in local life. Like the Mevlevi dervishes,[2] Konya demands a kind of initiation into its secrets.

After the preliminary steps, the city will gradually give you all it can for now and eventually reveal its past. Like a beautiful woman who knows how to love, she wants to make you a gift of her childhood and youth that took place far from you. From the intermittent free-roaming memories she narrates, you will see how the woman, whose beauty and maturity you now admire, was once a charming child, a little later a bashful girl, then a woman in the first throes of her love affairs but still without experience, and now you will love her as a very different creature for the qualities she had in times you never knew, her fascination, her charm, her strangeness, her fears and alarms, her torments. Similarly, when you linger nostalgically before Konya, recognizing its past and its power, you will love it even more with its new identity, and you will scarcely believe in your good fortune that it all belongs to you.

Since you were unable to place the adventures you read about in your school books in any framework, a different crowd of people came to life in the world of your imagination, wandering there like rootless shades with their weapons and victorious armies and sad fates. A crowd of names of sovereigns and viziers press about you like heavy, old swords, their hilts and scabbards rich with jewels, the steel inscribed with verses from the Koran or couplets from the *Şehnâme*, Selçuk names plucked like precious stones from the Koran, the *Şehnâme* and the *Oğuz*[3] epics. All the splendour and pomp of Moslem Asia is contained in these names, many of them titles and nicknames bestowed by the caliph, crowning them with reminiscences of their native lands and of battles they had won, and clothing them as it were in rich kaftans laden with pearls and in fine armour encrusted with gold and silver.

We tell ourselves, 'Here in this city men have lived who, within two centuries and in the middle of ill-omened events that sometimes overturned the course of destiny, yet managed to conquer this country, secure the birth of a new nation and a new language, in spite of hatreds, calamities and passions that made every historical event a blind struggle.

'In the disastrous years when Byzantine raids and expeditions by the Crusaders threatened total destruction, Kiliç Arslan I[4] took his lightning passage through Anatolia and made Konya his capital. Perhaps at the very spot where I am standing he stood and reflected and made hard decisions. It was to this city he returned after the dubious outcome of the little-known victory at.

'When the army of the Third Crusade seized Kiliç Arslan II's[5] capital, he negotiated for peace with the legendary commander Frederick Barbarossa in the inner citadel we now call Alâeddin's Mount. On account of a disagreement with his sons, the sultan was unable to keep his promise to the Crusaders whose army of a hundred thousand, already reduced to half by hunger and low morale, subsequently set fire to the city before they departed, to be completely decimated on the Taurus slopes. From the hill, in a summer house of which not even a single stone of its ruins remains, the sultan watched their retreat.

'When Gıyaseddin Keyhüsrev[6] realized he could not withstand the forces of his older brother, Rükneddin Süleyman, he entrusted his two sons to the people of Konya and fled the city. But he returned on news of his brother's death and the city vowed allegiance to him. Alâeddin Keykubad's life would have rotted away in the fortresses near Malatya if his elder brother, the cruel but ailing Izzeddin Keykâvus, as great a warrior as he, had not died of consumption. The city gave him a magnificent welcome on this very plain, with carriages bearing five hundred tents, carpets and precious materials unrolled on the ground. Women hung out of windows to watch the sultan's progress.

'It was here that this great sultan prepared all his tactics, his cleverly planned political moves and his important expeditions. Here he welcomed Celâleddin Harezmşah's ambassadors and rejected with proud and calm dignity Hülâgu's proposals that Anatolia should come under his domination. When finally his foolish weak-willed son, Keyhüsrev II, persuaded his ministers to poison him, his corpse was brought here to the city of Konya to be buried.' And so continue our endless reflections.

Now the great portrait gallery of Selçuk history unfolds before you. Alongside the sultans are a crowd of viziers, masters of ceremony, tasters, emirs and officers of the guard – Sadeddin Köpek, Seyfeddin Ayba, the emîr Mübarizeddin, Celâleddin Karatay; the last, a slave who was given his freedom and converted to Islam, rose to become a vizier, and in letters and edicts written to him by the sultans, he was addressed as 'God's saint in the world'. And there is Sahip Ata, a patient man, a ruler who knew how to protect himself in times of crisis, who enriched Anatolia as far as Sivas with a number of monuments and now lies in his own mosque in Konya. There is Sahip Şemseddin Isfahanî, who always refused honours when they were first proposed, got rid of his rivals by means of plots contrived by others and, finally, at the insistence of others, married Izzedin Keykavus's widow, thus becoming an Atabek or regent; he was always hypocritical, always a tear in his eye, a poet, calligrapher, musician, very learned, a writer, a man of taste. And then there is Muinüddin Pervane, a powerful warrior and great scholar, not loath to play three or four cards at once in the internal political intrigues of the Mongols and Egyptians, making and unmaking sovereigns, clad in all the virtues and decadence of an era in decline.

The image of Alâeddin Keykubad arises and stands out in the middle of this procession as one who combines all the features of Selçuk history and artistic pleasure. A strong, young warrior, happy harbinger, two centuries early, of Mehmed III[7] and Sultan Cem,[8] subtle politician, from time to time a poet and perhaps architect – he is thought to have drawn plans for the Konya fortress as well as for Kubadâbâd[9] and Kubadiye – devoutly religious, cruel at times, unbelievably impatient, but always a man of impeccable taste, forward-looking, the classic model of a complete civilization. At six years old, he had the right to ascend the throne, but escaped from Sultan Sencer's palace where he had lived as an imprisoned hostage. As head of a new state, inheriting a burden which might swallow a whole life, he continued the work of Kılıç Arslan I, who, in the midst of the violence of the Crusades, had begun to turn an invasion with unknown consequences into a form of liberation. Alâeddin Keykubad followed his policy with a thousand subtle and delicate poetic touches. Selçuk history had first looked for the ideal ruler in his father Gıyaseddin Keyhüsrev, then in his elder brother. But in Alâeddin it found the perfect fruition of its civilization. After him, his son would be but a pale shadow and history's search would pass only to viziers.

II

The history of the Anatolian Turks is caught between two fearful events. First, the Crusader expedition of 1097 which began as a reaction in the Christian world against the conquest of Anatolia by Sultan Süleyman, son of Kutulmuş. During the first expedition, the most dreadful of all, the new principality or 'beylik' not only lost Nicaea, its original capital, but also part of the land it had just captured. In fact, at first the Byzantine Empire even regained a kind of vigour and drove its forces once more into the Anatolian interior. Moreover, the impulse to settle, which had certainly begun around the major centres, naturally stopped. The long life and survival of nomadism, which has always played a major role in Anatolia's political and cultural history, is certainly the result of the Mongol incursions. But perhaps the First Crusade and the other expeditions which followed, including the Third Crusade of 1176, though not so great as the Mongol invasion, also played a part in its origins.

For two centuries, the harbours of Syrian ports became a perpetual battlefield that forced the caravan routes to change course; the Crusades had created a new form of economic life. With the capture of the harbours of Antalya and Alanya, the Selçuk principality was now open to the Mediterranean and, with the capture of Sinop and Samsun, to the Black Sea. Throughout the Crusades, it commanded all eastern trade.

The silk and spice routes were largely under its control. The fortress-like caravanserais you can still encounter at every step along the great old routes in today's Anatolia were once built to protect this trade. Anatolia was never as rich and prosperous as it was at this period. Luxuries and artworks nourished a whole feudal society and an aristocracy of bureaucrats. On the other hand, the crusading armies which trampled the Byzantine lands wherever they went in Rumelia finally took possession of the Byzantine Empire for a time, but far from restoring its old might to this Rome of the east, as was first hoped, only hastened its downfall and facilitated the growth of the first Turkish state in Anatolia and of the empire which was to follow.

The Mongol invasion was altogether different. A torrent from every corner of Asia swept before it all the tribes and peoples it had ejected from their homes and became a for-midable force. Seizing all it could and wrecking everything in its way, for more than a century this juggernaut continued to create havoc like those fierce ocean storms that keep turning on themselves.

With his shrewd political diplomacy, Alâeddin Keykubad succeeded in resisting the Mongol terror for a while. Between him and the Mongols, there was a short-lived state created by Celâleddin Harezmşah.[10] But it was not easy to deal with him or with the wild warrior tribes whose power he relied on. On Celâleddin's death, the Harezmşah state disappeared, and among the tribesmen, now left to their own devices, fierce confrontations arose.

The main force which fed the Babâîl revolt in 1241, a serious threat to the Selçuk state, was the Harezm tribe, no mean warriors, unwilling to accept authority, in search of a beylik for themselves and free pastures for their herds.

The Baha İshak[11] revolt was harshly overthrown with a force which completely suppressed any further growth of the Selçuk state. And immediately after, in the battle of Kösedağ[12] in 1243, badly conducted by the weak, incapable Keyhüsrev II, the rule of the Mongols in Anatolia began. It was the start of the era of interventions and of taxes that increased from year to year until, finally, a year after Mevlânâ's death in 1274, the real occupation took place.

Hence, sandwiched between two important events in its history, the new empire had only one and a half centuries in which to put its affairs in order, establish political unity and become the actual owner of its territory. Despite difficulties arising from its structure, in this brief time the Selçuk state dealt with these issues successfully.

In fact, a great part of the Turkish population was still at a more or less tribal stage. On the frontiers, some tribes were almost independent, always ready to interfere in the affairs of the state and make its life difficult. On the other hand, the great feudal lords, inheritors of earlier centuries of conquest, tried to share power with the sultanate. Once they were abolished, the era of disputes began. As there was no single agreed law of succession in the Selçuk system, the Selçuks either divided the state among members of their family or else in a general assembly chose one of their line as ruler. Struggles for possession of the throne were interminable. Even a great leader and monarch like Kılıç Arslan II was subjected towards the end of his life, and at the hands of his elder son, to the condition of a slave. Then he took refuge with his younger son Gıyaseddin Keyhüsrev and shared the throne with him. This harsh custom of succession continued until Alâeddin Keykubad's era, the most peaceful period of Selçuk sovereignty. When you think that this monarch, who gave his era a great name, was poisoned by his own son at a public banquet and that the emirs and viziers who participated in this incredible crime had been nurtured by him and had been his brothers in arms for 18 years, you can see the epic achievements of the Selçuks from a totally different point of view.

In fact, these commanders, emirs and viziers lost no opportunity to lay hands on power, and it was only when a rapacious ruler came to the throne that, through fear of death or from personal interests, they submitted to the bit.

After the battle of Kösedağ, the era of the Pervanis began, an era of shadowy young figures, of children who would never come of age, of viziers, emirs and regents nominated and confirmed by the İlhanid rulers, whose authority had more weight than even the sultan's, an era of incessant intrigues, internal strife, tribal discontents and rebellions resulting from ties to two separate centres of authority. Greedy, ambitious princes subjected the state to external interventions. Some sought sovereignty from the Mongols; others rose to power with the help of the Byzantines. But this chaos seems almost normal if we consider the medieval allegiances of subjects to princes and the ties between the ruling families.

With its endless intrigues, rebellions, treasons and deaths by poison, dagger and bowstring – it was customary for princes of the ruling family to be strangled with their own bowstring – with the personal politics of aristocrats rapidly replacing one another as they fell from favour and of viziers, many of them great scholars, Anatolia lived through something like the end of the Middle Ages. The rough and sensual Keykubad II was poisoned at a banquet by his tutor on an expedition against the Golden Horde. Kılıç Arslan IV was strangled at a feast – undoubtedly with the approval of the Mongols – by Muinüddin Pervane, who had put him on the throne in the first place. The perpetrator of this treacherous deed was the vizier Muinüddin Pervane, conqueror for the second time of the Sinop fortress and who made great efforts to withstand the results of the Mongol occupation. For a time, this vizier, himself later murdered by the Mongols in 1297, seemed to be the real ruler of Anatolia. The last words between the vizier and his prince are recorded in one of the most horrific pages of the chronicler Aksarayî.[13]

In fact, the last to enter the palace of the Mongols or the last to return is always a little more powerful when he leaves and for some months, if not years, has acquired the right to dominate others. On their part, it is the policy of the Byzantines, and the custom of the time, never to send back empty-handed anyone soliciting their help.

This is a period in which every movement, unjust or not, even the best-intentioned, gave birth to the most frightful results. Tax after crushing tax descended on the Anatolian people, particularly on the settled landowners cultivating their fields. Grabbing loot was the natural daily activity. Debts incurred in the Mongol palaces by princes and ministers, who went to the Mongol headquarters in search of powerful positions, increased several times over and, according to agreements, had to be paid by Anatolia.

Amid this chaos, a kind of mysticism flourished – anarchy itself. Anatolia had always been drawn to Sufism[14] and had never been fully satisfied with Sunni Islam, the state's official religion. Now, the Alevî[15] beliefs increased as well as the dervish paths of the Melâmî, the Kalender and Hayderî sects, which integrated beliefs and relics of Shamanism with the Moslem religion. Belief in the Mahdî,[16] so dangerous to the world of Islam and so threatening to its political stability, took root at this period.

This secret dervish spiritual condition that was to give birth to a duality that has continued in Anatolia until now has played both positive and negative roles at different periods of our national life.

But it is better to listen to the words of İbn-i Bîbî describing the condition of Anatolia at the time: 'The land of Rum has remained in a state of chaos. In this beautiful country which once sheltered the poor and gave a home to strangers, there have been so many troubles and afflictions it is no longer possible to breathe in peace.'

So wrote İbn-i Bîbî on the death of Alâeddin Keykubad.

Nevertheless, a desire for a powerful state and ties to the dynastic family had begun to take shape. A corpus of elite army commanders, emirs, lawyers and great scholars did their best to preserve the authority of the state and resist foreign interference; some came from illustrious local families and Moslem theologians, others from Moslem countries including Arabia, and particularly Syria; some had fled the Mongols independently and had taken refuge with the Harezm tribe, or were brought to power much later by the Mongols to work for them and become loyal subjects; and from far and wide, viziers were swimming in their gold and jewels, the spoils of war. These last were sensitive artists composing poems and quatrains in answer to the great Iranian poets and Sufi mystics who wrote tearful poems in Persian mourning their own sorrows and the sorrows of their country.

III

What was Konya like? How did it come to be known as a capital city just at a time when a new nation was taking shape in a country of such harsh conditions? What were its ideas? We don't know. Certainly in the beginning, the influence of the absolute rule of the feudal system and the aristocratic viziers and then the Mongol interventions which adopted the same apparatus, more and more from the middle of the thirteenth century (1243), gave Konya very little opportunity for its voice to be heard. The ethnic face of the city is almost unknown to us. But we guess that in Konya, as in some other medieval Anatolian cities, alongside a large section of original Turkish people were numerous other communities of Georgian, Byzantine, Syrian, Egyptian, Iraqi and Algerian and Latin merchants, Harezmi mercenaries from Constantinople, the debris of the Crusades and members of local tribes. The class of ulema and sheikhs was equally diverse. If we consult the register of names come down to us from the chroniclers İbn-i Bîbî, Aksarayî and Eflaki,[17] we discover a bizarre mosaic. All of Central Asia was there, and a little also in the Mediterranean regions.

Undoubtedly, customs, traditions and manners of dress were influenced by this diversity. We mentioned above a number of holy men throughout the empire who were not in agreement with the Sunni faith, or who only assumed its outer forms, which certainly gave life in Konya a varied aspect. The medieval Moslem custom of growing long hair in beards, moustaches and eyebrows, or of cutting them off altogether, modelled the human face, making it a kind of mask that belonged to a trade or a religious belief. Clothes and headgear also varied. Non-Moslems wore the garments of their people. The marketplaces and narrow alleys of old Konya overflowed with a colourful diverse crowd. But from the time of Alâeddin Keykubad, the main accent outside the ruling class was an 'ahî' style of dress. Despite a few minor reactions, life was tolerant and open to discussion. Every eccentricity was excused on the grounds that it had a flavour of Sufism.

As for the palace, it was in constant contact with Constantinople and the Latins on the Mediterranean coast and in the south and also with the İznik dynasty. The Selçuk sultans, who took Byzantine brides and sheltered in their palaces in times of trouble, were noted for their breadth of outlook in many matters. It is said that even little chapels were provided in the palace for some of the Christian princesses.

But there were plenty of internal disputes in this great Islamic centre. The Sunni faith conflicted with the beliefs of the Shii and the Sufis, Islam with Christianity, the culture of the people with Moslem culture, the Turkish language with Persian. Of course, the Sunni ulema kept a careful eye on the palace, on the Sufi elements and on the possibility of subversion in the various trades and professions.

The court and the ruling class had become so penetrated by Iranian culture that relations with the hinterland and the tribes were difficult. In this thirteenth century, all the Asian elite had come together in Anatolia, driven by the Mongol occupation, including those who had fled but failed to reach Egypt or Syria or the west, and those who were reluctant to change their environment and culture. The official language and the language of poetry was Persian. It was the great Iranian poets who directed taste and wisdom. A little later in Anatolia, this culture was to reach its zenith in Mevlânâ.[18]

All the documents agree that the medieval city of Konya enjoyed great prosperity until the Mongol invasion, even to the end of the thirteenth century. It was not only trade that nourished its wealth but also its great arts and crafts.

What a pity that we have only the merest indications of the Konya market. Like all the markets in Anatolia at the time, the old Konya market was run by the ahî, an organization which dominated the Istanbul market even until the era of Süleyman the Magnificent. We know it was introduced to the Selçuk court by the caliph Nâsır himself, a move that perhaps originated and gained strength from his wish to give new blood to the Abbasids by adopting a mystic movement that had already been in existence for some time. İbn-i Bîbî relates that Alâeddin Keykubad believed that it was Sheikh Şehabeddin Sühreverdi, a great scholar closely connected with the history of the '*fütüwwa*', who had granted him his sultanate. He also narrated the dream of Keykubad the sovereign on the night when Emir Seyfeddin Ayba brought him news of his brother's death in the fortress of Kezirpert. After Alâeddin's accession to the throne, the sheikh brought him, on behalf of the caliph, the insignia of the *fütüwwa*, his baggy trousers and belt. Like the palace, the market and the craft workshops were also ahî.

In the chaotic period that followed the death of Gıyaseddin Keyhüsrev II, advice and help in all important matters was always sought from the ahî and the 'young' of Konya who were part of the government. Sahip Şemseddin Isfahanî appealed to the ahî when he wished to get rid of some of his rivals. When the Mongol army besieged Konya in 1291, we know that the governor of the city was an ahî named Ahmed Şah Kazzaz.

At this period, we guess that the people of Konya, whether local Moslems and Turks, refugees or guests, as in all medieval cities, were divided by disputes of class and lived in their own way among themselves. But we can guess also that under the pressure of events, a kind of public opinion was beginning to take shape. Perhaps for this reason and from fear of the partisans of feudalism, the Selçuk sultans preferred to settle some of their internal problems in Sivas and Kayseri rather than in Konya. Even a ruler like Alâeddin Keykubad with all his resolution, when the old emirs abused their influence by thinking they had the right to share power with him because they had helped him to the throne, preferred to execute them in Kayseri.

But a capital city is always the capital. However much it is intimidated to remain silent, it still speaks. After the death of Kılıç Arslan, Konya, which had witnessed so many raids by him, certainly did not remain indifferent to the fierce struggle that broke out among his 11 sons, whom it claimed and regarded as 11 branches of the sultan's tree. Her heart suffered like a mother's. Konya was besieged for months for the sake of Gıyaseddin Keyhüsrev, and when he could no longer withstand the forces of his elder brother Rükneddin, she certainly could not look on coolly when he went into exile with two of his sons. For a long time, Konya followed closely the story of these princes at the Byzantine court as well as the victories of his elder brother, and she was there when little Kiliç Arslan was crowned and when Gıyaseddin returned from exile with his two sons. Later, she saw and grieved for Kiliç Arslan imprisoned in a castle, waiting for death. But when the armies were ready for combat and their banners were ready to fly, things changed. I would have loved to share in Konya's rejoicing on the victorious day when Antalya and Sinop were taken. And the day that Alâeddin Keykubad's splendid array entered the city, what a magnificent spectacle it must have been.

But what sorrow the city must have felt when the sultan's body, poisoned by his son or the followers he had nurtured, was brought there as a corpse. How profoundly it must have been moved to see what a great change had taken place in its lifetime, to know that it would never see the old days again and that a mechanism capable of such a fearful crime would one day drag the city to disaster, destroy its empire, kill its commerce and ruin the market.

Like every Eastern capital, Konya sometimes saw all these events as a distant spectator of its own destiny, only to see even worse tragedies in the future, and wept like a Greek chorus, or sometimes rejoiced. And from time to time, when she realized she was in trouble, she took up arms. This is undoubtedly the meaning of sentences we came across in İbn-i Bîbî and Aksarayî such as 'The people of Konya loved their prince'.

IV

Even in the middle of raids, wars and internal disturbances, it is strange to find that under the Selçuks, great building projects were undertaken. From early in the eleventh century until the end of the thirteenth century, or, if we consider the style until the end of the fourteenth century, opportunities were certainly provided by the feudal society and its aristocracy of viziers to collect wealth, and thanks to economic growth, hundreds of mosques, tombs, religious schools, hospitals, hospices, inns and caravanserai were built.

The great spacious caravanserai that suddenly appear before you today with the magic of the Arabian Nights, from the solitude of the steppes, illuminating, in so many different ways, towns like Konya, Aksaray, Ermenek and Niğde or Divrik, Kayseri, Ürgüp and Sivas, Ahlat (victim of the Harezm raids), Erzurum and Sinop, and the fortresses of Antalya, Alâiye and in the towns of Eastern Anatolia, were all built in these three centuries, astounding us with their complex histories.

It is impossible to describe in detail the workshops, or all the qualities of the architecture that acquired new characteristics as it changed in the hands of a master architect, or of its philanthropic founder, or through the nature of the materials used, the wealth or lack of stone, or the technique of tiling – elements surviving from tribal or local traditions, from climate to climate, beylik to beylik, city to city. Those who wish to know more can consult the great work of M. Gabriel, the tireless researcher of Anatolian monuments.

Selçuk architecture was at its peak in the era of Alâeddin. As well as the Keykubad palace in Kayseri and Kubadâbâd near Beyşehir, and the pavilions at Alâiye, he rebuilt the inner fortress of Konya. Today we know it as Alâeddin's Mount. Unfortunately, all that remains of the buildings constructed by the ruler, who was himself an architect, is only the name and a few ruins. The great Sultan Han, which I would so like to see completely restored, is from his era.

In constructing a roof, architects hesitated between the arch and the dome. Except for some wonderful works that seem to have been born complete with their own style, we surely cannot consider that this architecture, which is sometimes content with very simple rules for the interior of its buildings, solved all its problems. But, undeniably, there is a wealth of research stretching from Andalusian forms to the gothic, which, in the monuments of Ahlat,[19] stretches all the way to styles from ancient Iran and the Caucasus.

The façade of their buildings reached the highest peak of Selçuk architecture and possibly resulted from the narrow streets of medieval cities. Architecture took as a model the tent which still played an important part in popular life. Builders, growing more ambitious, tried every possible mode of carving and working stone on the façade of their buildings. An examination of the rhythm of the great doors, and the fountains and walls on either side of them, shows how the Selçuk masters' taste for detail competed with the idea of mass. Often, Selçuk architecture seems to wish to imitate the sculpture, which religion forbids. In the façades of their buildings, it is endlessly searching for effects. From every artistic school, little medallions, suns, stars, corniches, water channels, pendants casting light and shade to play above the door, jutting corners like lanterns on either side of the entrance, bouquets of flowers, garlands and arabesque panels often leave little space for any inscription on the façade and reduce the search for it to a game. The very artistic calligraphy called 'the Selçuk Kufic script' with its shapely hieratic lines – or 'forms' – give the façade the appearance of a tribal kilim or of woven designs on cloth, and sometimes if the proportions are big, they become a bas-relief. Other times, peerless workings on stone evoke, rather than a sculpture, a kilim or shawl woven like a book, or the page of a medieval manuscript.

The façade of the Ince Minareli (the Slender Minaret) made by the orders of Sahip Ata is like a huge sultan's tent woven from fine mohair.

For decor, it has simply verses from two chapters of the Koran (the sura 'Yasin' and the sura of Victory) which interweave exactly over the door in an exquisitely made knot. The doorway, almost unique of its kind, frames the modest entry as though it wishes to express the wretchedness of the human condition before the greatness of the word of God. In the period when the Sultan Han caravanserai and the Karatay Medrese were built, we suddenly witness a change, which may denote a new religious sensitivity, compared with the façade of the hospital in Sivas and the Çifte Minare (the mosque with two minarets) in Erzurum. Inside, the wide-vaulted recesses and the walls are adorned with glazed bricks and enamel tiles. In the brick constructions, as in the minarets, the exterior was decorated with coloured tiles. The true tone of the jewel-like Selçuk tile was a mixture of deep emerald green and very dark blue. From windows crafted like a cage made from a single block of stone, light was skilfully directed, filtering through coloured glass and falling on the walls in an orgy of colour. The ambitious, proud and pious viziers who had these buildings constructed, but who swam in blood, wished to have everything about them in the finest, most artistic taste. None of the palaces of the sultan and his ministers as they once existed are intact, and if it were not for the writings of Aksarayî, we would never know of the oppression and tax burdens imposed by the Mongols, or that the villas of rich merchants and landowners were built with the same fastidious artistry and taste as the religious schools and mosques.

The ornamentation of the Sırçalı Medrese (1242), that elegant octagonal building built of glazed bricks like woven straw, and the tiled ceiling of the Karatay Medrese (1245) that gleams like a little Milky Way with hundreds of suns and stars are all that remain to us of that artistry. Walking among the sketchy traces of ancient Konya (like an archaeologist) we can only imagine an unrecognizable Konya. When we think that only

150 years ago the royal villas on Alâeddin's Mount still existed, we can understand the real significance of the decline of an empire and the civilization that underpinned it.

V

Mevlânâ and his father came to Konya in 1228, during the reign of Keykubad, the year when the Sultan Han was built near Konya. A little later, the fortress of Konya was repaired as well as the forts of the frontier towns and the residences of Kubadiye in Kayseri, and of Kubadâbad in Beyşehir. In addition to the ruins of the summer house on Alâeddin's Mount, whose last surviving remnants have disappeared before our very eyes, the mosque which was his and which he had repaired, or perhaps altered in 1227, and the tomb of the Selçuk sultans, there still remain today the three great masterpieces of Selçuk art: the Sırçalı Mescit, the Karatay Medrese and the Ince Minareli. In Mevlânâ's lifetime, he witnessed the sad fait accompli of the Mongol occupation, the ill-omened period after Gıyaseddin Keyhüsrev's reign, when all the sultans who came to the throne were children and the Atabey viziers took over the reins of power as regents. It was in these years that Mevlânâ's *Mesnevi* and the collection of his poems, *Divan-ı Kebîr* ('Great Divan'), appeared.

Without further ado, we can safely say that their simultaneous appearance meant that Konya was searching for its own identity through its architecture and its soul. The Selçuk renaissance was like spring pushing up green shoots under timeless oppressive blizzards.

According to Eflâkî, when the Karatay Religious College was complete, Mevlânâ and Şems[20] attended a meeting of the ulema at the college. He even participated there in one of those naïve disputes of the Middle Ages. When Mevlânâ was asked, 'Where is the most important seat of honour?' he answered, 'For the one who loves, it is in the embrace of the lover,' and he rose from his seat and went to the door where Şems had, immediately on entering, squatted on his heels, and sat by him.

Şems did not like crowds much and did not want to be seen in the forefront. Eflâkî says that from that day, the fame of Şems began. If you consider that the Karatay Medrese was finished in 1245, the truth of this tale becomes dubious; or perhaps the one in question is Salâhaddin Çelebi, whom Mevlânâ chose as his friend after Şems.

When Alâeddin's funeral was held in Konya in 1237, Mevlânâ was 29 or, according to my friend Abdülbâki Gölpınarlı, 33 or 34 years old. He was 38 in the year of Baha İshak's revolt, 40 in the battle of Kösedağ. The arrival of Şems in Konya occurred between the two fateful events.

After Şems's first residence in Konya and his escape to Damascus, Mevlânâ said to Sultan Valed, his son, 'Why do you sleep, Bahaeddin? Get up and look for your sheikh!' His words were like a flash of lightning illuminating a dark night. *Get up and look for your sheikh, find the truth and yourself!* Did Mevlânâ know that his insistence on Şems's return would lead to his death? A great friendship jeopardized by the East's metaphorical turn of speech, and a terrible drama.

Who was Şems? What was he like? Where did his wise words come from? What else did he teach Mevlânâ as well as his philosophy of the unity of existence that spread everywhere at the time? All sources agree that his arrival in Konya began it all. Until then, Mevlânâ, famous as a teacher and scholar, in spite of an interest in Sufism which was very natural at the time, had lived in the world of forms. After meeting Şems, he became deeply involved in mystic meditation, taking part in the dervish dance and in poetry but living beyond the worlds of forms and appearances. Konya was filled not just with the exuberance of the dance but with a new soul.

How I would like to know more about the man who is seen as the sole cause of all these events than what comes to us from the one work left on him, the *Makalat* – it is sad that we are reduced to knowing and seeing this holy man who suddenly emerged from the darkness of the period only through the collection of legends or in the light of his Divan, this travelling dervish who rejected the world with a single stroke of the pen, accepting no argument, even as he clashed (give or take a few differences) with a man like Muhiddin Arabi, regarded as the most revered in his own world.

But the legends in their dervish simplicity tell us nothing today about the manners and customs of their lives. We, the tired offspring of two civilizations, do not wish to dwell on their pivotal words and the problems they address; we move on. As for the 'Great Divan' (*Divan-i Kebir*), it is impossible in its dazzling light to see things as they were. Mevlânâ does not talk of Şems but of Love.

How often I have thought of him, Şems, in the daydreams and thoughtful hours I passed inside the courtyard of Mevlânâ's tomb in Konya or in the dervish convent of Sadreddin Konevi, and wondered about the role played in the story by tale or truth. Was this man truly so influential? Was it from him that everything came to Mevlânâ, one of the greatest poets of the East? After Mevlânâ met Şems, did he become a shaman-like character overflowing with inspiration as he danced the dervish dance? And what was said about the death of Şems? Was the blood of this beloved master shed by Mevlânâ's son, by some of his fellow citizens or by his disciples?

Certainly his personality had a magnetic quality. And perhaps Mevlânâ and Şems in face-to-face communion with each other said much that differed from the reports in the hagiography. Perhaps he never spoke at all (in one of his stories, Eflâki has Şems himself say that he would not speak in public). His mere presence, his looks and his silence impressed everyone around him. To begin with his name, Şems of Tabriz – at that time the name which means 'sun' was fashionable but, in his own case, had a special significance – everything was mysterious and enigmatic, including his death. For us, everything turned his countenance from the essence of darkness into a mysterious illumination. The collection of legends report a phrase of Salâhaddin Çelebi, who influenced Mevlânâ after Şems's death, almost as deeply as Şems himself:

'I am the mirror of the lord Mevlânâ. He sees his own greatness in me.' This is the sentence that may best explain the relationship between Şems and Mevlânâ.

Mevlânâ is a poet. Although he rejected poetry as of no importance, he remains one of the greatest poets of the Orient. Just as we find in Dante, the Middle Ages of the West with its horror of suffering, its sense of social order or disorder, its yearning for compassion, its thirst for justice, all the wisdom of the Islamic East, its ecstasies and passion for union with God, are contained in Mevlânâ's 'Great Divan'. Ancient Asia's longing for eternity cannot accept the laws of human destiny. A philosophy of union must not be an escape from life – as it is for many, even the greatest – only in losing itself in divine love does it find life and humanity.

Mevlânâ's world is a world in motion in which everything revolves round God, who is the creator of love and light; it aspires to him, is lost in him, is born from him and divided from him, then is reunited with him and with everything else. All things long to be one, to respond to each other. There is no difference in this world of perpetual confusion between the killer and the victim, the lover and the beloved.

Undoubtedly for the world of Islam, all this was not new. Ever since Hallaç,[21] the Sufi way of life had become part of Islamic life and poetry. But Mevlânâ spoke in a different mode.

Even in the past when love was sacred and came from a different god, nobody had spoken of it like Mevlânâ. He spoke in a language of flame. The 'Great Divan' was like the burning fire into which Abraham was cast: seen from without, a consuming fire; seen from within, a rose-garden.

If you keep in mind when his poems were written, they are like the last prayer rising from a sinking ship. All existence is present in an all-encompassing sob that goes straight to God. Anatolia, destroyed by the bloodshed and hatred of its many conflicts of faith and custom, aspires to a prayer or invitation that echoes all loss. It runs, limping like a wounded animal to drink from this well, and is restored to life. For this is the voice of hope and forgiveness. I wonder if 'forgiveness' is the right word here. Mevlânâ considered that evil does not exist. He saw that the drama of evil lies within man himself and his destiny. He saw in the world only the possibilities of goodness and love.

> Come, whoever you are, come
> Whether you're non-believer or Jew or idolater, come
> Our convent is not a convent of no hope
> Even if you broke your promise to God a hundred
>   times, yet come.

Over Anatolia, whose inhabitants lived in caves and hollow tree trunks for fear of Mongol tax collectors, and in the famous famine 699 years after Mahomet found not a single blade of grass to chew, over Anatolia blighted by every kind of plague, the voice of Mevlânâ blew like a spring breeze. Crushed by so many calamities, men felt reborn as they listened.

The first response came from the yellow mud of the banks of Sakarya. The voice of Yunus Emre suddenly appeared like a lone flute in the great orchestra of sounds rich with the signs of spring and the hazy landscape. Certainly he was expressing the same thoughts and emotions as Mevlânâ. He too was a man who proclaimed Love but he had taken more from him than words. And his tune changed with his instrument. As the Turkish solo continued, the splendid orchestra coloured with Persian poetry gradually died away, as though to form a musical base which left only a few colourful notes to the voice which was taking its place.

Yunus Emre, who was Taptuk Emre's[22] disciple, did not have the richness of Mevlânâ. His poetry is dry as the stone of a fruit. This village dervish does not write his verses but carves his teeming thoughts on the rough bark of a tree. He is utterly himself, the earth which comes to life, surrounded by a community of the faithful. Although he has little knowledge of Oğuz Turkish with what confidence he proceeds, how clearly defined are his imaginings! One might suppose that in Yunus's poems, words are the essence of the thing itself.

One of the major differences that divide them is the place of death in their worlds. Yunus comes from the generation whose destiny is described by Celâleddin Rumi: '*Those who come after us will suffer much, but their children will have peace.*' In fact, Yunus grew up when the Mongol invasion was at its height. To find a vision of death like his or the great poet Seyyad Hamza's in his one poem, we must look to the mysticism which embraced northern painting in the sixteenth century like a black wave.

But Yunus is not defeated by death. He sings:

Why fear death –
Fear not you are eternal.

Every moment we are born anew
Who can get tired of us?

Perhaps to deny its reality in the end, he accounts for every turn of death's wheel. The tree of death in Yunus is the endless wheel of becoming. And, like Mevlânâ, he looks at man's inner being.

If I didn't declare my love
The agony of love would strangle me

What drives you mad
Is still in you, within.

If you consult his Divan, when he met Mevlânâ, he joined in the gathering and their whirling dance. And according to tradition, Mevlânâ read his *Mesnevî* to the dervish from Sakarya, who listened respectfully but at the end of the reading said,

'With respect, my Lord, it is beautiful, very beautiful, but a little long. In your place I would have cut it to just two lines:

Wrapped in flesh and bone
I appeared as Yunus.'

The couplet may or may not be by Yunus, but it is very fine. It is in true Bektashi[23] style, which loves to simplify a story. But Mevlânâ's philosophy of unity is not so brief. The *Mesnevi*, although it is long and didactic, is a book of many beauties. It is one of the most attractive books from the East, with its stories of animals, birds, viziers, peasants, merchants and folk tales. And Mevlânâ is one of the best storytellers in the world, so good that when I think of the Mesnevi, rather than imagining the book, I think of a building like Sainte-Chapelle, stained glass abounding in pictures of men and animals, part imaginary, part caricature, part the 'forbidden' realistic. The 18 couplets which head the work, their echoes scattered through the poem, illuminate this world of colour, or rather this purified East, its profound wisdom and its realism which is almost imaginary with the light of a yearning for unity.

Mevlânâ's philosophy of love and longing is concentrated in the 18 couplets, along with all his mystical teaching. Few other works are so laden with the future. Our sensibility's eternal longing for unity is symbolized in Mevlevi music by the music of the 'ney', from the hymns of İtri[24] to the works of Selim III and Dede.[25] When Mevlânâ wrote the 18 couplets and stuck them in his turban to read to his friends – for a poet is always a poet, however spiritual he is – he gave birth to a whole line of musicians and poets which came to a head in Şeyh Galib.[26] Yahya Kemal acknowledges his debt to him when he declares:

Like the celestial bodies in that divine night
We are the glorious interpreters born from the word
    'Listen!'

It was Sultan Veled[27] who essentially established the Mevlevi order as a way of religion. But its ritual protocol, refinements and training belong, like its music, to a later Ottoman period and to Istanbul, in particular. Undoubtedly, it represents the peak of our culture. It formed so much of our identity, from the delicacy and good manners that invisibly shaped us, the flower of a civilization, to the forms of our sensibility.

The Mevlevi religion does not allow excess either of humility or of esteem. It is an adventure that takes place among equals. And equality governs not only the religious order but the world beyond also. For to use an expression much favoured by contemporary philosophers, it concerns man's place in creation.

> You who are the quintessence of the world, look after
>   yourself
> You are human, the apple of Creation's eye.

Şeyh Galib's couplet is the perfect medium for the Mevlevi greeting. Man looks at man – he looks between the eyebrows, for that's where we must look – and sees God and honours him. Şems never explained his relationship with Mevlânâ so well and clearly as in this salutation.

It was in Konya on the Night of Power just before the closing down of the dervish convents that I watched the Mevlevi ceremony for the last time. There are few rituals that speak with such symbolism. There is meaning in every posture, every attitude, every movement, every step. Their way of wrapping themselves in their robe, their awakening at the first note of the ney (death and the Day of Judgement), the spread of the arms and their way of locking their feet (in the Mevlevi ceremony, every dervish becomes the sacred sword of Ali), everything is profound and significant. As for the *sema*, it is one of the most beautiful dances in the world. It masters the atmosphere of the sacred, a ballet that mirrors the mystery of creation. A pity that it was never painted by a Degas.

Before me, turning in the tremulous light of candles, men alter, glide and, almost separated from their material bodies, become true martyrs of love; their wide-open arms, their necks bent in acquiescence like purified souls, they rise to the heavens as they spin and spin.

The next morning in the market, I saw the men I'd witnessed the night before when they danced the sema now going about their business, and I was amazed to recognize one of my students in the lycée who had taken part. I imagined they had flown away before the harsh wind of the '*rast*'.[28] Even now I grieve that I could never join these men who knew the secret of resurrection after death and experience their ecstasy.

During my years in Konya, I was profoundly engaged by the poet Şeyh Galib, who had spent a year of his Mevlevi initiation in the Konya convent. A poem, which I imagine he wrote at the height of his art, describes all the symbols of the Mevlevi ceremony and the spiritual adventure of the Mevlevi order:

Someone drunk with love has come from the tavern
Another dazed and bewildered has come from sight
    of a flame
Some have come from a world of light like the sun
Others have returned to the land of unity
My eyes lit on a group all with conical caps
What grandeur! What majesty! What forms of
    blessedness!

They speak the language of silence their words like
    storm-tossed seas,
Lovers tell the secret of love without words
In the trance every breath tells of my sorrow's reason
It declares all the symbols of love without tongue or ear
My eyes lit on a group all with conical caps
What grandeur! What majesty! What forms of
    blessedness!

Angels envy the delicate Mevlevi modes
Angels have no tambourines or drums or reed flutes
The sun and moon and the starry sky are on their
    dance-floor
Above all in their midst are Rumi Mevlânâ himself
My eyes lit on a group all with conical caps

What grandeur! What majesty! What forms of
　blessedness!

Together they revolve in absolute unity and ecstasy
Everyone moves alone like the sun or among the many
At the centre of motion a point which is absence of self
They found a lover's union in the beginning and end
My eyes lit on a group all with conical caps
What grandeur! What majesty! What forms of
　blessedness!

Konya possesses yet another treasure which might not reach
the heights of Mevlânâ's music but has an equally profound
effect on us – its folklore, which we can consider a Selçuk
epic. It was in that city I learned to recognize the folk songs of
Central Anatolia, with their burden of exile, fate, weariness of
the flesh and the loads of pain and bitterness.

I used to sleep in a little room on the top floor of the old
Konya lycée. At any hour of the day, the melancholy songs
of prisoners from the nearby prison mingled with the voices
of children playing in the garden or with my work, sometimes coming from the wretched houses of ill-fame on the
other side. I loved especially to hear them in the hours when
the Takye Mountains flushed in the evening light. And also
towards morning when the noise of carts carrying fruit and
vegetables to the city woke me up. In the cold, leaden autumn
mornings, the songs would enter the dreams I had hardly left
behind and draw me with their torture and suffering like the
faces and bodies of dearly beloved women who had known
oppression and cruelty.

I first heard the songs of Central Anatolia in Konya at the
time of mobilization. It was at the end of summer in 1916.
We occupied one of the little houses behind Government
Square, whose walls of sun-dried brick were whitewashed
and whose wide porch received all the autumn sunlight.
There were very few young and middle-aged men left in
the city. One evening at the station where I'd gone for some

reason – why, at such a late hour, I don't know – I met a convoy transporting troops from one front to another. Under the smoky lamps in the baggage trucks, a crowd of pale, exhausted-looking young people were crammed together and were singing one of the mournful songs which burned like molten lead. No complaint could have been more dreadful. Actually when I came from Kerkük to Konya as a youngster of 14 or 15, I had seen so many tragedies behind the scenes as a result of war. But the real meaning of what I'd seen happen around me meant nothing to me until I met these poor people who were going open-eyed into a life of neglect and suffering and death, and who were pouring their impossible dreams and longings into the night of that station like a froth of blood. It was only when I heard their singing that I understood the silence of neighbouring houses, and why the women and children I met at every step had faces marked by grief but were even more beautiful in their epic loneliness. Yes, and it was only after I met them as I came down from my evening walk on Alâeddin's Mount that I understood how the dog howling so piteously in the dusk had suddenly hushed a whole town.

Among the women of the Konya prison, there was one whose face I'd never seen but whose voice I recognized. I used to wait for her voice in the evening hours. And I particularly longed for her song, 'My armful of roses in the vineyards of Gesi'. To hear this strange melody is like swallowing a handful of poison unaware.

Sometimes she sang the shameless dance tune that begins with 'The little dog stops anyone entering your bedroom'. I've never come across any other songs of ours that, by its rhythm and melody, comments so openly on carnal pleasures, as though composed by a saint under a curse who had spent his life in prayer and worship but one day committed a sin and, unable ever to forget it, failed to find his way back to Islam and passed his days in deep repentance. Through the burning sin rises the smell of scorched flesh as it tries to fly to places now inaccessible.

When I listened to these songs I was always reminded of the title of the splendid book written by Maurice Barrès on Spain, *Blood, Sensuality and Death*. How sad that when I visited the world of pleasure again, the magic had vanished – What laws govern the composition of a tune? Impossible ever to know.

Anyone who wants to write the Anatolian novel must surely start from these folk songs.

The songs I heard in Konya did not all originate from there. And the dances I watched in the city festivities or in the vineyards of Meram were not all from Konya. Although it's the real centre of Western Anatolian folk music, it is difficult today for an amateur like me to distinguish the voice of Konya. But I heard it in the Konya evenings on the slopes of Alâeddin's Mount and on the Meram roads. I heard the barefoot children whistling as they passed me as I stood admiring the stonework that formed such an artistic garland of the two verses of the Koran before the door of the Slender Minaret. Now when I hear folk songs on the radio, or from time to time hum to myself, memories mysteriously return and Konya suddenly springs to life again. I find myself walking those paths, sitting in the low-ceilinged cottages in the vineries or standing before the door of a mosque or medrese, while at night the starry sky above me changes suddenly and becomes the imperial black tent of Alâeddin I, inlaid with gold, embroidered with silver. In that city enamoured of music and dance, the scene of Selçuk epic and drama that gave birth to the *Mesnevi* and to the mystic odes of Mevlânâ, I relive the joys and sorrows that filled the days of my past and the hours of its people.

Notes

1. Meram – A fertile, well-watered area near Konya, remarkable for its delightful orchards and gardens.
2. Mevlevi dervishes – One of the four orders of dervishes. The 'Whirling Dervishes' was founded at Konya in the thirteenth century by Rûmî.
3. Oğuz – Originally a Turkish tribe that migrated westward from the region of the Altai Mountains to the east of the Caspian, where they

came under the influence of Islam, giving rise to the Selçuks who conquered Anatolia in the twelfth century AD.

4 Kılıç Arslan I – First of the Selçuk sultans. After he was defeated at İznik and driven back to the Anatolian plateau by the First Crusade, he made Konya the capital of the Selçuk centre.

5 Kılıç Arslan II – His reign (1155–1192) was marked by confrontations with the Crusaders, the Byzantines and with several powerful feudal lords of Anatolia.

6 Gıyaseddin Keyhüsrev I (1204–1211) – In 1207, he captured Antalya from the Venetians, opening up western commerce to the Selçuks. He was responsible for the building of several hans.

7 Mehmed III – Reigned from 1595 to 1603. Noted for his interest in the writings of mystics and his struggle with Iran.

8 Cem Sultan (1459–1495) – When Mehmed II died in 1481, Cem tried to seize the throne but was prevented by his brother. He fled to Rhodes, France and Italy, where he was held prisoner and died mysteriously, perhaps by poisoning.

9 Kubâdâbâd – Summer palace of the Selçuk rulers, near Lake Beyşehir.

10 Celaleddin Harezmşah (??–1231) – He fought against the Mongols across much of Asia, establishing a short-lived realm in Western Anatolia.

11 Baha İshak revolt – Dervish Baha İshak, a Turcoman preacher, in 1241 led a social, political, religious, anti-establishment movement that was finally ended by his hanging.

12 Battle of Kösedağ – At this battle in 1243, the Mongols defeated the Selçuks, which resulted in anarchy and in the widespread destruction of Anatolian cities.

13 Aksarayî – A thirteenth-century chronicler of the Selçuks.

14 Sufism – The Moslem spiritual quest to be united with God. It took the form of poverty and renunciation and its disciples were known by their mendicant habits of rough wool.

15 Alevi – A minor but widespread religious sect who, in Turkey, followed Ali, the Prophet's son-in-law.

16 Mahdî – A prophet who would come at the end of time to convert the world to Islam.

17 Eflakî (1290–1360) – Poet and mystic, one of the great names of Selçuk literature. His book on the Whirling Dervishes is an important source for the history of the Mevlevi.

18 Mevlânâ Celaleddin Rûmî (1207–1273) – The great Anatolian mystical poet who originated in Persia. In Konya, he became a disciple of the theologian and Sufi Veled. There, he created the order of the Whirling Dervishes. He wrote a long poem of 45,000 verses, a mystic epic consisting of stories, extracts from the Koran, prophecies and legends, as well as collections (Divan) of poems dedicated to Şems.

19 Ahlat – Originally an Armenian town near Lake Van. Seized by the Arabs, it remained Moslem in a Christian surrounding until it was taken by the Mongols.

20 Şems – A wandering dervish who arrived in Konya in 1244 and stayed with Mevlânâ for several months. After he left for Damascus, he was assassinated, it is suspected, by the followers of Rumî, who were jealous of the strong influence he had had over their master.

21 Hallaç (858–922) – A Moslem mystic accused of heresy and of creating miracles in public, and put to death in Baghdad.

22 Taptuk Emre – Yunus Emre mentions him several times in his poems as his master in wisdom.

23 Bektashi – Haci Bektash taught that the four gateways to religious knowledge were revealed to Adam by the Angel Gabriel. 'Hakikat (truth and reality) is my spiritual state'. 'Tarikat (The Way) is my actions'.

24 Itri (??–1711) – Musical composer to five sovereigns. Also poet and historian.

25 Dede – Head of the Mevlevi convent of Galata for 20 years. Best commentator of Rumî's 'Mesnevi'.

26 Şeyh Galib (1757–1799) – One of the great mystic poets and a member of the Mevlevi order. His best-known work is a Mesnevi of 4,000 rhymed couplets, named 'Beauty and Love'.

27 Sultan Veled – Rumî's eldest son, poet and founder of the Mevlevi order.

28 'Rast' – An oriental melody.

4
Bursa

I

Of all the cities I've ever known, I can't think of another which has inherited so much from a certain era as Bursa. The 130 years between the taking of Bursa and the conquest of Constantinople in 1453 not only created a city which was completely Turkish through and through but also established unalterably, and for ever, its spiritual aspect. Whatever changes, disasters, periods of neglect or stages of good fortune it underwent, it has always retained the atmosphere of that early period when it was founded. It speaks to us from there and communes with us in its poetry. As the era was essentially a miraculous period of heroic and spiritual deeds, Bursa can be described as possessing the purest touchstone of the Turkish soul. Evliya Çelebi understood this truth so profoundly that he described Bursa as 'a city that transcends the material'. Clearly, he was not only content with the city's visual impact but also realized its true nature, and parts of his writing on Bursa overflow with the emotions of popular love poetry.

Grand Vizier Keçeci Fuad Pasha,[1] who was almost never mistaken in his judgements, stamped the definitive seal on Bursa's past when he described it in another way as 'the *prologue* to Ottoman history'.

I have visited Bursa often, and the first step of every visit finds me inside a history which is like a legend. I lose almost all sense of time, and I am always overcome by the integrity of the lifestyles of our forefathers who, entering the city for the first time, recreated it as an entirely Turkish city. Fortune first smiled on them with their victory over Bursa and they loved it so much, embraced it so sincerely, that its stones and earth are still full of the bright traces of the exalted passion that gave it form. The feeling that the city belongs to a particular period is so powerful that one can imagine thinking, 'In Bursa there's also a second Time'. Alongside the time in which we live, laugh and enjoy ourselves, work and make love is another Time very different, much deeper, unrelated to the clock and the calendar: a creative and indivisible Time which, like an eternal season in this city's atmosphere, is regulated by art and history and a life lived with passion and faith. This Time, which belongs to things that often seem old-fashioned to us, and to beauties which, seen from without, we imagine are of no account in our daily lives, cannot compare with time as we know it, but it beats in the pulse of a city which is enclosed in its memories like a beautiful woman of another age who lives only in the past.

How often, returning to my hotel from a long idle stroll, have I imagined fearfully that in some unknown quarter, a fine membrane or a crystal dome will suddenly crack, and that a Time accumulated beneath, a Time which belongs to my memories and their surrounding landscape, a Time with a thousand and one characteristics that are not of today, will carry everything away like great waters bursting their dykes. I believe that anyone familiar with Bursa will share this illusion of mine; history has made its mark so deeply and powerfully on this city. It is present everywhere with its own rhythm, its own particular delight, and springs up before us at every step. Sometimes a tomb, a mosque, a traveller's inn, a tombstone, here an ancient plane tree, there a fountain, with a name or a view reminiscent of the past, and a light of past days shimmering above them permeates all with yearning and catches you by the throat. It enters your conversations and your business and informs your daydreams.

It is names that create the most amazing chance events. Is it because they have come from the great source that we call language, which summons our true spiritual self into being, that they enrich us with all the secrets of the magic around us? You can never forget these names once learned; like little friendly dreams, they find their way into your hours of solitude, they compel you to make friends with them, to force open mysterious caskets and get to know and enjoy their secrets. Willy-nilly you'll repeat them: 'Gümüşlü,[2] Muradiye,[3] Yeşil,[4] Nilüfer Hatun,[5] Geyikli Baba,[6] Emir Sultan,[7] Konuralp[8]' – Are they actually names of a certain neighbourhood or locality of the city, or are they the names of people who lived just like us at a certain time? All have special colours, special lights and the very nostalgic pleasures of regret and melancholy that belong to the past and are culled from that distant legendary country we call the past. They all draw us into long meditations on life and time and revolve in the mind like a little star, and with their golden reflections lengthening and shortening, they toss about miraculously complex architecture in the waters of memory.

Gümüşlü, for example, is the name of the old Byzantine monastery where Osman Bey is buried. Is it because I know the historical reality that whenever I hear these three syllables I see before my eyes an enchanted mirror held up to the dawn? Or is the gleam merely a result of the complex created by the syllables? What secret of the Turkish language is hidden here? How did the colours of dawn come to tinge the bluish white of the word *gümüş* (silver)? Undoubtedly, the conquerors of Bursa were able to entrust to one word only, like Gümüşlü, with its three syllables which resemble a dream of the future, the memory of the man who, for nearly half a century, paved the way for an exalted religious faith. The letters *ş* and *l* in Turkish always create the most beautiful harmonies. When we pronounce *yeşil* (green), we find the freshness of a meadow, mingled with the good news of spring at any hour of the day, like paint squeezed on a palette. This word has clearly come from our early ancestors and their nomadic spring pastures in Central Asia. But in Bursa, the meaning of 'green' is very different; it means the compassionate face of eternity, a transient hour of peace that comes as a reward. As soon as you mention the Green Tomb or the Green Mosque, death alters the face it wears in our imagination; it says, 'I am the silent immutable sibling of life. I hold out a garland of peace and repose for the brow of the transient mortal who has performed his appointed duty.'

II

While I was still a child in primary school, I would hear my father tell stories of Bursa, a city he loved, and in my imagination, they would merge with the names I came across in my history book. And suddenly, the page would come to life before my eyes; it would deepen and fill with light and colour. At the head of the list of names were Konuralp and Geyikli Baba. I had learned about the former at school and heard tales of the latter from my father who had visited his resting place. For me, Konuralp was always a hero at the centre of a great tumultuous battle, his stern, sunburned face dominating a crowded scene. I saw him on his black horse, racing like the wind, always chasing victory and fortune in a Holy War. For me, he was the legendary hero, surrounded by hoofbeats that poured like torrents through the night and by cries of victory, his banner waving over the screams of the wounded and the dying.

As for Geyikli Baba, he is one of the Khorasan warrior saints who turned the capture of Bursa into a great legend and made the birth of the new Turkish state seem like a new religion. Like the shepherds in the Gospels who came to visit the child Jesus in his cradle and piled gifts of treasure at his feet, some came from far within Asia, led not by a star but by their sheikhs, and some left behind not only their homeland but their throne and the crown to which they were born. They built hermit-cells around Bursa, still a Byzantine city, and besieged the city with their miracles and strength of soul, and then joined young Orhan's army bearing weapons so heavy that no one else could use them.

Among them were men like Hacı Bektaş who were an inspiration to Anatolia and Rumeli, and those like Karaca Ahmet,[9] whose names were given to a whole district of Üsküdar. But I knew nothing of them at the time, so I had no idea that Geyikli Baba had forced the gates of Bursa with a rock weighing 80 *okkas* (about 13 stone) in his hand and wearing only an animal hide. But at the sound of his name, I would see a strangely embroidered prayer mat spread before me and myself on the threshold of a story I had never heard. What lay behind it, what mystery unravelled, what secret was handed like a golden apple to the one who leapt over the threshold? This I never knew. Now at this lonely hour of night, cheered only by the sound of water by the road that goes to Çekirge from Muradiye, I think of them again as in my childhood: Who was this Geyikli Baba? What was he like? What did he teach these innocent believers who gathered around him? What mystery of life and soul did he reveal to them? What remains to us of his services? And who is Konuralp? Did he ever love? What sort of things pleased him? When he looked at the narcissus flowers opening every spring on the Bursa plain, or when he watched the sun sinking every evening over distant mountains, what did he think about? In short, who were all these heroes whose names recall for us those first steps taken in the newly conquered city?

The poetry and charm of names, strange and full of secrets, trailing our dreams behind them, sudden fountains in our mind that suddenly sing the story of times when 'dream and action walked hand in hand', they are the gold and silver and crystal caskets that take us back through time to the perfume we call the past. The artistic part of our spirit is surely fed by daydreams of them. One alone of these names fills Bursa with all the beauty of a spring season. It is Nilüfer (lotus), the white flower of victory and good fortune. With this woman who fell one day into the arms of the young Orhan, her beauty a prize for heroism, the smile of Love, in defiance of life, appeared on the stern features of the founding era. Unfortunately, we know little of her life and character; even İbn Battuta,[10] the Arab traveller who says that he met her, gives us only her name. But her name denotes also the flower of fortune like a frame which may contain illusions of happiness and love.

Nilüfer Hatun's is not the first woman's image to appear in the turmoil of the founding of a new state. Before her was Osman Bey's love for Mal Hatun, daughter of Sheikh Edebali. In fact, the Ottoman adventure begins with a love story.

Sheikh Edebali was a Moslem jurist from Karaman. Tradition relates that he hesitated a long time to give his daughter to Osman Bey but finally accepted him as his son-in-law when Osman described the famous dream he had the night when he was a guest in the Şeyh's house and they lay side by side on a bed on the floor. This was the dream: a crescent moon emerged from Şeyh Edebali's breast and, growing to a full moon, entered Osman's bosom. Then, from Osman's belly (and, according to some stories, between the two of them), a mighty tree grew up, from whose roots sprang the great rivers of the Tigris and Euphrates, the Nile and the Danube. Its branches sheltered three continents. So it was that Osman saw in his dream the whole victorious history of the Ottoman Empire.

As the historian von Hammer was the first to observe, this dream was exactly like the dreams of old ruling dynasties and replicated Jacob's dream in the Old Testament. But it is undeniable that Osman's marriage added a moral force to his gradually increasing strength of arms.

Perhaps, too, the marriage was an event that united the new principality and that hospitable organization that was so widespread at the time in Anatolia and in neighbouring parts of Syria. It is certainly a fact that Şeyh Edebali owned great possessions, including a hospice that welcomed itinerant travellers. If you recall some of the names of his relatives, you can guess that he belonged to an Ahî brotherhood. When İbn Battuta was travelling in Anatolia, he almost always met up with an Ahî and became his guest.

The fine hospice in İznik with its five-doored portico and well-proportioned dome is connected with the lady Nilüfer. With this hospice and the mosque of Murad Hüdavendigâr[11] at Çekirge, we leave behind the element of retreat in Selçuk architecture that includes too much colour and detail. The galleries over the mosque door and the twin windows separated by a single column are the first experiments in rhythm of a new architecture, as are the portico of the hospice and the plan of the dome.

Orhan's love for his wife and her great affection for their son Murad I has linked her name forever with the history of Bursa and İznik.

But it is not the only love story in this era of legends. It was the daughter of a Byzantine prince, in love with Abdurrahman Gazi, one of Orhan's relations, who opened the gates of Aydos citadel to the Turks. Actually, this period is itself legendary, with its dreams foretelling good news of the future, with its exploits of love and heroism and its stories of sainthood. And our first great poets are our chroniclers, like Aşık Paşazade, Neşrî[12] and Lütfi Pasha,[13] who tell these legends bit by bit in such pure and simple language.

The true centre of the legend is the saintly countenance of Orhan Gazi who, with his own hands, lit candles in the mosques he had had built and personally distributed to the poor and to strangers the first food he ordered to be cooked in the hospices. All this spiritual strength and morality flows from him. The starting point of an empire not only began with him but was strengthened by the addition of his profound mercy and compassion.

Von Hammer, who sometimes forgot the mission he had undertaken as historian of the Ottoman Empire, insisted that in the early stages, the Western world and Byzantium, with a little effort, could have saved the situation, but when he came to write of Orhan, he suddenly softened and his style altered as though he was describing a holy man. Indeed, in strength of arms and splendour, Osman equalled the Khorasan warriors. It is they who are the true continuation of Orhan, like much that belongs to that era.

But I preferred to imagine him in his own little hospice in Bursa or in his tumbledown mosque in the market. Some evenings, I pass by the little mosque or look through its door and see the hands that had forced open the gates of so many fortresses stretched out to light the candles, and my heart fills with happiness.

Murad I, Bayezid Yıldırım (The Thunderbolt), with a few different character traits; Mehmed I,[14] with so much intelligence and strength of will, who restored the empire after the 1402 disaster; and Murad II, who united simplicity with greatness, a first-class statesman and man of war, both poet and lover of the arts, are more or less like future reflections of Orhan. But why look only in princes for this continuation? For a century and a half, Orhan was the model for the whole empire.

In the century that followed its foundation, Bursa was like the old sultanas of story, forgotten by the men they had loved and helped in their great undertakings, growing old, wandering sad and alone through the rooms of an empty palace and watching in little silver hand mirrors their hair turning white. Who can tell how much Bursa grieved when Edirne was chosen as a wife equally loved, and how it wept when Istanbul was preferred? Right until the affair of Cem, every time the corpse of a dead sultan or murdered prince was brought to the city, the heart of this former beauty must have been wrung with grief again. 'They live far from me; it's only when they're dead that they return. It is my fate from now on to mourn for their deaths,' she said. Yes, as Muradiye spread with the increase of little tombs, Bursa realized she was remembered only on certain occasions.

Of the Bursa of that great era and the centuries that followed, almost nothing has remained, except a few major works of architecture, some tombs and mosques and part of a house said to be the birthplace of Fatih, though scholars hesitate to date it earlier than the eighteenth century. The fire of 1271, bemoaned by Keçeci Fuad Pasha as the 'prologue to Ottoman history which has been consumed', almost completely swept away the inner palace and all of Bursa. The mansions of the nobility and the treasures accumulated over five centuries of history were all lost. As for Bursa Palace itself, through indifference and neglect it was already a ruin at the beginning of last century. In his work on Bursa, the historian von Hammer concluded that the plans could easily be recovered from the remains. Today, the name of Gümüşlü evokes only memories for historians; Osman Gazi and Orhan Gazi lie in exile in the utterly soulless buildings erected in the pompous official style of the Tanzimat period and, by a fearful irony of fate, are marked by a novelty decoration of Sultan Aziz at their heads.

But every part of Bursa still sings with light, the sound of water fills it like a divine dream and, under its light, refugee children come from all parts of the empire, play among the musical waters like children of the era when it was founded. And perhaps little girls even now sing folk songs close to airs of that time, and the tiles of the Green Mosque rejoice with colours gathered from a fifteenth-century garden.

III

When Evliya Çelebi had described the fountains of Bursa at some length, he concluded by remarking, 'Bursa, in short, consists of nothing but water.' My beloved Evliya! By these words alone, your name and Bursa are linked forever in my memory. You head the list of those who have enjoyed the poetry of Bursa, and if we want to make you happy some day, we'll name one of Bursa's springs after you. Through its mouth, your soul, pure as a waterdrop, will tell us the story of this lovely city's adventures throughout time. Yes, Bursa *is* a city of water that recalls a surprising character who entered the history of Bursa in a rather unusual way. Kara Çelebizade Aziz Efendi,[15] the *sheikhülislâm*, or mufti, was a scholar with a strange soul who behaved with great inhumanity when İbrahim the Mad was deposed and assassinated. In the early years of Mehmet IV's reign, he could not refrain from reproaching him before his ministers. Despite his intelligence, sensitivity and nobility, he was a difficult man unable to get on with others, who loved success but, on account

of his harsh temperament, failed to maintain it. In this city
of waters to which he chose to be exiled, he spent a large
part of his wealth in creating the fountains which gave him
unique enjoyment. He had built these fountains before he
even thought that there was any need for such a pious deed,
and they are still called the Mufti Fountains by the people
of Bursa. When I read this story in books, I was a little
surprised and even laughed, but when I went to Bursa and
heard the sounds of water holding up their enchanted mirror
over the city to reflect every moment of the day, I gradually
acknowledged that Kara Çelebizade was right. Now I recognize and love him in quite a different way. From that moment,
he remained for me in the foremost rank of men with sensitive and subtle souls whose lives are permeated by poetry.
Like an appreciative, but besotted and extravagant, lover who
overwhelms the woman he loves with jewels and diamonds
that reveal her beauty even more, he bestowed on the city, of
whose beauty he had become aware, garlands and chandeliers
composed of the sounds of water, strings of pearls poured out
for the mornings, and, for the exile of evenings, necklaces
alight with the glow of huge jewels. He wanted a passer-by to
understand at any hour of the day, by means of his fountains,
the heartfelt cries of his unhappy spirit, condemned to die
far from his native city where he was born and bred, an exile
alien to life and action. This voice should tell them of the
great turning points of existence, the beauty of the seasons,
the transience of life. It should speak of the bewitched eyes
of desire and the cruel tyrant death, and in the lonely hours
of the night plunge deep into bitter guilts and murmur of
perfidious fortune and the rough hands of fate. And perhaps in his long, painful hours of isolation, suspicious of
everyone and everything, he tried to harmonize the notes of
the 200 fountains like the strings of a dulcimer; sometimes
from the phantom music he drew golden-tongued songs that
recalled moonlight nights on the Bosphorus, and sometimes
he sought in it an echo of the muezzin's prayers that made
mornings in Istanbul so luminous. He assigned to it the cries

that would render the story of his life and the howling storms that erupted in his unhappy soul; then, suddenly, he dedicated everything to the loveliest of cities, to Istanbul, for whom he longed but whom he knew he would never see again.

Poor Aziz Efendi! Now I seem to see him in the Bursa streets, followed by a little crowd of architects, master builders and fountain engineers working for the Bursa pious foundations, indicating, one by one, where the 200 fountains should be placed. Undoubtedly, he lifts his head every now and then, and thinking of the crystal arcs in Bursa's open air and of their meeting points and of the harmonious world which will be erected in the sky above Bursa, he smiles proudly like an orchestral conductor or the architect of an inner world.

Every time I visit Bursa, I think of him and sometimes I am amazed at how the meaning of a life can be completed by events that come together so strangely.

One of those who came and settled in Bursa in the seventeenth century was İsmail Hakkı Efendi,[16] a sheikh of the Celveti religious order, a very hard-working, well-intentioned man. As we know, the second period of the Celveti order began in Bursa with Muakkad Dede and his disciple Üftade.[17] But its real fame throughout Turkey lay with Aziz Mahmud Hüdayı Efendi, the most influential sheikh of Ahmed I's reign. İsmail Hakkı Efendi, who played a major role in the events that followed the defeat of Vienna, particularly in the reaction of the people and the market during the great uprising that resulted in the murder of Siyavuş Pasha[18] by rebels, an uprising that continued throughout Süleyman II's reign to end in the deposition of Mehmed IV, was the disciple of Osman Fazlî Efendi,[19] the sheikh of Atpazarı. Osman Efendi was one of the most attractive, honourable and courageous men of his time. He didn't hesitate to rebuke the sultans in the firmest terms, and often in the mosques he lost no opportunity to preach sermons that often exceeded the limits of criticism. Certainly the feeling of discontent stirred up by his sermons played a part in Mehmed IV's dethronement. But after Siyavuş Pasha's murder, he became an ordinary councillor of state.

There is nothing more contrasting than the historical role of the *ulema* and the sheikhs of Islam. On the one hand, they agreed to the harshest despotism in order to forestall and repress rebellion. On the other hand, while they were occupied in mystical meditation, uttering truths at the most unsuitable times, they were responsible for doors opened wide to intrigue and anarchy. After the murder of Siyavuş Pasha, what part did Osman Fazlî Efendi play in intervening in the affairs of state – a man whose virtues and moral qualities were above suspicion? What part did he play in electing the command of Osman Pasha 'The Nephew', who was virtually the captain of a band of brigands? That is hard to decide, but it is impossible to forgive his bitter criticism of the essential fiscal policies of Fazıl Mustafa Pasha, the one and only hope of the state, who straightened out its affairs in his brief viziership and regained Belgrade, Niş and even all of Rumeli. As though that wasn't enough, he wished to join the army with his followers and participate in the Holy War. At a time when nearly everyone was expecting the coming of the Messiah, when the army was in a state difficult to control and when anarchy was imminent, it would have been playing with fire to permit such an attractive personality to join the army. Whether or not he wished it, Mustafa Fazıl Pasha[20] was obliged to banish to Famagusta the man whose honour he trusted and whose criticism he acknowledged when he himself had complained of the imposition of taxes. İsmail Hakkı Efendi, who went from Bursa to visit his sheikh in Cyprus, relates in his *Silsilename* how the sheikh summoned the soul of Mustafa Fazıl Pasha, who had died fighting at Salankamin, and reproached him bitterly.

Undoubtedly a naïve belief in a person, which can even go as far as lying on their behalf, has undoubtedly a good side to it. But how sad that the life of an empire is so different that it specifically demands cold-blooded decisions. It is quite amazing that Hakkı Efendi, who had lived through so much himself, altered the death of Fazıl Pasha in his *Silsilename*, saying that he died among his close attendants. This was certainly meant to deprive him of a martyr's reputation. Ah! This seventeenth century, how alike they all are, holy men, doctors of theology, viziers and ministers, brigands! In İsmail Efendi's works, there are a number of naïve inventions which reveal this side of contemporary attitudes. It seems he stayed awake until dawn working on his famous commentary. At that moment the cock in his garden cried to him, 'Greetings, İsmail Efendi!' Similarly, writing about Hacı Bayram, he declared that angels in heaven had quoted some couplets of Şeyhî, one of his disciples, the poet who wrote *Hüsrev and Şirin*. No, Evliya Çelebi is not alone in this!

In the time of Mehmed Pasha (The Diamond), İsmail Hakkı Efendi joined the army and was even wounded in a fight. The biographer Mehmed Ali Avni Bey says that after that event, the writer of *Silsilename* wrote a national hymn for schoolchildren which still remains in his collection of poems.

IV

They say that the East 'possesses the secret of death'. But even in the East there are not many countries that overcome death as successfully as we do, giving it a distinctive image and protecting it from all kinds of casual familiarities. And we do it with such artless elements: often a tomb simply built, elegant and carved in wood; sometimes a plain, unadorned sarcophagus draped with embroidered cloths or a cloth of plain green, a turban, a horse plume, enough to assure eternal life for our forefathers. On the monument built with such poor materials, all that reminds us of the individual life is a name. Yes, a single name from the remoteness of death revives the memory of a life, like a dead star that continues to send us light from space where it is one of millions. The little monument which appeals to our imaginaton was made more for Death than for the dead within and has created almost a third Time, like a bridge easy to cross, suspended between Eternity and the time lived in the middle of old Turkish cities. The dead bore witness from their simple mansions to all our street life. We shared everything with them, our times of Ramazan and festivals, our holy nights when the minarets were illuminated, our great victories, our joys and sorrows.

In other nations, there are many who contemplate death in a far more imposing way, creating the tomb as a little exhibition of abandoned worldly blessings, reducing a life that now belongs to the next world to the condition of a museum of a dreaded future. They have exhausted all their arts and inventions in overcoming their deep fears of mortality, but not one has managed to tame death or soften its terrible reality as we alone have done.

We feel our terrible common destiny at the tomb where 'Çelebi Mehmed lies with his wife and children', in the middle of a regret as melancholic as sweet-scented roses in an evening garden at the end of a fine day. But lost and melted in the quiet air and in the unfading seasons of the tiles, it is transformed by the shadowy moonlight pouring through the windows, for the love of life and art has taken it for its own.

For those who lie in this tomb and in others like it, what lies behind the curtain is undoubtedly a dream in which regret for lost blessings is experienced as only a sweet drowsiness. They sleep in their tombs after a turbulent life as though washed in soothing waters. As we stroll by their tombs, we sense a tranquillity which their lives never knew for a single moment, surging in waves around us like a great sea. What gives us the illusion of peace is certainly art. People who struggled all their lives and never hesitated to spill the blood of strangers and even of their own kindred share in the fate of a saint, thanks to the talents and compassion that moved the hands of great artists and architects.

Leaving the tomb, I entered the Green Mosque described by André Gide as 'the height of spiritual perfection'. Gide, whose prejudices impelled him to look at everything he saw in Istanbul with a jaundiced eye, was much softened in Bursa. I could never understand his strong antipathy. Apart from any question of beauty, if he had attended closely to the distress of the people among whom he travelled as a guest and observed the calm patience and submission they showed throughout the poverty and pain he described, he would have found an endless treasury of poetry. But it is clear that Gide came to our country not to look with his own eyes but to dislike whatever Barrés and Loti had liked. There was so much to be seen, loved and pitied in this land, on the eve of the Balkan disasters! A great nation wronged and suffering in its pride, its rights and history. At the time, André Gide found our countryside destitute and joyless, our art a random confusion, our people ugly. His superior eye looked with disgust at the distress around him and he passed it by. Children of a future France, who experience the great disaster which is the present, will understand how ridiculous this inhuman behaviour was, when they read *La Marche Turque*. How sad that for nations, as for individuals, certain misfortunes are only understood through personal experience. Nevertheless, I love Gide for what he wrote on Bursa. He was the writer who best understood the Green Mosque. He caught wonderfully the mosque in its full light, with the landscape stretching, as though deliberately planned, to its foot. A new feeling of deep and humble reverence enters the lines, and here he captures the shiver of delight he never experienced in Süleymaniye or in the mosques of Istanbul. From then on, he almost speaks with the language he would use of the Panthéon. The Green Mosque deserves his admiration and even more. It would be an exaggeration to say it is the most excellent example of our architecture. But it is certain that in this mosque a technique evolved which inspired one of the most beautiful and subtle ambiguities that opened the way to the splendour and magnificence of Bayezid and Süleymaniye. The tension between two different ways of understanding results in a smile of pure pleasure. Like taking a final look back while we move forward into the future. But a look full of awareness! In passing through a mixture of stages, tradition has become enriched and enlarged. For this geometry to appear in one day in such a simple guise, in such clarity of proportions, the old order of Asia was displaced, civilizations mingled, whole communities underwent profound changes. As soon as we pass through the door, the human soul, described by Neşatî as 'the cryptic riddle', finds one of its most natural elements in the green atmosphere that encloses us. Everything here tells us the secret of the power that in 30 years recreated the recently captured Bursa as a Turkish city, from which then sprang the genius of Süleyman Dede. It is only when we stroll round the Green Mosque and other works of the period that we realize in Emir Sultan's tomb, built by Selim III, and in other similar buildings, what greatness was lost. These products of rich material and feeble design, like a meaningless, empty phrase that tires the mind, declare their weakness eventually and proclaim, 'I'm a total nothing!'

So Emir Sultan lies here in imperial state frozen in spirals of gilded stripes. There is no sign of the mystical sense that infuses other architectural works, making out of stone a living creature and reaching the eye like a window into the heart. Undirected light creeps over walls and paving stones like a dead thing. It is no longer the focus for the heart swept by great winds of the spirit, described by the poet Yunus (the last of that name) in one of the pearls of Turkish poetry:

Emir Sultan's dervishes
Their business only prayer and praise
Rows of birds of paradise
On Emir Sultan's tomb

The old tomb and Emir Sultan's mosque was one of the centres for Bursa life which gathered round it from time to time. Evliya Çelebi never tired of praising the splendour of the tomb. The door was adorned from top to bottom with silver scales, silver rings and handles of silver. There were thresholds of silver and carpets of silk. The ceiling was hung with jewels and bejewelled objects and the saint slept in the richness of a Thousand and One Nights, lit by hundreds of candles and lamps of gold and silver. Every spring a great crowd gathered in the tomb to celebrate the Festival of the Judas Tree. The celebration made me wonder if anything remained of the old religions and beliefs whose broken monuments and little tomb figures we see in their hundreds in the Bursa museum. Or is it just a festival invented by our victorious forefathers to bless the newly conquered earth? Wherever it comes from, the name of this Turkish holy man has survived in Bursa throughout history and has mingled with a tradition very similar to 'nature worship'. I personally like Emir Sultan's role in this, for in our climate, if any flower is celebrated more than the rose, it is the flower of the Judas tree. Every spring, it comes to life on the edge of our cities, ecstatic and colourful, like a Dionysian dream. Its exuberant joy illuminates everything, announcing that nature has awakened from a deep sleep and the world has changed again; it sings of spring. There is a Judas tree that shoots up on its own between the ruined walls of the Manavkadı Mosque, a little mosque like a broken fragment of an old morning prayer, stuck there on the ramparts of Istanbul. Ever since it was first shown to me, I went at least once every spring to pay it a visit and watch the languid light of the lamps that gave me the feeling that they were gathered from the city's morning. Between the dead who sleep beside it and the neglected ruins of the past, this Judas tree symbolizes for me the eternal desire that love of life be continually renewed. I am especially touched by its humble site that dominates the landscape.

The generous feast of life and desire that appears spontaneously every spring gives heart to the dead who sleep by Emir Sultan's tomb. They say that in the old days, a company of villagers and the sick gathered in the tomb and were joined by the neighbouring Ahî. And when Emir Sultan became enamoured of Yıldırım's daughter and carried her off by force, he killed all the soldiers Yıldırım sent to retrieve her in rather a bloody way, even for us. As one of the great heroes of Bursa's love stories, he has the reputation of giving moral support to lovers and of facilitating marriages.

Perhaps it's Emir Sultan's face that most stirs the imagination of the Turkish people of the fifteenth century. Hoca Sadeddin,[21] in his *Tarih*, Taşköprülü, in his *Şakayık-ı Osmaniye*, and Beliğ,[22] in his *Güldeste*, all have legends to narrate about him. The following is one of the three stories in Beliğ's collection: One of Emir Sultan's followers asked him to prove his miraculous powers. Emir Sultan struck the earth with his stick and water gushed forth. A second story refers to the building of Emir Sultan's tomb. According to Beliğ, one day, Hoca Kasım, a wealthy man from Bursa, presented Emir Sultan with a new kind of head-gear called an *arakiye* (a soft felt cap to wear under his turban). Emir Sultan gave him a coin in return. That day, Hoca Kasım was strolling through the market when he saw a huge diamond for sale for 30,000 dirhem. He was annoyed when he realized he hadn't enough money. But counting what he had in his wallet, he saw that he had more than 30,000 dirhem, so he bought the diamond and sold it again the same day to a Jewish jeweller who offered him 130,000 dirhem. Knowing all this was the proof of Emir Sultan's miraculous powers, Hoca Kasım used the money to have a cell built for a recluse, which still exists in the same place and later contained the tomb. The third story has a different charm. One day in the year 1032 – about 200 years after Emir Sultan's death – a stranger who enjoyed walking with a huge lion came to Bursa. One day, he wished to visit Emir Sultan's tomb. Chaining the lion firmly to a post, he entered, but the lion soon broke its chain and came through the tomb door, dragging his chain like a demented lover and visited Emir Sultan with tears flowing from his eyes. Then he returned to his place and waited for his master.

They say Emir Sultan addressed nearly everyone in the same friendly and familiar way.

According to legend, Emir Buharî, one of the Prophet's descendants, received permission from him at Medina to visit the centre of the new empire. He made the whole journey with a lamp on his head, and when he reached Bursa, the lamp could be seen burning for three successive days and nights.

At the door of Emir Sultan's tomb that looks towards the Green Mosque lie the seraglio women of the unfortunate Murad V, and overhead are Persian-style inscriptions by the last calligraphers of Bursa.

Today in Bursa, Emir Sultan's tomb lies in a neglected condition matched by the piece of architecture above, in contrast with the surrounding countryside which is exceptionally beautiful. It is curious that such lifeless architecture appeared at the same time as there was a renaissance of Turkish music. It is hard to accept that the architecture of the Emirgan Mosque, the barracks and the Tanzimat kiosk at Topkapı was contemporary, with the spiritual enlightenment so richly present in the solemn Turkish music of the dervish dance and rituals, and at a time when Dede's musical fame was legendary. Just at a time when Turkish architecture was at a low ebb, music was undergoing a complete revival. But perhaps this was its final blaze, like a splendid evening generously bathed in its own blood.

The Tanzimat era and the periods that followed were undoubtedly constructive in a general sense. But the architects of the Tanzimat era were happier to build than to create. The difference between the two is apparent in all the works of the time. In the general framework of our cities, a number of works can be immediately recognized as inappropriate and reveal that architecture does not merely consist of using a certain material for a certain function.

Our ancestors did not just build; they worshipped. They wanted their strong religious faith to pass into the materials. In their hands, stone came to life, a portion of their soul was chiselled into shape. In the Green Mosque, everything prays – walls, domes, arches, altar, tiles; in Muradiye, all is contemplation, and in Yıldırım, it hovers over the plain like an eagle ready to launch itself into the depths, in its thirst for heaven. Throughout, all sings one single spirit.

Ah, those old masters who transformed everything they touched and the miracles of art that created a new world from the most primordial element. Our forefathers' miraculous faith changed the face of Bursa and Istanbul. In half a century, they were transformed into pure Turkish and Moslem cities. Within the space of 20 or 30 years, the Eastern Roman ruins of Bursa and Istanbul were completely eliminated and replaced by an architecture of subtle invention and gentle features, jealously aware of the beautiful materials it used, suited to the climate of a city built from similar elements, with its mosques, religious schools, colleges and hostels. While art suddenly altered the general appearance of the hills of these cities in their splendid framework, a second victory was won, street by street: little tombs, whose green windows smiled with promises of eternal life, and fountains that surpassed those of Istanbul and Bursa. Fifty years after the capture of Bursa, poets grew up among the children of Bursa, and when Fatih, who had captured Istanbul at the beginning of his reign, was brought to this city in his coffin, it had become pure Turkish, with its traditions and neighbourhood names, its saints' tombs, its life of poetry and art. As the first generation of children born in Bursa and Istanbul to Turkish parents grew up, they saw their own family tree spreading. When Bursa mothers of the first period spoke of the age of their future warriors, they would say, 'My son was born the year Orhaniye or Muradiye was built.' And they would offer up vows to mosques of the same age as their sons to ensure their safe return from their long, exhausting campaigns.

V

That day, I spent all morning wandering from monument to monument in the city and saw, as usual, many beautiful objects and savoured many pleasures. But I failed to experience the intense satisfying shiver that overwhelms the spirit when the veils between ourselves and ordinary objects are removed, leaving us nothing strange or alien. I had made this last journey to winkle out the secret of Bursa's countryside and, if possible, to learn a lesson from it. But the harder I searched, the more it escaped me. Stones, trees, works of art, moments, all shut themselves away and excluded me from their confidence. Gradually, I began to see only death around me, and I said to myself, 'What remains but eternal ennui?' At that moment, everything except death seemed to be only a childish remedy for escaping boredom. Love, art, desire, success, all toys of our sick vanity and revolving behind them the great wheel of destiny. How could I think of anything else on a day when even the sound of water, the most beautiful expression of this city, held out an empty glass to my daydream?

For a moment I fell into the illusion of searching for my own memories in the city I loved so much. And I wondered, 'If I went to the Hüdavendigâr Mosque again, could I recover the smile of the beautiful young person who walked with me here five years ago in the evening gloom?' This tender smile had shone like a fresh rose at dusk in the old place of worship, and as I watched it, I felt the surrounding air illumined bit by bit by golden reflections as at the sudden birth of a star, and filled with a music-like thought. This laugh was a dedication gleaned from sun and light, and all that we have loved and consciously abandoned, to 'Death', who lies dormant in all the stones, dreaming of the past. I was sure that there, for a moment, the souls absorbed by those silent stones found themselves happy and fragrant as a young rose shoot newly opened, thanks to this laugh. But if I went now, I'd find no trace of the laugh, and when I die, the only witness of the memory would be lost.

As I walked on, disturbed and depressed by the thought, a driver I knew suddenly appeared and almost forced me into his car. I proceeded a little longer to contemplate my wretched loneliness in the little mirror placed as an ornament at my feet. Now I no longer looked about but abandoned myself to thoughts rising in me like ill-omened music. 'Why am I so upset about this?' I wondered, 'why must I want life to continue, why do I have such violent longings? What's the point of it all? Even if I drank all the fountains of life dry, what would remain? At the bottom of every glass we enjoy drinking there's always the same demon with his cold, indifferent eyes with their ash-coloured pupils devoid of light fixed on us and laughing at our drunkenness . . . the powers that so control our lives, however much they conform to our desires, can't rescue us from death. The whole of creation is a game trumped up for his own amusement by a bored god of enormous and unique power. In the midst of life's blessings, this ennui of the spirit is our biggest inheritance from the creative impulse. We conquer countries, give them works of miraculous perfection, leap from one emotion to another that gives our every moment illusions of eternity, and in the briefest intervals that divide them, we come upon the cruellest irony. It arrives most unexpectedly, squats before us, glares into our eyes ... How often I've felt its damp turbid breath on my brow just when I thought I was furthest from it. In the flesh I stroked, in the rose I inhaled, in the drink I swallowed, there was always that poison. When I woke from the happiest, most delightful sleep, didn't I find that grotesque demon in my arms like a creature of black lea- ther? Perhaps it is he who creates for us the real rhythm of time; who measures our minutes, long or short, according to his own desire, and drives us into the yawning mouth of death, every little push a wake-up call. In the end, he drags time's harrow over us with satanic laughter and closes the oven door.'

In the country coffee house where I was sitting, these dark reflections might have continued but for the old proprietor who cut them short with a graceful movement of one hand as he arranged a chair for me and with the other suddenly threw a glorious red rose into the little fountain before me. All in a moment, the hour and the scene were painted with the freshness of spring. Where had that poor old man learned such an artistic gesture? In this poor man down on his luck, what genuine good manners, what a tradition of beauty, continued! By his gift I was suddenly restored to the world of values.

From where I was, I could see the plain in all its immensity. What I like best of the Bursa plain is the way it does not stretch interminably like the plains of Muş or Erzurum but is just vast and wide enough for the eye to take in its beauty, more like a work of art. All is fertile. It seemed as if nature had wanted to load every part with fertility, then, from a sense of proportion, had given up. The distant mountains and strange massed shapes that remind us of ancient things and embrace us like an ancestral dream, with their narrow shady valleys and little pastures that press charming villages to their bosom, left an imaginary feeling of happiness as they stretched away to

the distance and framed the horizon. Far away in the background, dark lilac-grey ghosts added their own outlines to the
gentle vault of the sky. Here and there the sun gained depth,
opaque and misty, and occasionally broke through, like a tink-
ling crystal chandelier.

Without attempting to discover the vanishing point of the
plain and surrounding mountains, I try to name the places
where every year, Lâmii, in his famous poem, marched his
spring army of three columns to chase away winter:

Ab-ı hayat Yaylağı, Molla Alanı, Saru Alan, Kurt Bılanı,
Doğlu Baba, Şakın Efendi Pınarı, Kırkpınar, Binyaylak,
Karagöl, Hızırbey yurdu, Kuş Oynağı . . .

I can't remember them all, and I've forgotten their order.
But it is certain that the story or folk tale brings spring winds
to the plain in three columns.

Ah, the colours of our mountains that change with the
light and the hour! The real garden of our soul comes from
you! On that sad day when I looked at you, I experienced
some of your tranquillity passing into myself. A bee traces
an invisible path round me. Suddenly I remember Eşrefoğlu,
not for himself but for the answer Kul Hasan[23] gave him
250 years after his death:

A bee flies here and there
Flitting from flesh to flesh,
The beloved escapes, flies from us,
We are the bee, the honey is in us.

For one line of the poem, Kul Hasan substitutes:

We are the garden, the rose is in us.

After the defeat of Vienna, it was very difficult to use such
language. But what really attracted me was that 250 years after
Eşrefoğlu's death, Kul Hasan could disagree with him. It means

that the power of Death is not absolute. Eşrefoğlu was Hacı Bayram's son-in-law and lies in Bursa, but where? I must have been shown the spot, but it has escaped my memory. Also, I was never able to visit the village of Kestel that Mehmed IV gave to Şeyh Vani Efendi.[24] After the rout of Vienna, Vani Efendi lived in Bursa as an exile. I wonder if he met the Mevlevi whom he had oppressed so harshly or the Bektaşi dervishes whose convents he had closed down for a while? After the Feyzullah Efendi[25] episode, he certainly had a share in the bloody revenge taken on Feyzullah's family, even on his cats. A late and quite unnecessary cruelty. But in this light before the beautiful plain, isn't it better to look at birds tracing mysterious shapes and symbols in the air, rather than to think of Vani Efendi? Two pigeons stand side by side on the rim of the basin like a poetic metaphor for love, perhaps attracted by the rose thrown by the coffee-house owner when I came here. They will sing love songs as long as the rose sways in the moving water. I want to think of nothing. I'll remain, happy to drink in the moment and the light from the great vessel of emerald known as the plain of Bursa. 'It's best,' I say, 'to renounce wordly things and give our hearts to the power of beauty.'

As I gradually relax, the scene and everything around me grow distant. I remain face to face with the rosebud swaying in the moving waters in the little pool and with the sound of water suddenly all about me. I feel that this sound of water creates an invisible second city above this city. An imaginary, more fluid architecture, but as present as everything we see, covers all. It mirrors all life in its colours of the rainbow, but more unsullied, more crystal clear. Perhaps this is real time in the absolute sense and now I am living in an abstract world.

Now I realize that the pigeons flying around me a moment ago, whose fantasy of flight I admired, belong to this transparent world and are the same as the dreams that slip from there into our world. In that other world is everything, our past, our longings, anxieties, joys and hopes, all with their own characteristic colours.

The scene before me I admired a little while ago, the distant villages that give us the longing for escape or freedom, the young cypress trees standing guard at the gate of the Green Mosque, the dead asleep in their little unadorned tombs, all the names in my memory, every one with their different hours and seasons, my childhood and my past, the smile I sought in vain in the mirror of the Moslem refugee's little car and which I know I'll find again in the Hüdavendigâr Mosque, the woman gathering with a new piety every moment of life's joyous seasons, there, side by side, hand in hand, in the world woven by the sound of water, all are alive exactly as they live in my imagination.

Now in Bursa I have learned that the second Time created for us alongside real time is different and deeper than our real time. The sound with its echoes that embrace its environment and repeat for eternity the essence of everything it touches, this mirror forever reflecting our thoughts and seasons, is an enchanted mirror that gives us three simultaneous tracks of Time. The mirror of art is no different.

Notes

1 Keçeci Fuad Pasha (1815–1869) – A diplomat, grand vizier, poet, critic and linguist, he wrote the first Turkish grammar.

2 Gümüşlü – The old Byzantine monastery, burial place of Osman, known in Turkish as the 'silvery dome'. This building was destroyed by the earthquake of 1855.

3 Muradiye – The Bursa quarter of the tombs and the mosque built by Murad II. Among the ancient trees lie twelve 'türbes' (tombs) from the fifteenth and sixteenth centuries, including some remarkable personalities of Turkish history, e.g. Prince Cem, Murad II and Mustafa Şeyzade, the son of Sultan Süleyman.

4 Yeşil – Literally, 'green'. Here, it signifies the Green Mosque in Bursa built by Mehmet Çelebi, son of Bayezid I, and the Green Tomb. Both mosque and tomb are remarkable for their beautiful blue and green tiling.

5 Nilüfer Hatun – Daughter of a Byzantine governor, wife of Orhan I and mother of Murad I. She built a bridge over the river that flows through the Bursa plain. Her name signifies 'water lily' or 'lotus', the symbol of victory.

6 Geyikli Baba – A legendary hero of the thirteenth century who fought for Osman, founder of the Ottoman Empire, and for his son Orhan. He rode on a stag and wielded a heavy wooden sabre. His tomb in Bursa is beside a mosque and a convent.

7 Emir Sultan – A famous sheikh of the fifteenth century who came to Bursa from Bokhara and who married a daughter of Bayezid I.

8 Konuralp (thirteenth century) – He fought alongside Osman and Orhan Gazi against the Byzantines and other feudal landowners of Anatolia, capturing several towns for the Ottomans.

9 Karaca Ahmet – Lived in the sixteenth century, a member of the Bektaşi order and the hero of several legends. His tomb in the Üsküdar cemetery attracts many visitors.

10 İbn-i Battuta (1304–1369) – A famous Arab writer and traveller who explored the whole Islamic world of his time.

11 Murad I (Hüdavendigâr) (1325–1389) – The third Ottoman sultan. Under his leadership, the Turks advanced west as far as Serbia and routed the Serbian army at the battle of Kosova, but he was killed by an enemy soldier.

12 Neşri – Was nominated by Bayezid II as official Turkish historian. He died in 1490.

13 Lütfi Pasha – Grand vizier for two years under Süleyman the Magnificent, whose daughter he married. He left more than 20 works dealing with history, literature, politics, religion and the lifestyle and conduct of the viziers.

14 Mehmed I (1384–1421) – Fifth Ottoman sultan, also called Çelebi Sultan. As one of Bayezid's six sons, he had a long struggle with his brothers for the throne. He is buried in Bursa's 'Yeşil Türbe'.

15 Kara Çelebizade (1591–1657) – Historian and poet, he was known to have been involved in the troubles that led to the assassination of Sultan İbrahim I. A few months after he became the head of religious affairs, he fell out of favour and was exiled to Bursa in 1650.

16 İsmail Hakkı Efendi (1635–1725) – One of the great sheikhs of the Celveti order. He wrote several religious works and a collection of poems.

17 Muhyiddin Üftade – He succeeded Hacı Bayram, founder of the Bayramı order, and saw in a dream that his disciple Mahmud Hüdaî Efendi would follow him.

18 Siyavuş Pasha – Mehmed IV's last grand vizier. He was murdered in 1688 by the Janissaries who dethroned the sultan.

19 Osman Fazlî Efendi (1632–1691) – Disciple of İsmail Hakkı of Bursa, mystic and poet. He became sheikh of the Atpazarı Celveti convent in Istanbul but fell out of favour in the palace and was exiled to Cyprus where he died.

20 Fazıl Mustafa Pasha (1637–1676) – He came from the famous Köprülü family and held the post of grand vizier for two years. He died of his wounds in the battle of Salankamin.

21 Hoca Sadeddin (1537–1599) – Chronicler, especially well known for his historical account of the beginnings of the Ottoman Empire until the reign of Selim I.

22 Beliğ (1668–1730) – Historian and poet from Bursa, best known for his *Güldeste* ('Garland of Roses') or the 'History of Bursa'.

23 Kul Hasan – Little is known about this Bektaşı poet of the eighteenth century.

24 Şeyh Vanî Efendi (d. 1685) – A famous orator, interpreter of the Koran and Mehmet IV's religious tutor. He was held to be one of those responsible for the Turkish disaster at the siege of Vienna, stripped of his honours and exiled.

25 Seyyid Feyzullah Efendi (1638–1703) – As the *sheikhülislâm*, he was ordered to carry out reforms of the ulema, becoming the most powerful statesman of the Ottoman Empire.

5
Istanbul

I

When I was a child, my father and I made the acquaintance of an old woman in an Arabian city. She often fell ill, and when the fever began, she would recite the names of Istanbul's springs:

Çırcır, Karakulak, Şifa, Hünkâr, Taşdelen, Sırmakeş . . .

As these names squeezed through her taut, dry lips and under her tongue that was heavy as molten lead, her lustreless eyes came to life, her whole face grew attentive as though she was listening to things inaudible to us and her hollow cheeks filled out with concentration. One day, her son-in-law said to my father, 'It's her medicine, it works like a charm . . . as she tells over the names she begins to recover.'

How often by her bedside during our visits I have seen her free herself from the deepest sleep, like someone raising the stone lid from a cellar, just to recite the magic names. The windows of her room were quite obscured by dark green branches to protect it from heat and the sirocco, and as the names seemed to fall one by one into the dim depths of a well filled with crystal clear water, I was spellbound. These sparkling gemlike names revived a thousand images in my childhood imagination.

All around me, the air was full of the sound of water, the chink of silver bowls and crystal wine glasses, the flutter of pigeons' wings. Sometimes, my dream became more concrete. As the repetition of names raised goose pimples on my skin, I seemed to see the familiar Istanbul fountains, the water carriers leaking the illusion of coolness from their damp, black, greasy goatskins and the little fountain of our neighbourhood, with its simple decorations, that under the drooping acacia tree assumed the look of a young bride every spring. And sometimes the flood of greenery round the reservoirs which we had visited only once came to life before my very eyes, and for a while I imagined this dim and green-lit room as a swimming pool where we all swam like strange fish: the sick woman, myself and those around us.

What happened to the woman eventually, I don't know. But a bit of me still believes that after her death, she became a water spirit.

It was only years later that I was able to interpret the melancholy that made every spring of water a source of yearning.

For the woman, Istanbul was the city of the cool, crystal waters of health. Just as for my father, it was the city of peerless mosques and muezzins with beautiful voices and of learned reciters of the Koran. This devout Moslem's only revolt against fate, his one anxiety, was his fear of dying far from Istanbul. In such an eternal sleep, he feared he might meet with much that he disliked and that was even immoral, including alien modes of chanting prayers from the Koran.

The variety of appearances that a city takes in our imagination is well worth contemplating. It not only changes from person to person but from generation to generation. Undoubtedly, our ancestors who lived in Üsküdar[1] and Anadoluhisar at the beginning of the fifteenth century regarded Istanbul merely as a country to be conquered, and on Istanbul evenings when they watched it from Sultantepe and Çamlica,[2] they were looking at the treasures that Eastern potentates would sooner or later share as booty. But for those who came after the conquest, the city became the pride of the Islamic world and of the whole empire. They boasted about it and its beauties and graced them daily with new monuments. The finer it became, the more they saw themselves as fine and noble reflections in its magic mirror.

The period of reforms, the Tanzimat, regarded Istanbul in a completely different light. It saw in the city a crucible for a new synthesis, born from the union of two civilizations.

For our generation, Istanbul is now a very different place from that of our grandfathers, or even of our fathers. In our imagination, it does not appear swathed in silver and gold robes of honour, nor do we see it set in a religious framework. Rather, its name is illumined for us by the memories and longings evoked by our own spiritual state.

But this nostalgia is not an emotion that belongs only to the past, in conflict inevitably with our modern life and with our good sense. One channel of this very complex feeling reaches right to the heart of our daily lives and dreams of happiness.

So much so that it is from our very nostalgia that Istanbul's real face is born and it is the simplest characteristics of the city itself that nourish the feeling in us.

This is scenery that inspires our daydreams with very different ways of living and arouses various emotions in us. The real Istanbul is the city not only of mosques and minarets enclosed within walls but also of such diverse geographical locations with their own particular beauties as Beyoğlu,[3] Boğaziçi, Üsküdar, the shores of Erenköy,[4] the lakes at Çekmece,[5] the Reservoirs[6] and the Islands,[7] all inside one city.

So, naturally, an inhabitant of Istanbul yearns for a place other than that of his daily life. At Göztepe,[8] as you are enjoying a summer morning under a rustling tree, a tiny sensation, goose pimples, from nowhere will wander over your skin, a vision or even a child's song will suddenly summon you to some village on the Bosphorus which you left only yesterday, disturbing your peace of mind, calling you from a far, distant, other world. You are in the throes of work in Istanbul and suddenly you want to be in Nişantaş;[9] you are in Nişantaş and you must see Eyüp and Üsküdar, come what may. And sometimes you remain just where you are because what you remember and desire is all of it.

We are moved to momentary longings and flights of escape by the beauty of nature, a work of art, our lifestyles and a host of memories. Every inhabitant of Istanbul knows that a Bosphorus morning is an entirely different delight from any other neighbourhood's, and the heart of anyone who watches the lights of Istanbul from the heights of Çamlıca at dusk is filled with a unique sadness. On moonlit nights, the difference between Sarıyer,[10] only a hundred fathoms further on, and the gulf of Büyükdere[11] is as great as the difference between the Bosphorus and the open Sea of Marmara. With a few strokes of the oar, the man whose daily bread is poetry leaves his familiar dreamworld and enters a harsh, legendary Argonaut night. At every hour of the day, the lakes at Çekmece have a completely different beauty from the neighbouring seashore.

These lakes by the open sea are just like a little song compared with complex musical compositions: they share a melody but as soon as the scale changes, how great the change in character!

The sun on the lakes that are like old-fashioned hand mirrors resembles an old master who enjoys using his talent only on landscape in relief; every reed, every blade of grass, every wingbeat, all contours and colours dissolve in a single silver gleam.

But the change goes even deeper; as in a medieval landscape of a Book of the Hours, the work patterns of human beings, their times of idleness, their thoughts and despairs differ according to place. Imitating Paris in a half-hearted way, Beyoğlu reminds us of the poverty of our lives; the neighbourhoods of old Istanbul and Üsküdar with their last vestiges of values inherited from a self-sufficient world create, unknown to us, a wholeness of spirit and alter our dreams and desires. At Boğaziçi, in Üsküdar, in Istanbul, face to face with the Süleymaniye mosque or the fortresses on the Bosphorus, on Vaniköy[12] pier or in a coffee house at Emirgân, we often become quite different people. Which inhabitant of Istanbul, roaming the woodlands of Beykoz[13] or the hills behind Bebek,[14] hasn't longed for a rich studious solitude as a defence against the desiccating demands of 'the real world', and who hasn't donned, if only for one short moment, a protective armour of steel?

There is certainly no likeness between our thoughts as we lean in contemplation against the walls of the Bayezid or Beylerbey[15] mosques and the thoughts induced by the riot of evening lights on the shores of Tarabya[16] – a place still alien to a part of us. In the former, everything slips straight into our hearts and gives rise to a nourishing sadness.

In the other, we are without any deep-rooted yearning. Around the little mosque, of whose architectural quality we are rather doubtful, we find the complete old Istanbul of our fathers. When we talk with them, the people here now are not so very different from people in Tarabya, but they seem to have withdrawn into themselves and to be living in a dream of the past. The young girl here is just like any other girl, bored with the emotional poverty of her life, admiring the same filmstars and satisfying her appetite for life with cheap newspaper installments, but she seems, if not more beautiful, nearer to us, and a daughter of a different, richer world, for she inhabits streets and squares where we imagine there are echoes of the music performed in all the little palaces and summer houses and villas from which we know Mahmud II[17] witnessed magnificent equestrian displays.

Even death wears a different face in these parts.

As we contemplate all these changes in our imagination, an Istanbul is born that opens like a rose, petal by petal. Every major city, of course, is more or less like that. But Istanbul's special climate, the conflict between the north and south winds, and the various conditions of the soil emphasize differences between neighbourhoods that are rarely known elsewhere.

Thus, Istanbul continually exerts its magic influence over our imaginations. To know the good and bad sides of the city where we were born and where we live now is natural. But Istanbul has a certain artistic way of life, a delicacy of taste, a healthy culture of its own. Everyone of its inhabitants is more or less a poet, for even if he doesn't create new forms intelligently and decisively, he lives inside an imaginary magical drama that extends from history to daily life, from love to the dining table.

When he thinks, 'October and November are here, the bluefish season will begin,' or 'It's April. The Judas tree blossom must be out along the Bosphorus,' he manages to transform the present moment into a legend. The people of old Istanbul lived inside this legend and only there. For them, the calendar was like Hesiod's *Book of the Gods*. Days and seasons unrolled before their eyes in a dream that took colour and smell from their particular neighbourhoods.

A pity that this realm of poetry no longer rules our lives as in the past. Now we are more often seduced by longings for foreign parts – Paris, Hollywood – even for the Budapest and Bucharest of yesteryear, and every day, the lights of Istanbul grow just a little dimmer in our hearts. But the neighbourhood quarters of Istanbul remain there, complete and whole like one's native country. One day for sure, the great rose of the past will summon us.

II

Every great city changes from generation to generation. But Istanbul has changed in a different way. In every generation, a Parisian or a Londoner remembers his native city and feels a sadness at how it was 30 or 40 years ago, as he confronts its many strange new customs, its new forms of entertainments and its new style of architecture.

In one of his finest poems, Baudelaire exclaims, '*The old Paris no longer exists, how sad that a city's shape alters more quickly than the human heart*'. I think he was one of the few poets in all of French poetry who bitterly regretted the changes in Paris.

A well-known theme voiced by French writers after World War I is their nostalgia for the Paris of 10 years before.

Istanbul did not change in the same way. In the interval of 15 years between 1908 and 1923, it completely lost its old identity, which was swept away by a constitutional revolution; three great wars; a great number of successive fires, large and small; financial crises; the abolition of the Ottoman Empire; and our eventual acceptance in 1923 of a civilization on whose threshold we had stood hesitating for a hundred years.

Before 1908, all the wealthy from the southern Mediterranean parts who wished to live within an Islamic framework of art and entertainment would come to Istanbul. The rich farmlands in the European and Arab provinces and their huge productive estates nurtured the summer palaces and lodges on Çamlıca and the shores of the Bosphorus and those soon to be built at Kadıköy or even further afield. They planted gardens and woodlands. It was their wealth that assured its complete renovation when the city was ravaged by fire in the following 30 or 40 years. The flow of money increased particularly in the period after the Tanzimat. In the reigns of Abdülmecid, Abdülaziz and Abdülhamit, an important part of Egypt's wealth, profiting from European methods, above all, was pouring into Istanbul, while the summer palaces, pavilions and city mansions had close ties with the local guilds and markets, the real base of the city, a tradition which could be described as despotic but with a very local flavour.

Today, names like Saraçhane (Saddler's Market), Okçular (Archers), Sedefçiler (Mother-of-Pearl Workers), Çadırcılar (Tentmakers) only indicate neighbourhoods, but 70 or 80 years ago, there were crowds of small artisan workshops and studios, busy as beehives and important to the life and comfort of the city, supplying a delicate handwork that gave a flavour of the arts and crafts to everyday objects. These markets formed the real backbone of the city, most of them a complete answer to our specific lifestyles. It was they who nourished Istanbul and still made up the city's inner core.

Despite the 'Capitulations'[18] that opened wide all the doors of the Ottoman Empire to foreign goods and customs taxation, it was thanks to those markets that the empire survived. The Great Bazaar and the Bedesten[19] were the treasure house where business was carried on. In the seventeenth century, even before Europe had tasted the 'Thousand and One Nights' in Galland's translation, it had already experienced in the Bazaar and the Bedesten the whole ambience of the tales, and their dream had come to permeate their daily lives.[20]

A colourful mass of humanity flowed through the markets. Differences among races, languages, even continents, and various religious cults could be recognized at first sight by their diverse garments. All the ancient East was there in those streets. Men from Turkestan, with their neat, rounded beards; high cheekbones; faces drained by godliness and abstinence and hands clasped in long-sleeved woollen cloaks, had settled in one corner of the city like a sick stork separated from its flock – how many years had passed since they set out on their pilgrimage to Mecca? Chinese Moslems who had married in Ayvansaray[21] or Hırkaişerif and now had a family of children, but with bodies still unaccustomed to our garments; Caucasians in black fur caps, their waists tightly clasped by silver-buckled belts; Yemenites swathed in long white cloaks that remind the old pilgrims to Mecca of Mt Arafat; finally, a crowd of negroes whose gentle natures and sad tales of slavery had found for some a home among our contemporaries; a throng of elderly 'nannies', eunuchs and tutors whom the children teased at a distance, calling them 'daylight lanterns', but to whom, on the contrary, they were firmly attached at home; some gabbling Turkish from the back of their throats like a turkey laying an egg, some squeezing out nasal syllables of broken Turkish as though their noses were clamped shut and some who knew no language but their mother tongue but managed to survive, thanks to certain possibilities that only big cities can offer. In short, a crowd whose real fellow citizens could only be found in our markets or in the shops of wealthy bird breeders of the time.

In the past, the negro, who could be found almost anywhere in Istanbul, even in middle-class homes, we see now as a necessity of Western life, in jazz bands or at the door of every big hotel: with foreign fashions he has re-entered our lives, like a very exotic import.

How odd that nowadays we pay teachers to show us dances that were once performed in every major household to entertain women and children but which were often abandoned halfway for superstitious fear of the disturbing ecstatic effects of the dances.

Yes, Africa certainly used to play a far greater part in our lives than it does today!

For one month a year, this crowd was at its height at the Beyazıt fair. Here was every kind of turban, astrakhan headgear, fez, clothes embossed with the latest relief from Sargon, a complete oriental Babel, closely packed, chattering in every tongue, a sea of movement in the almost metaphysical atmosphere of Asia and the Orient which emanated from the smell of a thousand mingled spices.

This motley throng should not just be seen as a *'pittoresque'* element; it also relied on the economic possibilities of the city. Behind it lay a large part of world trade. All of the Mediterranean and the Black Sea came flooding into Istanbul, which, until the year 1900, was acknowledged to have one of the finest harbours in the world. The whole Bosphorus and the shores of Marmara were full of vessels of every kind, under every flag. All the travellers of the time who spoke of Istanbul's harbour compared it with London's. Lamartine in 1833 and, in 1850, the English traveller Dallaway[22] emphasize the similarity.

When it all ended along with the particular civilization on which it was founded, Istanbul began to live by its means of production, which required time to develop. In short, a city of great consumers became a city of small producers. The Istanbul of the future is bound by the laws of production and the forms they will take. There is no doubt that developments in the country, its geographical situation, the richness and potential of its soil will surely present the city with an entirely new life, a life in which people can enjoy the freedom to work. After a rather lengthy transition period, the Istanbul of today seems to be moving in this direction. But when it does realize the wide and prosperous age we desire, we must not completely forget its past, for that is one of the great adventures of our soul.

III

Istanbul's past was a fusion of great and small, significant and insignificant, old and new, local and foreign, beautiful and ugly, even by today's standards vulgar, the result of a melting pot of innumerable elements. Behind this synthesis were the institutions of Islam and the Ottoman state, and a whole raft of economic factors revolving these two pivots on the wheel of poverty. For two centuries, this fusion had resulted in economic production drying up in nearly every field. Hence, Istanbul from without was seen as rich and imposing and, thanks to its reputation for living with taste and enjoyment, as still uncorrupt and original, although in reality it was quite poor. Its survival was due to its squandering the last remnants of its legacy of a glorious past and to its reliance on a whole chain of traditions and customs. A particular lifestyle, including the wearing of religious robes, gave life an integrity, blessed all it touched and created a miraculous unity. Every import that passed through customs became part of Islamic life. The English mohair worn by a senior judge, his lady's headscarf made of silk from Lyon, a desk in the French style inscribed with Ottoman calligraphy, a lamp of Bohemian workmanship, all became 'Islamized'. When a rococo clock, just arrived from England, was introduced into a hybrid room furnished with mirrors, vases of flowers, marquetry and Louis XV-style Ottoman and cambric cushions, it was at once absorbed by Islam for it began to tell the time according to Moslem chronology. Like a convert to Islam who has earned the right through an intense religious education to wear the robes of a Doctor of Moslem Theology, or like the convert Hançerli Bey, who, at Keçecizade İzzat Molla's assembly, is said to have succeeded in silencing genuine Moslem doctors with his knowledge of the Koran and the Hadiths.[23] Several artefacts that seemed of local origin were, in fact, manufactured abroad.

In my childhood, nearly every home in Istanbul had a table clock that sang at the beginning of every hour 'His robe is red' or 'Passing through Üsküdar'. These were the shoddy goods peddled at the time. Then coffee cups turned up decorated with the red flag and inscribed '*Souvenir of Istanbul*' or '*Liberty, Equality, Justice*'. Yes, the Orient of our childhood was partly manufactured abroad and stamped with the local middleman's mark. It was the same long before our childhood, but it all became part of a world so subjective that we hardly noticed. In a big orchestra, separate instruments are indistinguishable. For it was our inner self that drew the bow across the strings and created total harmony. It was the city itself, our architecture, our music and our way of life, and finally floating over all and absorbing all, our time and our calendar, composed of the feelings, sorrows, joys and dreams which were ours alone.

It was impossible to wander even in the remote neighbourhoods of old Istanbul and not experience this feeling of time, not fall into its enchanted well. It was a strange time, like a half-open door that stood between this world and the next, laden with prayer and submission to God, bestowing an air of 'mağfiret' or God's forgiveness, a yearning for the purest simplicity, transporting all it encountered to the frontiers of the divine and enveloped in spiritual colours so opaque that a hand might touch them. When the inhabitant of old Istanbul looked at his face in a mirror of the time, it appeared like a shadow intoxicated with the smell of the hereafter, at a great distance, almost unreachable. The old Istanbul quarters lived as it were within this time, close to the dead who lay in the cemeteries of the *medrese* and the little neighbouring mosques, sharing with them their sorrows and joys, hardly breathing, like an ancient tree whose trunk is throttled by rings of climbing ivy. In these neighbourhoods, the day moved through the five phases of the *ezan*, or call to prayer, and according to the hour, resembled a colourful, grand and sometimes diverting entertainment. Although there was no formal record of any ceremony, the day followed an immutable etiquette of customs.

The cries of the street pedlars were one of these. In the old quarters of Istanbul, these cries punctuated the day from beginning to end and coloured the hours. Like a pretty woman arranging her hair in a cheap mirror, the neighbourhoods bowed to these cries as they spread far and wide and prepared to welcome the unchanging stages of the day's journey.

Behind the latticework screen that sifted the fierce summer noon, mote by mote, right into the interior, a tree of street cries suddenly grew branches, sprouted shoots and fruits of song unrelated to any wares, clung in clusters to mirrors swathed in embroidered napkins, to gilded texts on marbled paper under dusty glass, to kitchen shelves where shining copper lids were ranged in order, to lamps made ready for night by the stairheads. Then the cries scattered leaf by leaf to far-off streets. Sometimes two or three street pedlars suddenly met and a little forest of cries would spring up.

Now there are no more old pedlars of lamps and lamp chimneys, no one selling *simits*[24] or water bottles or glasses and plates. The simit pedlar no longer carries a lantern at night: he doesn't even know how to compose a *mâni*, the Turkish folk quatrain. Sellers of *macun*[25] have been replaced by a locust horde of dirty children selling caramels. Only the yoghurt seller survives like the aged maples and pines that, all alone, watch over the gardens of some old summer houses. But I wonder if his voice accompanies the procession of the seasons as it did in our childhood. For the former inhabitants of Istanbul, the yoghurt from Silivri meant the end of winter. As summer began with wreaths of cherry branches and winter with the footsteps of the *salep* and *boza* merchants, their cries through the streets, followed by the fresh smell of meadows and fermenting images of bleating lambs, began the kite season, at that time a very important part of the city's life.

My favourite pedlar was the *lambacı* (lamp seller) who passed by every afternoon with an overflowing basket on his back. His was a strange street cry. Inflating his mouth like a balloon, he would dwell on the first syllable of the word '*lamba*', then swallowing the final '*a*' as though wanting to erase it completely at one gulp, he would exaggerate the final syllable of '*şişelerinin*', then blow out long breaths in every direction as his mouth reduced every bit of glass in the world to dust. He was the man who sold light to our neighbourhood. His were the lamps we bought, by whose light I listened to stories and read on winter nights, and on summer nights with moths fluttering round them; by the stairs, in the corridors and courtyards, they watched over the solitude of the whole house and listened to the creaking wooden floors when we were all in bed.

Their cries supplied the chief colour and pleasure to nights in poor neighbourhoods where entertainment was scarce. The change they actually brought about was not merely a musical interval that marked divisions of time. But they also illumined the silence of nights that were full of fear and foreboding.

What kind of shiver can be raised in a young person of today by the street cry of a pedlar passing in the night? To a modern ear ringing with the cacophony of a gramophone on the top floor and a radio alongside, a pedlar's cry can only be valued in relation to the price of his goods. To experience that gooseflesh shiver, we must go back to the former nights of Istanbul, when fire and every kind of insecurity obliged the citizen to stay in his home, alert as a mountain traveller.

Tanbûri Cemil's[26] 'Lullaby' is hardly a musical masterpiece, but if you can find the disc, listen to it carefully. It conveys in the liveliest way the intimacy in a community whose economic stability wavers, whose religious foundations have begun to crumble and whose traditions, once its pride, have disintegrated. The tanbur conveys the whole atmosphere with an imitative music that is scarcely art. I'm sure our former Istanbul did not consist only of melancholy emotions and sensibilities but enjoyed more pleasures than we imagine. Like Hüseyin Rahmi's[27] novels that make fun of every phase of our lives, the lullaby too was perhaps composed to divert. Nevertheless, in the world of the poor, a dark shadow had begun to loom over the lives of these simple and well-adjusted people who looked for happiness through spiritual harmony. In fact, a spontaneous melancholy was born of certain elements of life, like one evening in the theatre when we watch an empty stage. The oil lamp, the street half-lit by gaslight, the voices of beggars, the watchman's cudgel, the fear of fire, the mournful whistle of ferryboats and the strange psychological states caused by too intense a religious life nourished sadness in an almost mathematical way. Whatever it was, it existed and thickened the atmosphere about us in an almost tangible form. When we lost it and found ourselves shaken and stripped bare, we realized it had played a large part in our lives.

Do you remember a little article by Ahmed Rasim[28] called *Sokaklarda Geceler* ('Street Nights') that appeared in 1913 in *Nevsalî Milli* ('The Nation's New Year')? The piece shows all the magic of Istanbul nights alongside the misery of local life. Now totally lost, or surviving only as a fragment, the old Istanbul quarter still lives on there, talking in its sleep.

Very few have leant over their city like him, registering all he heard like a recording machine.

Once I met Ahmed Rasim. He was enjoying a morning *rakı* in a seaside tavern on Heybeli Island. I began to speak of the feelings that had gathered in me over the years. He looked at me with bleary, bloodshot eyes and changed the subject completely. But for a moment he seemed to listen, then suddenly asked, 'Do you like my *bestenigâr*?' A little surprised, I replied, 'Yes, very much.' Was I right to be surprised, I wonder? I had looked for the writer and found the musician. It might have been the chronicler who appeared. The story of *bestenigâr* is a whole other part of our former life. In his youth, Ahmed Rasim gave music lessons to the female slaves of Sadullah Pasha – a famous military commander in Abdülhamid's time, whose mansion was then at Çemberlitaş and is now the head office of a pious foundation. One of the slaves was a lovely young girl called Nigâr, loved by the poet, who also admired her talents as much as her beauty. She died of tuberculosis.

Hence his poem that began, '*I am the music of Nigâr that sets hearts on fire,*' was put to music and became an elegy for the girl. This little song, one of the most beautiful in the style of Dede Efendi's famous elegy on his own daughter's death, was a turning point in the development of our musical sensibilities.

It is not only this melody that has disappeared from the old Istanbul. The very character of the neighbourhoods is lost. You can read about the old quarters in Neşet Halil. In his profound and beautiful writings, you will discover the secrets of all the Istanbul neighbourhoods, presented with a bitter regret closely linked to his love for the new way of life. Today, the neighbourhoods are no more. Only scattered here and there throughout the city are some old, poverty-stricken former inhabitants, old inhabitants who endure countless difficulties as they wander from district to district, sometimes emerging from hidden corners to ask news of each other, to drink their coffees and recall the past. For me, they are the real poets of Istanbul. Their faltering feet wander in search of past time, at the corners of apartment blocks which are without style or elegance, on asphalt roads whose sides are still empty of buildings, seeking in vain in the faces of children of old acquaintances. But these pitiful relics left behind by the caravan search in vain and peer confused in every direction. Today's neighbourhood is not as it once was, an organic community closely bound by strong ties, but is simply a section of a municipality. The neighbourhood has gradually been replaced by a high-rise block of flats, a little tower of Babel where a different radio station blares from every window, the inmates ignorant of who live above or below, indifferent to the living or the dead.

Now they are only a memory, those Istanbul quarters where a herd of humanity used to live packed closely together, instinctively aware of danger, a part of their values disappearing every day in the dusty streets overhung with vines, where children used to learn the latest songs of the city from the sweet vendors. Strangely, we too, like the neighbourhoods, have lost the ability to live and enjoy a communal life.

In the Istanbul of old, even in my childhood, every class, rich and poor, enjoyed life together. Moonlight excursions, Kağıthane parties, outings to Çamlıca, picnics by the Bosphorus – almost all ensured the city's communal way of life. They were customs derived from the Middle Ages when enjoyments were few. Until recently, they continued as shared pleasures, but changes in the economic laws, the decline of taste, the divisions between us, a few more each day, and the influx of new, foreign fashions and desires opposed rightly

130

or wrongly to the old turned Istanbul into a city where its people no longer shared entertainments. There was no longer inherited wealth to finance moonlight trips, and for some time we had begun to find Kağıdhane rather commonplace. Büyükada replaced Çamlıca, and Sunday picnics added little to the city's diversions. We live in an age when foreign cinema controls our entertainment. We gather together in the dark. Songs accompanied on the guitar by the astoundingly intelligent, daring and devoted son of a millionaire railway tsar are sung to a lovely laundress on a moonlit night in Honolulu. The next morning, we hear them whistled by shop assistants on the shores of the Bosphorus, we listen to their ludicrous howls, we admire a woman's dress and make-up and a man's capers – in short, a heap of idiotic absurdities.

Not until a fruitful new life returns its own particular appearance to the city, and not until we live our lives creatively again, will the people of Istanbul surely cease to amuse themselves in solitude.

IV

Today, one side of our lives is like a theatre wardrobe. There is nothing more melancholic than seeing Hamlet's black costume, or Ophelia's robes or King Lear's beard, out of their context. It is only works that are great in their unity that can help us to overlook the discord in such an experience.

Recently, I happened to come across what were perhaps the most pathetic remnants of a festival. I was hurrying on business from Fatih to Beyoğlu. In the recently opened avenue, the car suddenly came to a stop under the Valens Aqueduct.[29] We had apparently met with one of the festival carts. At first I didn't recognize it. In a wooden cart dragged with great difficulty by a horse so incredibly gaunt that all his bones were visible, and so elongated that I thought the animal would never end, about 10 young girls dressed in red, green, pink, orange and sky blue were singing a strange tango air and clapping hennaed hands in celebration. With their motley clothes that looked even more crass in the grey overcast air, their carts of rough, unpolished wood, their horses with emaciated jutting muscles, more like a caricature of an endless locomotive, and their rudimentary songs and joyless gaiety, they seemed more like something from an eerie ghost story. It occurred to me that if I looked closely, I would meet something old and decayed which would disintegrate and scatter into dust. I met several similar carts along the way, but in spite of their frequency, I couldn't get used to the experience. And the thought that there is no longer any real place for festivals in our society gave me little comfort.

In the old Istanbul of the past, festivals were completely different. On the morning of a bayram, even the sun rose with an almost spiritual difference. In our old lives, the almanac had a religious, almost mystical significance. The city made ready for the bayram several days before and if the Sugar Bayram was approaching, it consisted of one massive preparation for transforming the Ramazan celebrations, which suddenly turned into revolving wheels and merry-go-rounds and carousels, with horses and their shiny Circassian saddles and silver whips and a thousand surprises. The festival locations gave the city a colourful aspect very different from that of everyday life. The supreme ruler of these days was the child. There was no connection at all between the bayram I had just seen and the bayrams of the past.

A few years ago, I saw the last roundabout in Kadırga Square. The old friends of my childhood had become so worn, so wretched! The horse's ears drooped, two feet were broken. The giraffe had lost its elegance, its long neck reduced to the size of a piece of string. All the animals were sick and miserable, like victims of a new strain of leprosy held in time's underground cellar. They were looking at me as if saying,

Ah, see how we are now, the last remnants of a dream.

I turned my eyes to the crowd around me: they, too, resembled the last remnants of a dream.

No, Istanbul needs a new life, new festivals, new diversions, a new historical time. From now on, it is a city that earns its bread by the sweat of its brow, and everything must be arranged accordingly.

V

It is not only Istanbul's past that gives rise to such thoughts and feelings. Dadaloğlu writes:

The dying die; it's the living who remain and belong to us.

When a civilization, or indeed life, moves on, much is lost and disappears, but there are also kingdoms that have dominion over time. What is distinctive and fine in a culture is the way it clothes the spirit in unchanging colours. Architecrure, ever since the Ottoman Conquest, has existed in Istanbul for generations. The true Turk finds his Istanbul in this architecture.

There are very few cities that have surrendered to a single architectural style as much as Istanbul. Those who compare Istanbul with Rome, Athens, Isfahan, Granada and Bruges are justified. There is even an aspect of Istanbul which is slightly superior. For Istanbul is not only a city of many monuments and monumental works of art; its natural setting enhances their appearance, like beautiful women whose natural gifts are offset and enriched by ornaments and splendid garments. Seven hills, two or even three seas, if we include the Golden Horn, the various points of perspective and, finally, the continuous play of light that results from the tussle between the north and south winds, bring us at every moment the changing aspects of these works of art.

I have spoken above of the several separate cities that make up Istanbul and how their architecture and perspectives create such diversity. What a difference there is between the city of monuments if we look from the door of the Ahmediye mosque at Topkapı[30] that opens onto the avenue, or from any of its its empty sites, or beyond the several spots so frequently ravaged by fire, and compare the magnificent skyline; we can contemplate from a coffee house in Yedikule,[31] composed of great mosques merging with one another and with the fragments of wall along the seafront. Seen from afar, a country of minarets and silver domes allures the traveller approaching from the Sea of Marmara, but from the heights of Yeşilköy, it becomes an overcast, nebulous mirage. The Bosphorus seen from the outer courtyard of Süleymaniye gives the impression of having been planned as part of the mosque, a third courtyard designed by a master architect, spacious and wide, abundantly endowed with trees and water, very different from the Bosphorus we can contemplate from another hill or that we glimpse from the ferryboat.

And so the heights of Çamlıca and Üsküdar, the wide windy balcony of little Çamlıca, the slopes of Eyüp[32] provide us with our daily bread – a landscape of ever-changing appearances. In the words of Yahya Kemal, Istanbul is like the beautiful woman in his line:

I looked, you were twice as beautiful when you spoke.

The truth about Istanbul is that she is like a woman you don't love at all or like a much-loved woman whose every mood and detail you dwell on with passion.

Undoubtedly, after her landscape with its many beauties, her greatest attraction is her architecture. Around its white flower the dreamlike seasons revolve, deepening the melody of that silent orchestra with more colour and more intensity. For her, the seasons seem to compete with one another, the south wind and the north, night and morning.

She is the music of the hours and the dream that overflows with light. The true success of our old masters lies in their ability to create a union with nature. With the exception of the mosques of Istanbul, there is very little architecture where the mechanical function of stone and the enduring strength of form can be ignored; very few buildings surrender so delightfully as those of Istanbul to the play of light, to be reborn and renewed at every moment.

Those who confuse a crowd of statues in a cathedral with clever architectural effects may praise other arts as much as they like; my personal admiration is for those makers of monuments that stand simply as they are, like a naked human body; it goes to our architects whose divine sense of proportion has transformed prayer into a smile of intelligence and who have changed insensible matter into a hymn recited to the sun. We have forgotten most of their names and are so involved with trivialities that we have never once in our lives turned round to look at their work. These are the unknown ascetic masters who now lie under some toppled cypress, in some corner of the city which they fashioned inch by inch with such patience and faith in God.

They worked on Istanbul as though a jewel had passed into the hands of a good diamond cutter. Why shouldn't we praise them? There are few architectural works as fine as the interiors and exteriors of our mosques.

Of course, it didn't all happen in a day. For the formation of this pearl that emanates its own pure radiance, the Selçuk mother-of-pearl had to absorb centuries of past history and local traditions, then it had to be passed through the alembics of Iznik and Bursa, its shell gradually cast away and, lastly, its strength challenged in Nilufer's hospice, in the mosque of Bayezid I, in the Green Mosque, and in the mosque at Edirne,[33] with its triple-balconied minarets.

The architecture of the Ottoman Empire resembled the empire itself. In order to sit on the throne of kings, it selected from the capital's military headquarters and from the newly conquered cities many of their inherited traditions, trying out several refinements, and when at last Mehmet II's strength had reopened the gates of the great city, it took its place alongside Ayasofia, sure of its power.

The Byzantine Empire finally collapsed when the architectural complexes of Fatih and Bayezit settled on two of the hills of Istanbul, like a flock of soft white doves let loose from dawn, followed almost immediately by the plasticity of Sultan Selim's mosque, which conquered the third hill with ease and mastery.

The Bayezit Mosque is like a seed sown in the Istanbul earth. In itself it contains all its future growth and blossoming flowers, all its fertile seasons.

A traditional story I like very much tells us that when the mosque was completed, Bayezid II made it a gift of a pair of pigeons which he bought from a poor woman.

Evliya Çelebi is an inexhaustible treasurehouse of stories about the Bayezit mosque. When the architect could not decide where to place the *mihrâb*, which shows the direction of Mecca, and asked Sultan Bayezid in which direction it should be, the sultan said, 'Step on my foot!' As soon as the architect did so, he saw the Kaaba.

It was Sultan Bayezid who performed the first Friday ritual prayer in the mosque and never once missed his rituals of the afternoon and evening prayers.

Again, according to Evliya Çelebi, it was the men of religion and scholars who administered the mosque. Once a week they interpreted the readings. In Evliya's time, it seems that the mosque precincts were densely wooded.

The Bayezit Mosque with the hospice opposite was a complete group of buildings that included public baths and a religious school at the other end of the square. By having his complex built where Heraclius's Byzantine community had once been, Bayezid II changed the whole landscape of the city.

By the time Süleyman the Lawgiver came to the throne, Istanbul with its mosques, caravanserais, baths, religious schools, great palaces, fountains and tombs of saints was already a perfect Turkish city.

But this cityscape which, until now, had belonged to us was transformed by a genius.

And this genius was Sinan. His creative drive tempered by method, mingled century-old forms to compose Istanbul's skyline, using marble, limestone, porphyry, domes, arches and stalactites; he changed proportions, he broke down symmetry, he increased the size and width of everything, he multiplied their numbers and as though his genius could continue to infinity the experiences and discoveries of his predecessors, he brought forth new shapes and new compositions.

Every style of architecture collects around it a number of serious problems. When Sinan appeared, imperial architecture had two main problems. One was the dome that gives every building its shape and identity; the other was the monotonous uniformity of the side elevation walls. Sinan almost plays with both. He hangs the dome over the interior place of worship, so that the supporting buttresses are invisible. Outside, a half dome and a necklace of little domes are brought by his artifice to a near natural formation, in spite of their vast proportions.

As for the problem of the side elevations, he solves it in the construction of the Şeyzade Mosque. The variations he created by means of arches and pillars, and galleries and windows, are astounding. It is a rare genius who can combine so well the monumental and the graceful, the organic and the decorative. How does he break the rhythm and yet return to it again?

But his most amazing facet is the breadth of his creativity. While everyone is struck with admiration before the domes of Şeyzade, he abandons himself to the luminous emptiness of Süleymaniye and, in a single swift glide of his eagle wings, covers a part of Istanbul and half of the Bosphorus. From one heady flight, he passes to Edirne, the old capital, and builds the jewels of Selimiye's cascades. Meanwhile he conquers the whole of Istanbul with his mosques of Mihrimah, Rustem Pasha, Piyale Pasha, Kılıç Ali and Sokulu Mehmed Pasha, and with the theological schools, the aqueducts, tombs, fountains, palaces and pavilions and little mosques. Perhaps if he had been left on his own, his art, rich and comprehensive as the empire itself, might have created Istanbul as a single edifice with seven domes on seven hills, connected by arches and galleries whose secret was known only to himself, and which covered the valleys between. He might have planted huge trees with their rewarding greenery; on the gentle slopes he might have set pious schools and health hospices, and step by step he might have realized his dream of stone that would reach three seas and their shores.

But failing that, he achieved something similar. He broke the dream as though it was a jewelled string of stars, and beginning with his adopted city, scattered them to the four corners of the empire.

Happy era, when ringing hammer blows competed with the prayers of Islam's warriors and shouts of victory, with the clash of swords and hoofbeats! Everywhere in the great empire they are sculpting white stone and melting lead for the domes in gigantic cauldrons; skilled overseers, artisans, half-alchemists, half-saints who are watching by the porcelain-tiled kilns the seasons that will never fade, of carnations and pomegranate flowers, of almond and plum blossom, and belief in the union with God, being slowly fired along with the good news of victory proclaimed in verses of the Koran. Under flat bronze mallets, gold is being hammered to gild religious schools, hospices, caravanserais, hans, great palaces, the borders of public drinking fountains and libraries until it emerges fine as a butterfly's wing or like sheets of a glimmering greyish blue. A workman in the Süleymaniye courtyard busy transforming into stone a verse from the Koran, fresh from the calligrapher's hand for the unfinished mosque, looks up and sees sailing boats approaching the harbour like great seagulls. They carry huge marble chunks from Marmara and the islands of the Mediterranean for a mosque under construction in Üsküdar. The clamour of porters carrying timber logs just brought from the forests of Kastamono[34] resounds in his ears and mingles with the fresh fragrance of pine and juniper that drifts up to him.

I've often wondered if Sinan and Bâkî were friends. When Süleymaniye was being built, Bâkî was a young mullah, between 25 and 30 years old, who, for a year, had supervised the building works of the Süleymaniye complex. Perhaps it was here that he learned to manipulate Turkish so powerfully, when he witnessed the rise of an art with such maddening strength, whose rules were unfamiliar to him. When he returned from

Aleppo in 1572 with Kadızade, his teacher and patron, and had doubtless made his first Friday prayer in the mosque where he had once wandered among the foundations, he must have looked long at its finished arches, its pillars, its amazing mihrâb, at its doors like eulogies to victory, at its courtyard paved with marble which Evliya Çelebi tried to describe in language peculiar to himself, comparing it to crystal and its whiteness to 'the harem of white' or 'white pastures', and noting its spacious dimensions. Perhaps he ran to the architect who was the pride of an empire and clasped his hands.

'Blessed Sinan! Poet of stone which is silent and speaks volumes; you who have transferred our faith and your own living pulse to sleeping matter! You who dissolved light like metals melted in the most complex compounds, and from it cut garments for our victories! Not only have you created a mosque for this city which would be the envy of the whole world, you have reached the most difficult limits of human thought,' he said. But no, Bâkî could never have spoken in such inflated and affected language; he must have uttered words more simple and elegant, like a prayer.

They say that Süleyman the Lawgiver often took Bâkî with him on trips on the Bosphorus and the Golden Horn. While he was writing the wonderful elegy for his sovereign, and perhaps as they returned from their trips, he thought of Süleymaniye that never left the horizon and appeared before them only when they had passed the Bosphorus towers and were clear of Sütlüce. He saw it as a massive pile ready to take flight. Real architectural construction in our poetry begins with this poem.

The old Valde Mosque at Üsküdar, whose beauty we know from the poet Yahya Kemal, is one of Sinan's last achievements. At least the design and preliminary building are his. Built as a pious foundation, the mosque and its environment are still one of the most beautiful corners of Istanbul despite additions that conceal part of the landscape. The mosque which withdraws into itself has a very close empathy with its neighbourhood. It is a gift from Selim II to his beloved wife. But as royal custom did not allow the sultan to name his wife, the foundation act read, 'A mosque will be built at Üsküdar to honour the virtues of the mother of my son Murad, till the end of the world and the last judgement.' It is impossible not to appreciate its modesty. Selim II praised Sinan as one among equals like Bâkî, Sokullu,[35] Piyale Pasha,[36] Kılıç Ali Pasha and Hüsrev Pasha;[37] in this fleeting world, all were Selim II's heritage from his father.

Sinan was one of those artists who exhausted a complete tradition on his own and left very little for his successors to achieve. Like Phidias the Greek sculptor and Michelangelo and Palladio in the Renaissance era, who by themselves accomplished what would have taken the efforts of several generations to do over a long period so that art might develop at leisure, he managed in the space of a single life to fulfil all the great possibilities of our architecture. That is why his happiest apprentices were those who followed the call to India. They alone were able to give a true measure of their talents in a new environment and among traditions different from ours. Thanks to this change of location, it was easier for them to recall our architecture which had preceded Sinan.

Those who remained in Istanbul had a more difficult task. They had to work very patiently to break with tradition and find new solutions, in order to prove original after this giant who had discovered everything he was looking for, experimenting with every kind of proportion and inventing the most difficult combinations as though he knew them all by heart. In the seventeenth century when national life was at its peak and everything including boundaries seemed settled, to search for a new form was impossible, especially for a sacred edifice like a mosque. To us, the mosque with a single dome was like a cathedral to the Christians. We couldn't easily give it up. At the time, Turkey was self-sufficient. All eyes in the East were on Istanbul which was completely national in its tastes, a mirror of national life unstained by the slightest speck of rust. Every fashion and elegant grace, every kind of creative drive in social and private life, originated from there. All the elements of our lives were totally integrated; behind every life was such a luminous soul that not the slightest crack in its integrity could be permitted. We were closed not only to Eastern influences but also to influences from the West. In spite of their scholarly and religious studies, Arab tastes had not yet penetrated the Ottoman Empire. Moreover, even Persia, which had been an example to our literature for three centuries, had begun to be perceived as different and remote from us. The Ottoman Empire was 'the country of Rum'. Where there was no national culture there were only neighbourhoods. And the empire was proud of this law. In this situation, our architects could not abandon a tradition whose beauty and nobility they acknowledged. Thus, they kept within Sinan's orbit but occasionally returned to an era before him. Everything signified by the central and side domes had not yet said the last word. There were still many melodies of invention or skill to be sought for and discovered on this instrument. The architects of the seventeenth century and those of even finer taste who worked in the first half of the eighteenth century allowed none to be overlooked.

When we observe some of the changes in proportion made by the chief architect Sadefkâr Mehmed, who carried the torch of Turkish architecture after Sinan, we cannot claim that he was so completely different from his predecessor. The concept of the central dome that rises above four half-domes, and that is characteristic of Sultan Ahmed, comes from Sinan's Şeyzade Mosque. When Sinan was happy to seek new forms for every one of his works and was satisfied with simply noting his discoveries, he never returned to them again. Sadefkâr Mehmet made many changes to his master's discoveries. The most important of these is the series of little half-domes that give the exterior building a landscape of mountains carved step by step.

Most of the wall panels you see here in Şeyzade form the rim that upholds the rhythmic pyramidal structure. In this respect, Sadefkâr Mehmed may be said to be the greatest virtuoso of our architecture. It is the same inside the mosque.

In order to achieve the width he wants, the architect almost empties the building from within!

Sultanahmet's interior is a complete blue dream of spring; very few works of architecture weave a tissue of light with such delicacy.

The ceramics certainly play a greater role than the architecture but are still controlled by the architecture which directs light like the artificial cascades that give form to water; light is distilled through the architecture and finds its strength by reflecting off the walls and arches. As soon as we enter the mosque, an atmosphere of dream begins, as though we are held in a prism.

I believe that nowhere has the art of stained glass produced better or more perfect works than ours and that they can compare with great paintings. I am happy to find this light again, this colour of honey and yellow agate, the luminous green beside it and all those red tulips. Their colour sings to me like the sound of the old Koran reciters, which in my childhood elicited a unique intoxication, and when I turn my gaze away, a star-sprinkled blueness begins. Those who talk of Sultanahmet praise the beauty of its mosaics, but, personally, I don't separate one quality from another. The primitive ornamentation immediately emphasizes the mechanical aspect of the whole building. These ceramics are undoubtedly the finest of their kind, but the art of mosaic by itself is not to be compared with a great art like architecture. I have always preferred ancient calligraphy to mosaics. It seems to me more personal, more varied and to have a more charming atmosphere. I think we must stroll about Sultanahmet as though we were wandering on the hills of Kozyatağı or Eyüp on a summer noon, relaxing half-intoxicated with the light and the colour green, in the midst of the sound of mill wheels turning in the orchards or lulled by the hum of insects, or watching the moonlight over the inlets of the Bosphorus. One must take great care not to break the crystal palace of blue light around us with too much close attention.

These mosaics are indeed very fine. The reds of the pomegranate flowers, the purplish whites and the meadow greens are truly unique. But suppose they had not been created as separate panels but continued as a single design and a single wall. With no space between one panel and the next, the eye wearies! Moreover, if one panel breaks the rhythm and the next cannot pick it up, it has the effect of a garment made of the same colour but of different materials. I prefer the uniform garb of the Green Mosque. But it does not have Sultanahmet's free play of light. The interior of Sultan Ahmed Mosque[38] is like the paradise I dreamt of in my childhood.

According to Evliya Çelebi, the mosque's foundations were laid by Evliya Efendi, the sultan's imam and Evliya Çelebi's tutor; by Sheikh Aziz Mahmud Hüdayi Efendi of Üsküdar, head of the Celvetî order; by Judge Karasümbül Ali Efendi; by the treasurer Kalender Pasha; and by the minister supervising the mosque's foundation, Kemankeş Ali Pasha.

Sultan Ahmed in person removed earth from the foundations and carried it away in his robe.

Evliya observes that the mosque was erected on the ruins of the grand vizier's palace and that work was begun on the dome three years after the building was begun – he compares the mosque to a huge unpierced pearl. Noting the objects suspended in the mosque (he used the word 'chandelier' in the sense given by dictionaries of the time), he says they were worth a hundred times the Egyptian treasury, and he particularly mentions Cafer Pasha, a minister of Abyssinia, who made a present of six emerald lamps. It is said they weighed fifty *okka* each and were hung by golden chains from six-cornered chandeliers. Evliya says about these lamps that 'their tiny particles of emeralds are worth a Greek poll-tax'. But what is really fine in Evliya's account is revealed when he describes Sultan Ahmed, the builder of this mosque, as a prince of a 'courteous and gentlemanly nature'. The seventeenth century was a century that appreciated the arts. What Evliya writes about the mosque door made by his own father, who was chief goldsmith to the palace, is also very important.

'It is a decorated door without peer, with silver locks and hinges, a silver ring sunk in it, with designs engraved by hand, and tiny scraps of brass, metal and wood. Some say this door came from the Kızıl Elma (Red Apple) church in Estergon but they are mistaken. When the Austrian infidels took Estergon in 1013 they removed the said door and placed it at the entrance to St Étienne Cathedral inside the citadel of Vienna, calling it St Mary's Gate. As for the aforesaid door of Sultan Ahmed Mosque, it was made when our late father, Dervish Mehmed Zilli, God rest his soul, was chief jeweller to the palace; his name was included in the two inscriptions above the door, along with his titles and functions.'

How sad that from the time of its completion, in the reign of Mustafa I, a time which was the very essence of tranquillity, peace and contemplation, like music on a flute, this masterpiece witnessed an uninterrupted series of rebellions which lasted till 1826. Mad with rage and hatred, mobs beat down the door like seven-headed monsters and held bloody consultations under the porches in the courtyard. The bloodiest decisions on Canon Law were recited like prayers from the altars. It was towards this door that all the internal disorders of Ottoman history flowed until the suppression of the Janissaries in 1826.

The system of domes in the Yeni Cami[39] is like that of Sultan Ahmed. But its beauty owes more to perfection of detail than to its plan, and to its situation on the shore of a city, like a fairytale ship nearing but not quite reaching land. All through the seventeenth century, Turkey is to be found in the harmonious miracle of the arts with which it clad its architecture, calligraphy, gilding and bookbinding. Sinan is surely present here: even the side façade is almost a repetition of Süleymaniye but is more playful and sympathetic as though it was seeking connections with life. We know at first glance that though we are still within Sinan's orbit, we are entering a different climate. This music, this dynamic dance does not belong to the sixteenth century. Looking at the façade, we imagine we are listening to the melodies of the great contemporary composers like İtrî, Hafız Post[40] or Seyyid Nuh.[41] The door and windows, the arches, remind us of a lyric poem by Neşatî[42] or Naîllî.[43]

The New Mosque has quite a history. Everything in the seventeenth century has a past, a psychological adventure, a history closely linked with chance events. Holy foundations in a declining community, like individuals, gain a new independence. In time, changes of viziers, fires and various events resulted in assembling the New Mosque, but although the building began before the Sultanahmet Mosque, it wasn't completed till the reign of Mehmed IV.

Apart from the aspect visible from the sea, the situation of the mosque that Ahmed III caused to be built in the Üsküdar market to honour his mother, Hatice Gülnûş Emetullah, adds nothing to the city; to be admired, it must be seen at close quarters, exactly where it is, like a rose on the branch, shining in all the glory that belongs to that astonishing period in which it was built. It is the finest work of Ahmed III's era, unrivalled by the Sultanahmet fountain, the fountains of Tophane and Azapkapı, which create a continuity between the Tulip Period and the era of Mahmud I, and even by Ibrahim Pasha's hospices which are so elegant and so evocative of the true spirit of our Istanbul. It completes the seventeenth century, so rich in everything, even in disasters – for the Hekimoğlu Ali Pasha Mosque, despite all its many experiences, represents essentially a return to Sinan. The mosque of the sultan's mother has a feeling of richness and elegance, like the evening sun which gives no warmth, but a glow to all it touches, creating a melancholy splendour with the golden colours of nostalgia. The feeling particularly captivates a visitor, as soon as he enters from the outer courtyard into the beautifully adorned interior – like some fruit hidden in its skin – that breathes out an almost palpable fragrance like the perfume of a rose garden.

I love this mosque at evening time. At these hours, the elegant building is like silent music: as soon as you move away from the market hubbub into its atmosphere, you are in another world.

I went again this autumn. The mosque was deserted. Under the light of several lamps that did not quite fill the building but exaggerated the shadows, all the gilding and marble, the strange symbols, were shining like fearful mysterious signs from other distant worlds. A muezzin blind in both eyes, who had worked in the past in the Selimiye mosque, was wandering among the shadows and the otherwordly symbols, not a muscle of his face moving, groping for truths I had never sensed. Life is not only in what we see with our eyes. For the blind, everything is different, even movements of the mouth, perhaps because they lack the effect of light on their muscles, or perhaps the human countenance cannot be illumined by its own light; they are penetrated by a silence no sound can ever break, a tension perceived only in lifeless matter.

That evening, as I followed the silent enigma of the blind man who talked to me from behind a curtain of light, but did not see, the mystery around him increased. And so, continuing to ask his questions into his surrounding emptiness, he opened the door to the inner courtyard for me.

But the light I came into was no longer the light I had just come from, it was as though I had just entered a very different world that belonged to time rather than space, a world revealed by hands that apoke with time. Perhaps that is why the real contemporaries of the mosque seemed to be all around me.

Who was the architect of this mosque? We don't know. If one day we learn his name, we will undoubtedly number him alongside the names of Nedim, of Tâib[44] and of Tab'î Mustafa Efendi,[45] Ebubâkir Ağa[46] and the elegant Ali İzzet Pasha. But that evening, it was Tab'î Mustafa Efendi I most recalled, the composer of one of the irregular rhythms of Turkish music, called the Beyatî Aksak.

This little piece of his includes all the pleasures that give the Valide's mosque the feeling of a love offering. Perhaps I like this mosque so much because I know it is a contemporary of Tab'î Mustafa Efendi and his melody. For the little piece is one of several musical masterpieces which has survived its time.

When one stands by Sultana Hatice Emetullah's tomb in the market place beside the mosque, it is easy to understand the epoch. A similar tomb could not have been made in the fifteenth or sixteenth centuries. Those tender feelings, that feminine sensibility imbued with death, could only appear at a time when traditions were beginning to dissolve; they could only be born from a kind of childlike naturalism that began gradually at the end of the seventeenth century, a shape seen from afar like a great bird cage that took its final form in Ibrahim Pasha's time.

Sultana Hatice Emetullah, who shared her solitude with the lady Afife in the caged life of the harem, gave Mehmed IV two male children, who became successive rulers; she even accompanied Mehmed IV on his campaigns, giving birth to Ahmed III on Mehmed IV's Polish expedition; today she lies, not in a tomb, but with the assistance of a delightful bit of architectural fantasy, in a wonderful bridal chamber on a young bride's bed surrounded by soft tender grass and spring flowers.

VI

Istanbul is a city not only of great architectural works but also of little corners and unexpected views, and that is where her heart is to be found. Fine buildings provide the face seen from afar, but the other aspects fill in the portrait line by line and complete a framework of a thousand details of everyday experience and psychological states of mind. These, too, have a special architectural character of their own. But it is not an architecture that dominates everything around it, like the mosques of Bayezit, Süleymaniye, Ayasofya, Sultan Ahmed, Sultan Selim or the New Mosque; these little mosques give the impression of having melted into the privacy of the city; religious schools and fountains, edifices which are reduced to the most modest proportions in comparison with great and splendid fountains, they are not beautiful in themselves but as parts of the whole. Suddenly the ornamental slab of a marble fountain or a doorframe, or a white wall of beautifully carved stone, smiles at you in the most surprising place. Two cypress trees, an acacia or vine, a small unpretentious tomb or a cemetery you might mistake for a little garden makes a delightful corner. At first sight, you might compare it to theatrical or operatic decor arranged impromptu, but on closer inspection, you find it is a piece of the city's history. In the tomb lies a saint who died fighting on the day of the Conquest of Constantinople in 1453. The mosque was founded by an accountant in the time of Mehmed III, and the fountain was donated as an act of piety by one of the women from Abdülhamid I's palace. In the neighbouring cemetery, a great calligrapher or talented musician is buried under a communal stone inscribed with 'Only God is eternal'.

Few places are as attractive and pleasant as these little corners. They have come about through innumerable beliefs, traditions and natural good taste; they are the result of providence and even centuries of neglect. No pomp and circumstance, only generous nature, was responsible for the growth of the rose or the cypress or the plane tree, or flushed the Judas tree every spring, or hung the luminous bunches of grapes. Little by little they were shaped by time.

Secluded spots of the kind are to be found in nearly every part of Istanbul, in Üsküdar and by the Bosphorus. Some seem almost ready to fly up from the slopes where they lie with the sea just touching their feet. Some live in a genuine atmosphere of antiquity like remnants from the time of the Ottoman Conquest. In every one, trees, water and rocks converse with man like souls inspired to overflowing. They are our real landscapes, created from the lives of Istanbul's people, the work of men who look at creation through the concept of unity they carry in their souls. In very few places do art and architecture mingle so closely with daily life; such localities form the true core of the Istanbul 'neighbourhoods'.

Some among them include areas of authentic monuments, the result of a history of their time. As they succeeded one another, their development covered a whole part of the city. But little relics still survive at Ayvansaray, and especially at

Eyüp, long after the palaces of viziers and the sultan's sons-in-law have vanished.

All the cemeteries, tombs and fountains with their grills, inscriptions and sculpted tombstones, generous as the seasons provide their environment with materials and artworks of quality. The districts of Küçük Mustafa Pasha, Haseki, and Cerahpaşa, Topkapı and Silivrikapı are full of such monuments that regularly link the Golden Horn and the Sea of Marmara all along the ramparts.

Anyone going downhill one evening at Üsküdar, seeing only the Ayazma Mosque lit up in the distance, can enter a different timescale. The mosque of Abdülbâki in Sultantepe is in one of these delightful corners; a little mosque, unmemorable except for an inscription and two old tombs, beautiful only because it overlooks from a hill the whole countryside as far as Karacaahmet cemetery. If you pass through the very ancient Istanbul street, an avenue of cypresses, you cannot help being filled with a sense of curiosity when you emerge into the little mosque garden. Who is this Abdülbâki Efendi? The locals know him as the son-in-law of Aziz Mahmud Hüdayi Efendi.[47] But there is no trace of him anywhere. His name and the spot he chose for prayer, however, still survive. Those like me who love old things and places will go there occasionally and smell the ever-flowering rose bush in the garden and listen to the sweet chatter of little girls playing under its neighbour, the giant walnut tree.

Our old civilization was a religious civilization. One title only was awarded to a faithful member of its community when he died – that of an 'evliya' or saint. If he was beloved by the people he was considered a holy man and became a saint, which is why Istanbul is full of saints. In the first rank are those who died in Fatih Sultan Mehmet the Conqueror's army. Their achievements outranked those of the man who had died for justice and the state. From its commander who led the army, down to the last soldier, it was a sacred army, revered long before it planted its standards before the walls of the city. They were all saints. Today we read of the Conquest through Western eyes, and we criticize faults committed by Fatih during his lifetime: we examine them in the light of science and sociology. But our predecessors saw things very differently: they gave a sacred meaning to the national struggle that conquered Istanbul, they made no attempt to argue about theories of relativism. There are graves of martyrs nearly everywhere in the city, particularly by the walls. They are Istanbul's Turkish title deeds. Our lives in Istanbul began with veneration of the martyrs' tombs. It was with the first candle lit before their tombs that our ancestors overcame the deep but decadent spirituality of the Byzantines, full of pomp and expensive ceremonies and drowning for centuries in gold and silver. And places sacred to the people appeared everywhere. Then architecture arrived and embellished their sacredness with a little mosque, a little gilding and the colour green.

After the martyrs of the Conquest, a new kind of saint emerged: he played a major rôle in the life of the city, waging a continuous war between the purity of the soul and human passions – the elect called it 'the Great Fight'. He infused his epoch with love and wisdom won by constant vigilance, making his own experience useful to others. Such men were Yahya Efendi,[48] foster-brother of Süleyman the Lawgiver, Sümbül Sinan[49] and his successor Merkez Efendi,[50] and Aziz Mahmud Hüdâî Efendi who founded the Celvetî order and at the beginning of the seventeenth century ruled over all Istanbul.

Yahya Efendi was such a respected and courageous man that he was able to mingle with Süleyman the Lawgiver's private life. Like all learned men of the era, there were times when he experienced appointments, dismissals and advancements, or when he was angry with the sultan for years and never set foot in the palace. He lies between Beşiktaş and Ortaköy in a garden which he celebrated in a very peaceful poem.

During their lives, most of the saints prepared their last resting place as a house, a convent or a garden. Places where they had lived and worshipped became a kind of cocoon for them and a cemetery for those who wished to share in the spiritual life of holy men and to be near them. In Yahya Efendi's convent, divine grace assumes the appearance of a beautiful human face. Death is so close to life here that you can imagine you are on a mystic way or in a garden of love which is reached by just a few steps and terraces. Yahya Efendi's convent, with its specially inspiring atmosphere, must be considered one of the holiest places in the city.

The period takes great delight in gardens. At the time, the great poet Gâzâlî, nicknamed the 'Crazy Brother' on account of a very famous couplet and perhaps also of various encounters in his life, had a mosque, public baths and a garden built in Beşiktaş. The most sensitive of those who loved trees and gardens and who most appreciated Istanbul's climate was Süleyman the Lawgiver's vizier Siyavuş Pasha. He surrounded the pavilion he had built at Çatalca with a grove of Judas trees.

Sümbül Sinan took possession of the mosque of Bayezid II's vizier Koca Mustafa Pasha.

But best of all, let's hear about this district from Istanbul's supreme poet of landscape:

> In the contemplation of a view
> The next realm is so near a neighbour
> no wall divides it from our world.
> If you take a step you'll pass from one to the other
> andl meet the one you loved and lost.
> . . .
> O mystic night! Sümbül Sinan's soul
> burns like a jewel until the light of dawn.

But the mosque garden is a little Pantheon:

> Among inscriptions, ivy, trees and stones
> a light buried in calligraphy, Hâfız Osman
> illumines the black earth in this cemetery,
> he lies in his tomb haloed in holy light.

I wonder if visitors wandering in the atmosphere of the mosque garden remember that Koca Mustafa Pasha[51] was that barber of Bayezid II who, from his position as head keeper of the gates, attained the rank of vizier when he agreed to be sent to Italy, in order to poison Cem Sultan, and that perhaps he also played a role in assassinating a great warrior like Gedik Ahmed Pasha?[52] But the mosque converted from a church, the little cemetery, Sümbül Sinan's tomb and the plane tree beside it struck by lightning, its trunk wreathed in inscriptions by the great calligrapher Yesarî, create one of the loveliest views of Istanbul.

Undoubtedly, tomorrow this landscape will change. Tumbledown old mansions will be replaced by modern workshops or re-appear as stocking factories or similar places, and men with a different outlook on the world, who work by different rules, will come to inhabit the area round Sümbül Sinan, but the aura accumulated through centuries will still be preserved for us by Yahya Kemal's poem of love and pity.

Sümbül Sinan's successor, Merkez Efendi, lies near the mosque he had erected outside the walls, by a sacred spring he himself had discovered. It is sad that this Islamic 'asklepion' no longer exists; it shines among my childhood memories like a heavenly throne that emanates a dark, awe-inspiring spirituality. The trees that once made this place of pilgrimage so dark have been cut down, the convent cells round the courtyard have crumbled away, the well has been covered; in short, all the elements that created an air of mystery have vanished. The only remains are several of the dead in a bare unadorned room like a barracks and a dervish cell of fasting and prayer, its once-gilded grating worn away, overlooking the basin of the sacred spring.

Behind this grill, Merkez Efendi would plunge into deep meditation, reading the Koran from end to end, passing long, lonely winter nights until daylight, chained to endless prayer, watching the coming and going of the fish to which, as a child, I was taught to throw food, and the water from the underground spring, the colour of laurel green with violet streaks and silver, gleams like the eye of a frog.

The faces of these two men illuminated by the Koran, whose pages they pored over until their individual features dissolved into light, seem to us now like the divine opening chapter of the Koran, full of inspiration and compassion, the best and most beautiful aspects of our former civilization.

They were a softening influence on the harsh life of their time, like a tender smile on the sullen countenance of their era. They represented the finest models of Islamic tolerance and tenderness, sometimes to an absurd degree.

Just as Merkez Efendi's saintliness was only appreciated over time, so Aziz Mahmud Hüdayi Efendi, whose moral influence was as great perhaps as that of Prince Ahmed I, won deep respect only after the reign of Mahmud II. The Aziz Hüdayi complex below the Doğancılar at Üsküdar is an example of the lack of taste in the architecture of the Tanzimat era. What connection is there between Mahmud Hüdayi Efendi, a follower of Üftade of Bursa,[53] and these grotesque buildings, with their winter garden showcases, which ape the museum of ancient works opposite? They are models devoid of soul and meaning like the famous coats of armour of the second empire. It is among the foundations of the Sultanahmet Mosque that I dream of Aziz Mahmud Hüdayi Efendi's tomb. From time to time, I see him emerge from there, repeating the couplet I love so much, with an inconsolable melancholy:

Days come and go,
And fly away like birds.

Yes, days have come and gone. But they are still among us, those who bequeathed to time their marks of love and faith: their names and lives are still meaningful to our spiritual horizon. Now we no longer look for help from Sümbül Sinan in our wordly affairs, but we love and praise him and others like him, for their attitude towards life.

But even in their own time, did not the significance of these holy seekers bring a little honour to our nation's life?

A community who believed they were eternal conquered the afterlife through its sacred dead and, thanks to them, established its vast empire in Eternity bit by bit. Let us never forget that for them Bursa and Istanbul were cities as holy as Mecca and Medina.

VII

In addition to saints who were accepted and revered officially, who were respected by the sultans, who preached in the great Moslem mosques, in the mosques named after the sultans, and for whom special convents were built, there were other holy men, leaders of religious orders that were more or less separatist, often condemned to death along with their numerous disciples by learned men of the Sunni persuasion for disturbing the community with their mystical ecstasies. In those backward Middle Ages, when religion was everything, any reaction was possible. Anatolia had always been the mother of sects and religions. After the Babaî movement, the Alevi tendencies had developed, and nothing had managed to extinguish them. But the influence of the current mystics was equally strong in the Rumeli provinces, most of which had adopted Islam only recently, and whose population adopted a variety of religions. It was strange that from the sultans downwards – for example, even Mehmed the Conqueror – important men of state inclined to superstition nourished a love for the dervish sects. The single basic law of Islam, the agreement that there is only one God, facilitated the entry into its realm of many doubtful beliefs and interpretations. Of course, the economic conditions and insecurity of life accounted for this. Every great statesman, like the ordinary people, belonged to a sect. In the army, in the council chamber, among the people, they formed a brotherhood for self-protection, which brought a kind of balance to life. But when a sheikh who was approved for his morality, piety and mysticism was succeeded by a son or disciple who suddenly increased his ecstatic transports, the matter became very serious. When these influences infiltrated the army, most of whose members were Christians newly converted to Islam, violent measures of repression became necessary.

Now when someone is killed, a mausoleum is raised the next day, and a candle is lit on the same night and in the same place where he died. İsmail Maşuki, named 'The Youthful Sheikh' on account of his attractive youth and beauty, was the most famous of those sheikhs. The son of Pir Ali from Aksaray, he belonged to the Bayrâmi order but was beheaded in the Hippodrome, just beside what is now the Office of the Land Registry, and his body thrown into the sea. Later, a monument was erected for him there. When it became known that the waves had cast up his body at Rumeli Hisar, he was buried between Rumeli Hisar and Küçük Bebek.

In the seventeenth century, the Melâmî[54] order had found favour in Istanbul. Yahya Kemal has beautifully united in a couplet the poet Gaybî[55] and İdris-i Muhtefi,[56] two Melamî sheikhs who, according to their followers, had reached the height of sainthood:

> They conversed in their secret cell
> and İdris-i Muhtefî said to Gaybî

Although İdris-i Muhtefi was so famous that he held all Istanbul in his hand, and although he gave his era cause for alarm, he hid behind the pious, peaceful life of a very wealthy merchant who lived in a mansion belonging to Sultan Selim. According to an anecdote told by Atâyî, a witness who named him, this İdris possessed untold wealth. After his death, when they came to assess his estate, they struggled for a week and realized they could never assess all his separate investments and decided to divide them into categories.

Abdullah Efendi the Blond, commentator of the poems written in rhyming couplets called Mesnevî, and Ali Pasha, the 'second' conqueror of Mora, to whom the poet Nedim wrote his first great, beautiful long poem, were both members high in the hierarchy of the Melâmî.

VIII

If the magnificent architecture of former Istanbul has any rivals at all, they are its trees. But can they really be described as rivals? In fact, a tree is the most delightful accompaniment to our architecture and to all our lives. It knows how to offset white marble and carved stones as well as crumbling roofs and fountains with broken basins whose ornamental work was lost through neglect. It's like a paean to the sun.

All travellers to Istanbul comment on the beauty of our trees. The Istanbuls of Lamartine, Théophile Gautier and Lady Craven are full of trees and greenery, and a reader of Lamartine's *Voyage en Orient* often feels that the writer is describing a garden. Sometimes, as we see in prints and old engravings, a whole neighbourhood gives the impression it was built around a single tree, to emphasize the red colour and geometrical shape of a roof glimpsed through a green cluster of trees.

Our great architects never failed to set several cypresses and plane trees beside their buildings; the contrast with dense foliage created one of their finest compositions. Some went further and reserved a space in the centre of the divine geometry of the courtyard to a mosque or religious school for a cypress or plane tree to flourish, for a rose to blossom, for ivy to twine and twist. In fact, an old Turkish garden, such was its style. In Istanbul now, the best and certainly the only example of the unity of tree and architecture, apart from the gardens squeezed between old palace pavilions, is the courtyard of the Süleymaniye museum.

A wide-girthed plane tree or cypress always used to watch over every fountain, great or small. The day when light poured its blessed radiance over the sculpted marble, like fresh bread which might have been baked in the oven of the tree, it seems that architecture came into its own. Whether or not the architect or the pious donor saw the tree he had planted grow up, it was enough to know he had planted one. He knew that a tree entrusted to the earth is a gift of value, a talisman securing a neighbourhood, a district, even a whole community and all its religious beliefs.

Sometimes a fountain's cistern would form a terrace or a space for prayer. There is one with its little cemetery on the way to Balıklı. But my favourite is at just below Küçük Çamlıca where there is a prayer terrace and a flowing fountain dating from the time of Mehmed the Hunter.[57] To the side of this sacred terrace that faces the Sea of Marmara, the street named 'The Street of Two Eagles' rears up like the spotted back of an animal in the sun. Where did the name come from? Was it a souvenir, I wonder, of Mehmed IV's passion for hunting? Or of someone else who suffered the same passion? Or were the street and the fountain associated only accidentally? But this is certain, that Mehmed IV loved Camlica and had a hunting lodge and even a mosque built near that place of prayer. He came here to hunt in the difficult times before his dethronement.

Not only do the delights of architecture and the city benefit from trees, but the pure world of our classical poetry is also strewn with images of plane trees, cypresses and poplars, like carpet designs. But the real magic lies in legends. In a story I heard as a child, the prince met the fairy he was in love with but had never seen, in a prayer place such as I've described, under the kind of cypress tree praised by the poet Bâki for its height and grace, with a stream flowing from a spring below. He washed in the spring before praying, as he had been taught, said his prayers under the tree, and as he prayed he heard a voice repeating three times, 'Mesina, hold out one thread of your hair to Mustafa and accept him.' And three times from the depths of the cypress came the reply: 'I cannot, dear uncle! He is a human being and has been reared on raw milk.' But at the fourth time, a hair from the cypress appeared. At the end of the story, Mesina sent a prayer mat on which she had woven – from tears of course – a picture of the same fountain and cypress to remind her lover of herself for having been reared on raw milk; he had forgotten her, but as soon as he laid his head on the mat he heard the same voice and remembered, and returned to Mesina.

Two trees in particular have left their mark on the life and imagination of Turks: the cypress and the plane tree. The overall view of the city, especially from outside, owes much to the cypress groves like those at Karacaahmet, Edirnekapısı, old Tepebaşı and Ayazpaşa.[58] Some views gather around the plane trees in those atmospheric spiritual corners of the Bosphorus, and the cypresses of Eyüp once gave the whole of the Golden Horn its character. We owe the authentic melancholy of Istanbul's land and seascape to two trees, the fir tree and the stone pine, which both play a large part in developing our emotional sensibility.

My favourite is the plane tree. With its wide leaves, like fingers, and its friendly giant trunk, it reminds me of Peçevî's[59] tales of heroic fighters on the frontiers, who take up the word in councils of war and advise their generals on how to proceed.

And the truth is that every plane tree feels like a grandfather: they are the pride of our earth; perhaps it was from them that our forefathers learned their grave dignity, their mountain stillness. So I understand Yahya Kemal very well when he says that İtrî was educated in the school of the old plane trees:

It was from the ancient plane-trees
that the genius who gathered us together
heard our story that had lasted seven hundred years

Gradually Istanbul is losing her trees: it is not like our losing some old custom or tradition. Traditions vanish because others succeed them, or because they are no longer necessary, but the disappearance of a centuries-old tree is a different matter. Even if another tree is planted in its place it requires time to influence the landscape. And if it eventually succeeds, it cannot be the same tree blessed by our forefathers when they lived beneath it.

The death of a tree is like the loss of a great work of architecture. Sadly and inevitably, for a century or even more, we have become used to the loss of both. One after another, before our very eyes, masterpieces crumble into a heap of dust and ashes like a heap of salt that has fallen into the water; all over Istanbul, in every quarter, there are columns toppled, roofs collapsed, old religious colleges full of rubbish and charming little neighbourhood mosques and fountains in ruins. It would take little effort to restore them, but they deteriorate a bit more every day. They lie prone on the ground like the dead in an epidemic whom the living have not the strength to remove. The day that we realize that true creativity begins with preserving what already exists will make us happy.

How I wish I'd been like those old people full of passionate curiosity, who knew everything I knew in my childhood and never once forgot what they learned! I wouldn't only complain of the fate of trees here in Istanbul, I would make known to everyone all the gardens, all the little woods, from the reservoirs and even the Belgrade forest to Çamlıca, from İçerenköy to the Çekmeceler lakes. I would tell of the high trees that all alone guard a place of seclusion; the stone pines that resemble the free breath of lyric poems, their parasols wide open and carried high, the last remnants of Çamlıca's summer homes, filling our summer nights; the light fragrance of lime-trees; poplars whose pale shapes frame Istanbul autumns in panels of yellow amber; mastic trees whose names alone recall memories and character to the neighbourhoods; and one by one I would count the pretty vines that trail up the little stone steps of the coffee houses along the ramparts.

IX

The real inner landscape of Istanbul is created by the picturesque domestic architecture, composed of lines as soft as velvet and the rich colourful decor of its covered balconies opened or closed, its bay windows and jutting corbel supports, its eaves and canopies and open verandas.

It is sad that so little remains. After the Conquest, there was an immediate need for houses, and the first early neighbourhoods appeared, constructed of wood. The fear inspired by the great earthquake in the first year of Bayezid

II's reign and the subsequent shocks, along with the economic crises, accounted for the continued use of wood for building. Istanbul was always a city with many poor. It is strange to think that while we were filling Istanbul with wooden buildings which we thought suitable as city dwellings, the West had already given up wood for brick or stone, two centuries before. Nevertheless, the first palaces of the sultan and his ministers were wealthy mansions of stone. But however much the East loved building and excelled in it, they never knew how to preserve. To build the mosque of Sultanahmet, the palaces of five viziers were destroyed simultaneously. Of course, in this mosque we acquired a true masterpiece. But how sad that we know nothing about the palaces constructed in the era of Süleyman the Lawgiver, our most illustrious period. We can imagine how splendid they were from the remnants left to us of İbrahim Pasha's palace. Evliya Çelebi, whose information on these matters is often exaggerated, but in this case can be verified from his contemporaries, counted 39 ministerial mansions in Istanbul. Of these, he confirmed that 11 were built by Sinan. The palaces and wealthy mansions descended from the avenue of the Divan to Sultanahmet and Akbıyık and continued to the Sirkeci of today, then on to Kumkapı, Kadırga, Süleymaniye and Şehzadebaşı, and from there to Fatih and Edirnekapı, then by Aksaray to Koca Mustafa Pasha and Yedikule. The areas of Ayvansaray and Eyüp were full of similar mansions and particularly of summer homes. The terraces we now see bordering the modern Atatürk Boulevard, from Unkapanı to Zeyrek, are the gardens and estates of those great dwellings that once belonged to the sultan and his viziers.

In the mansions, then known as palaces, were kept, according to the owner's wealth, 60 or 70, sometimes 100, concubines and slaves and the same number of household servants. Treasurers, ministers of foreign affairs, army judges and Islamic judges all lived in the same style and splendour as the rich. On both sides of the Golden Horn from the sixteenth century onwards, some of these people had villas on both shores of the Golden Horn, the Bosphorus and at

Kadırga, and in the seventeenth century along both shores of the Bosphorus. On the hills of the Bosphorus and the shores of Kadıköy, stretching as far as Fenerbahçe and today's Moda, there were pavilions and vineyards in the gardens. Atâyi tells us that the mansion of the aforementioned İdris-i Muhtefi was as big and populous as a whole neighbourhood. Mehmed Ağa of Fındıklı reports that after the revolt of the Janissaries, which followed the dethronement of Mehmed IV and resulted in the assassination of Siyavuş Pasha, the palace was severely damaged, but he never stops praising its beauty and the workmanship of the doors and cupboards inlaid with mother-of-pearl.

All these grand palaces and mansions burned down every five or six years, some as a result of the Janissary revolts. Those that escaped the fire collapsed into ruins because of the poor building material used. Throughout the seventeenth century, when the Janissaries felt threatened, particularly after the assassination of Osman II[60] and the Abaza[61] revolt – that was the time when the phrase '*kul kırma*' spread among them – and when sometimes a Janissary, seeing the fire brigade at work, would calmly watch, completely indifferent, as the city burned. Often the fire was ignored in favour of looting. And sometimes it was the Janissaries themselves who set fire to the houses. After the revolt of the Janissaries in 1826, there were a few fires like that; in the 1650 revolt, Samsoncu Ömer quite openly incited the ringleaders to burn down the city. As a result of almost 30 years of fires, the city was rebuilt, but with every fire, a whole world of wealth went up in smoke, carpets, furs, beautiful woven materials, works of art, manuscripts and jewellery; in spite of the loss of their possessions, nobody thought of building in stone or widening the streets.

Even when opportunities arose to rescue the city from suffocation, they were overlooked. Raşid,[62] in his report on an imperial wedding in the time of Ahmed III, stresses the sultan's sense of justice and mercy when he had houses removed to allow part of the bride's dowry, a tree made of silver, to be brought to the palace at Edirnekapı, then had the houses rebuilt in exactly their original style.

As things began to deteriorate from the seventeenth century onwards, people, and especially statesmen, who commissioned large houses to be built, were not highly thought of. As for constructions of stone, oriental envy described them as 'structures too solid and threatening'.

On account of the custom of confiscating the goods and possessions of statesmen who died naturally or were assassinated, wealth failed to accumulate. And in difficult times, large houses of the kind were inevitably neglected. For these and other reasons, it is impossible for us to see in their framework the people who, for centuries, shaped our lives and gave us our tastes. We know neither Bakî nor Nefi's[63] house.

> Come beloved elegant as a cypress,
> take possession of our old house near Beşiktaş, it
> suits you,

said Nedim, half-jokingly of the house he wants to offer his lover. And if only the house had survived until today, where Nâilî, in the sweet melancholy of his couplet, waited for his lover, we would understand these poets differently:

> Oh, Nâilî, is it not worth worlds of painful waiting
> To see her little steps approach, like the moon
> When night descends?

Sinan, Itrî, Sadefkâr Mehmed Usta, Seyyid Nuh and Hâfiz Post are represented in today's city only by a name or a grave, should it still remain.

Every city changes once every 300 or 400 years. If the theory of cyclic civilizations is correct, a civilization takes five centuries to complete one cycle, and very little remains of the past. Accordingly, it is impossible to retain all the memories of the past, but in the same way we have also lost times much nearer to ourselves. Neither the summer palaces described in the *Sahilname'ler* ('Books of the Bosphorus'), which Selim III ordered his army officials to write, nor the mansions and pavilions at Üsküdar, built by Mahmud II where he stopped off on his cavalcade along the Asiatic shores, have remained with us.

The Üsküdar of the nineteenth century, with its mansions and summer houses, was nothing like the Üsküdar of the poem 'The Imaginary City':

> Indeed, the reign of Üsküdar the impoverished did not
> last long.

The pavilions and mansions built and furnished in the Tanzimat era, with their elegant lives so different from the past and their new tastes which we know about from a whole succession of memoirs, have similarly disappeared. When Sahip Molla in his youth went to visit Reşid Pasha, he saw him one morning wearing a yellow robe, a yellow jacket from Damascus and on his finger a topaz ring of the same colour; years later, whenever he passed the house in a Bosphorus ferryboat, he always pointed out to people around him the room where he had sat. Nothing remains of Fuad Pasha and Midhat Pasha's houses, which covered a whole neighbourhood at Şeyzadebaşı. Reşid Pasha's second villa, which he sold to the treasury for 50,000 gold pieces to cover his debts, has also vanished. Şirvânizâde Rüştü Pasha's mansion on the Ağa slopes seems to have been at Ekşi Karadut. The son of this Rüştü Pasha was the focus of a series of money scandals of the time. In his book 'The Young Ottomans', Ebüzziya[64] described at length a visit he paid him, when he saw his English-style furnishings and his library. In the final years of Abdülaziz, Murad V in his illness went as a guest to the Mermerli Yalı (the 'Marble Villa') in Üsküdar, for a change of air, and from there he wrote to Midhat Pasha a letter, whose story Ebüzziya relates in his book. The three houses belonging to Abdülhak Hâmid's family on the waterfront at Küçük Bebek, which he mentions in his memoirs; a big palace between Çamlıca and Bağlarbaşı, where Mahmud II stayed for a long time in his last illness; a villa also at Çamlıca which belonged to Fazıl Mustafa Pasha; the villas of Sami Pasha and

Abdülhak Molla; and Egyptian country houses which adorned the Bosphorus, the price of an empire's downfall were all lost by fire or similar disasters, and sometimes through lack of money and neglect. There is now very little to be found of the old Istanbul, with the exception of a few buildings like the Meşruta villa, which, seen from outside, today resembles a sick lobster; Kadri Cenanî Bey's villa at Kanlıca; part of the Mirgün villa at Emirgân; the police headquarters now at Akbıyık, once the harem apartments of Hamamî İsmail Dede's house; and the ruins of the big mansion high above Sütlüce, thought to have been the house of Şeyh Galip.

But you can still find a few corners and people in Istanbul that maintain the life of the past. Once when I was searching for some information about a sheikh living in the time of Mahmud II, I heard there were some souvenirs in the house of Hayrullah Bey, a descendant of Halil Hâmid Pasha, the assassinated vizier of Abdülhamid I. I was given the address of his house at Hırkaişerif, formerly a Şâhzeli convent. Although the house was in quite a bad state, it retained the style of the previous century. As soon as I opened the door, I recognized an atmosphere of an older time. The vestibule with banisters of a hanging storey, where old ceremonies once took place, where everything was so old and tidy that at every creak of the stairs one couldn't help recalling old dervish incantations like the roar of great waves rolling in one after the other. In the upper hall, there were a number of birdcages. I soon became friends with Hayrullah Bey. The tumour on his forehead and his white wide beard gave the impression that he was descended from Michelangelo's Moses. In all my life, I never met such an innocent and honourable man. He told me one day that when he performed his religious rituals in the morning, his birds also recited the prayers along with him. And at my request he showed me. As soon as he began to revolve before me, the wide hall was full of a storm of roses. What I saw that day was one of the most joyful experiences I ever had of our former way of life. From Hayrullah Bey I possess a letter written in the old style, with the same light touch and sincerity and humour as the letters he also gave me from the sheikhs. Whenever I come across it among my papers, I imagine I hear the song of his birds as they keep time to the rhythms of his dance and prayers.

X

How strange that after the Tanzimat era the fires that stripped our lives bare offered our citizens a kind of simple pleasure. As soon as the terrible cry of 'Fire!' was heard, the firemen appeared in their red jackets, shouting as they ran, half-naked and thin as the pikes they held, and curious people who loved to see this kind of calamity, including well-known beys and pashas, came out to watch. Among them were people driving carriages and, if it was winter, people in fur jackets who also brought an extra blanket as protection against the cold. There were even people who made coffee for themselves on spirit-lamps called '*kaminota*' as they watched. In my childhood, a highly respected pasha from Şeyzadebaşı went to see the fire with his horse and carriage. But the pasha who preferred tea to coffee had a samovar installed in his carriage.

I created a thousand fires from one spark.

If you observe the importance given by Naci to the words 'fire' and 'blaze' in his poems and to the titles of his books like 'The Spark' and 'The Fire', you may think that Naci himself, who wrote this line, was possibly one of these afficionados. They say that Nâbizâde,[65] the author of *Zehra* and *Kara Bıbık*, and İsmail Safa Bey, the great expert on Ottoman prosody before Fikret,[66] were well known as lovers of the spectacle in Abdülhamid's reign. I've been told by several people that when Safa Bey was a guest in Recaizâde Ekrem Bey's villa in Istinye – recently destroyed – he put great pressure on his host to go out at midnight to see the fire. It's sad that we have only one line in Turkish that describes this fascination with fire.

If only I had a fire, I'd warm my body.

Apart from a description by Namik Kemal[67] in his *Cezmi* – and it is uncertain if it was based on his personal observation – it seems as if in the whole of our literature fire does not exist. A few foreign observers were attracted by fire. Dallaway, who came to Istanbul in Selim III's reign, openly admitted the attraction and said there were few things as beautiful as a town in flames.

I too have witnessed several fires, one in my own neighbourhood. If I dare to comment and disregard its tragic aspect, I must say I don't much blame the lovers of this strange pleasure, beginning with Nero. The last fire I saw was the saddest. One night from the slopes of Cihangir, I witnessed the burning of Sabiha Sultan's old villa and the Academy of Fine Arts, once the Chamber of Deputies. In a flash, one of the finest buildings of Mahmud II's reign burned to ash between pillars of flame and smoke that rose to heaven in a maelstrom that buried everything under a rain of sparks and explosions that lasted more than an hour. Memoirs and art studies were reduced to ash and, above all, a collection I imagine will never come our way again, including copies of a Velasquez and a Goya, before which I used to stand every day in admiration and wonder for minutes on end. I still grieve for those two copies and for the broad, noble vestibule. Among the burned objects was a copy of Ingres's *La Source*, one of the finest works painted by Midhat, who undertook so many. As long as the fire continued, I was in a state of stupefaction, seeing the days of my own youth also going up in flames.

This terrible calamity gave birth to a very odd type of fellow peculiar to Istanbul, the colourful fireman, whose absence we miss a little because of the magic of what will never return. Like the Janissaries who were characteristic of the old Istanbul, a whole section of Istanbul characters after the Tanzimat era were called *Külhanbey*. Every book devoted to recalling Istanbul, beginning with Ebuzziya's 'Young Ottomans' writes about the *Külhanbey*, whose language and lifestyle could be as elegant and charming as the folk songs and poems of certain artisans and street pedlars, who were armed with knives and scimitars but could be easy-going as required, loyal, very disciplined among themselves, cruel beyond limits, respectful to honest women, always humble before anyone they had once respected, incredibly funny and satirical, masters of organization. They are different from the gangsters we watch today in American films, certainly less tough, less dangerous and more civilized. Their living depended on certain influential people and little personal enterprises. Some of them were small traders or artisans; most were fishermen or ran coffee houses or even pubs. As I have said, some had passed on their modes of speech and behaviour to certain artisans, but these were not considered true *Külhanbey*. If we can't describe the firemen's living quarters as the most select and of the highest class, at least they were the most mixed, including the sons of pashas and rich spendthrifts among them, and even some officials in the state departments. In a way, the life of a fireman was the only sport of Istanbul, the city without sport. They were always like quicksilver, ready for an uprising, and were especially loyal to each other in the face of adversity. In the late Osman Cemal Kaygılı's book *Semaî Kahveleri*, the story he tells of the death of Çiroz Ali, one of the great popular poets and singers around 1896, describes the type and all his characteristics.

It seems that Çiroz Ali had tuberculosis. When his illness got worse, he was sent to his uncle's house at Bakırköy for a change of air. Naturally, all the firemen's wards were involved with the health of their famous friend. The night before he died, İsmail Kâhya, captain of the ward at Defterdarburnu, sent a man to Bakırköy to bring warning of the event. Çiroz Ali died near morning. The messenger leapt on a hired horse, arrived at Defterdarburnu and greeted İsmail Kâhya with 'Long life to you!' (a euphemism for 'He is dead!'). Then, almost 200 firemen went from Defterdarburnu to Bakırköy and met up there with the same number of comrades. The firemen, including Christians and Jews, brought down the coffin from Bakırköy to the mosque at Eyüp at a running time of 70 minutes, an almost impossible timing. Ever since I read this story of Çiroz Ali's coffin flying on his friends' shoulders at a speed that astounded the whole city, he became for me a kind of symbolic image, like the colourful lanterns and the cries which gave news every night from the Bayezit fire tower of the disasters happening to Istanbul. He was indeed a creature from a fireman's mythology, the salamander born of fire and living in fire.

XI

One of Istanbul's greatest specialities was its old-fashioned Turkish coffee house with its basins and jets of water, praised by travellers of old for the decor on the ceilings, walls, shutters and the embroidered fringes, for the rows of pipes with amber mouthpieces ranged on the walls and for the most beautiful views of the city hung in the windows. In these coffee houses frequented by the middle class, artisans and Janissaries according to their district, and fishermen and boatmen if they were near the shore, professional storytellers recited their tales, poet-musicians took part in competitions and, on some nights of Ramazan, Karagöz[68] was played. We know that even at the end of the sixteenth century, not only high-ranking officials but also members of the educated class attended their local coffee houses. The coffee house plays a very important role in several popular tales.

Coffee houses were important meeting places for city people, as well as barber shops which, in 1826, were kept under tight control and sometimes closed down. Business men and simple, curious citizens who listened to stories full of the strange adventures of travellers returning from distant lands, or accounts told by the Janissaries and cavalry just back from an expedition, of things they had seen at the battles of Kanije or Oyvar, gathered there; it was here that public opinion was formed at moments of serious crisis. Evliya Çelebi, describing the Bursa coffee houses, mentions dancers and musicians: it is likely that places frequented by the Janissaries never lacked these entertainments.

Certain coffee houses were especially reserved for smokers of hashish and opium. A surprising number of master craftsmen are known to have met there. A popular anecdote reports that the coffee houses around Ağakapısı – behind Süleymaniye – an area which, after 1826, became the headquarters for the *sheikülislam* services, were used as meeting places for individuals who were ready to supply false witness, in return for petty sums of money: it seems that in order to be recognized at a glance, these highly respectable citizens, with their eyes heavily made up and their clean beards and turbans, stuck a thread under the large cups of coffee to which they were addicted.

Nerval writes that it was in a coffee house behind the Bayezit Mosque or, from his description, near the Copperworks or just below, that he heard the story of Belkis and Süleyman (called in his book 'Solomon and the Queen of Sheba') one of the most beautiful pieces in the book which best describes his inner world, *Voyage en Orient*. The story he tells of Belkis and Süleyman is very different from the one we know and seems to be related to the tradition of the Kabbala, but his description of the listeners is exact. Nerval, and more particularly Gautier, speaks of the Tophane coffee house by the sea, frequently represented in engravings by foreigners, like the café in the district we now call Tepebaşı, in the sixth quarter. Sometimes I reflect that Nerval or Gautier might well have met our well-loved poet Seyranî in these old coffee houses, and I'm amazed at the irony of fate. Several aspects of the poet Seyranî,[69] who was in Istanbul in the early years of Abdülmecid's reign, might have appealed to Nerval.

After the Tanzimat era, people and their taste for coffee houses changed. Coffee houses opened after the fashion in Vienna and Paris, with tables and chairs and walls decorated with mirrors. Istanbul gentlemen began to frequent them in the frock coats and starched shirts mocked in the folk song we still enjoy today, *Kâtibim*. As a result of the taste for newspapers which suddenly spread in the Abdülaziz era, some of these took the name *kıraathane* ('coffee house with journals'), and they spread from Beyoğlu to Galata, to Divanyolu and Bayezit. 'Arif's Place', in the time of Abdülhamid, became very famous when an individual called Bekir opened another *kıraathane* opposite Arif's. A verse of the time tells of a quarrel between the two rivals:

Last night two café-owners
had a fight
spectators said that Bekir
felled Arif with a single blow.

In the big coffee house at Parmakkapı, people came to hear Aşkî the storyteller and to watch the Karagöz performances of Hayalî Salim, one of the last great Karagöz puppeteers. He even tried to give new life to the Karagöz performance by introducing a curtain before the screen, as in the theatre.

All these coffee houses were frequented by people of the upper class, dressed in their sable furs. Since the beginning of the Tanzimat era, Bayezit had become the centre for Karagöz and Turkish theatrical entertainments. Nerval gives us a description of a Karagöz play he watched in Bayezit in 1840, in the company of the Minister of War, and in 1852, Gautier saw two Karagöz plays in one night. Later, at Ramazan and on Friday nights, musical evenings were established in these newspaper coffee houses. Thus, until the arrival of the Republic, old Istanbul did its best to keep up with Beyoğlu.

On the morning after my first night in Vienna, seduced no doubt by the magic of the name, I took breakfast in the Mozart Café and was amazed when the waiter placed before me a pile of newspapers, just as in the Istanbul coffee houses of my youth. The Viennese still persisted in a style we had borrowed from them. The newly opened cafés did not sweep away the old coffee houses and their entertainments of music and poetry overnight. It was only the arrival of tables and chairs that changed the scenery. For a long time, they continued alongside the others and were known as Semâî Kahveleri ('musical coffee houses').

Teahouses formed a third class, particularly in Şehzadebaşı, and here were gathered those who brought the taste for tea to the level of addiction. They were like the little cafés we see today in Italy and Spain. Istanbul gentlemen used to watch women taking their evening stroll, especially during Ramazan, just as they now do, sitting on the café terraces in Madrid and Seville; but at that time, they watched from behind glass. The evening stroll (which the people of Istanbul named the *passegiata*, after the Italian) was one way to enliven the old city of Istanbul after the Tanzimat period. They first began in Beyoğlu, in the reigns of Selim III and Mahmud II.

Foreigners used to drive their carriages along roads around the great cemetery that covers the Ayazpaşa area (where Tepebaşı is now) – and the little cemetery which overlooks the Arsenal – the limit at the time was the Asmalı Mosque. Women accompanied these evening outings on foot. A third place, then named the Büyükdere Way, specially in the albums of engravings and in the books of foreign travels, stretched from Taksim to Şişli, and one branch was a huge road that reached Kurtuluş, known as San Dimitri in European books of travel. In the early years of Abdülmecid's reign, some Moslems also began to take part in the *passegiata*. Moslems as well as Christians, and women in particular, often walked in the cemeteries, which were a little beyond the regular walkways and were regarded as city gardens. There were cafés alongside every cemetery. Perhaps the café described by Nerval in his *Voyage en Orient* and the tavern where he heard Rumanian music was near the Asmalı Mosque and was the café we see in the albums of engravings by Melling or Allom. The tavern where he ate and drank wine was at Ayazpaşa. We know from Théophile Gautier that the Moslem population were beginning to take their walks around Bayezit and Şeyzadebaşı. Commenting on Turkish women, Gautier says they were not so deprived of freedom, as was generally thought, but were at liberty to walk, provided they were accompanied by the eunuchs who supervised the harem; in the evenings, the wives of rich citizens and upper-class officials would drive their carriages in the

Bayezit vicinity. We know from references in Namık Kemal's novel 'The Renaissance' and Ekrem Bey's 'Love in a Carriage' that walks and excursions to some Bosphorus beauty spots like Çamlıca had already begun at this time. The Tanzimat reforms had certainly changed the life of the Ottoman woman. We learn from the earliest Turkish novels that by the end of Abdülaziz's era, equestrian trips beyond Beyoğlu still continued. Certainly at the time these riding expeditions began from Bayezit. But it was the carriage ride that gradually became the fashionable pursuit, acquiring its illustrious fame from the palace. Pedestrians also took part in these promenades, both in Beyoğlu and in the old city. The exhibitions that opened near the Bayezit mosque at Ramazan were meeting places for the distinguished and refined; Ramazan was the best season for the evening *passegiata* between Bayezit and Şeyzadebaşı. The smart ladies and gentlemen who came to hear the preacher during the leisure hours between the afternoon and evening sundown meal – two or three decades earlier, the vigilant Janissaries would not have allowed anyone to pass – undoubtedly took their walk on Çamlıca or by the Bosphorus with more care and apprehension. Indeed, these walkabouts were distant reflections of the horse and carriage excursions in Paris on the Grand Boulevard and the Boulevard Italienne in which even King Louis Philippe took part before the revolution of 1848.

The nights of Ramazan belonged to Karagöz, and in the old city, he would later share the favour of the public with the theatre. Karagöz was so special to Ramazan that its repertoire ran to 28 parts, except, of course, on the first night and on Kadir Gecesi[70] (The Holy Night).

The vogue for Şeyzadebaşı began when a taste for theatre developed, particularly after the Istanbul theatres moved from Gedikpaşa to Şeyzadebaşı.

It was in the teahouses of Şeyzadebaşı, especially in Reşid Efendi's, that Muallim Naci wrote his reflections in his 'theatre letters' to Fazlı Necip[71] on the callow followers of modern European fashions; they gave a truer account than the most exact statistics of the time of the economic situation of the city – the city's appearance dilapidated a little more every day, like the avenue itself, with a gradual encroachment of small businesses and workshops, ironmongery, car repairs, laundries and second-hand clothes dealers. It was from this teahouse that he inveighed against Recaizade's faults in language and his superior attitudes.

Those like me who have seen a Ramazan[72] night in their childhood in the open-air coffee house at the upper end of the Fatih mosque courtyard know what is meant by the *ulema* class of old Istanbul. The whole square was full of turbans. Whenever I read in Lütfi's 'History'[73] or in Cevdet's 'Memoirs' about the 'turban troubles' that preceded Abdülaziz's reign, I always remember that amazing crowd of turbans.

The Şeyzadebaşı teahouses were still surviving during the Armistice years of World War I. But we preferred to gather in the Sultanahmet coffee houses or at 'Ikbal' near the Nuruosmaniye Mosque. The Ikbal was first discovered by philosophy students, including Hasan Ali Yücel and Hikmet from the Higher Institute for Teachers; later, it moved to the residence of Bezm-i Alem, Valide Sultan, and is now the Istanbul Lycée for Young Girls. At that time, it was located in the old Fine Arts Academy opposite the Iştihat publishers.

After we began to frequent the Ikbal, it also became a favourite with Yahya Kemal. The premises where we met him to edit the *Dergâh* review was in the old office of the newspaper *Tanin*, just opposite the school, and they became a vital centre for us. Haşim[74] also used to visit the coffee house at certain times or in the evening, as it was very near the public debt offices where he worked. And sometimes Abdülhak Şinasi Hisar[75] would drop by, in despair over typing errors in the review. Mustafa Şekip Tunç, in his articles written for the *Dergâh* journal, added a very personal profundity that he owed to Bergson, to the nationalist tone of the magazine; Hasan Ali Yücel, Necmeddin Halil Onan and Ali Mümtaz Arolat, who suddenly abandoned poetry after writing a very fine collection of poems named *Bir Gemi Yelken Açtı* ('A Ship Unfurled Its Sails'); Mustafa Nihat Özön, who edited the magazine in his own charmingly sulky way, but who was an incomparable comrade; and, finally, Nurullah Ataç, Yunus Kâzım Koni and Zekaî, for whose untimely death I grieve as I write these lines – we would all gather in this coffee house where we would spend a large part of a whole day and night, apart from mealtimes. Mükrim'in Halil and Osman Cemal Kaygili, who worked for other journals, *Aydede* in particular, but who was at one with us, would sometimes come to Ikbal or to the Sultanahmet coffee houses or to the Yeni Şark Café by the mausoleum.

How many generations and how many different kinds of breeding and education came together here! Reserve officers, many of them disabled, bearing on their bodies and even on their faces the scars of several battle fronts, regular officers who left the army as wounded invalids, high-ranking soldiers who had never yet been to Anatolia (under Kemal Atatürk), several military judges from the era of Abdülhamid, half-mystics, half-pederasts, some keen on chess, some on checkers, and almost all bankrupt; irresolute high officials with gentle faces who had served at some time in second- or third-class positions; ultranationalists, Ferid Pasha's spies, alongside young journalists who admired Baudelaire and Verlaine, Yahya Kemal and Haşim, Nedim and Şeyh Galip. Our table was left of the doorway, but when Yahya Kemal spoke and our laughter grew louder and more excited, our circle widened until we occupied a complete side. Amid the sound of billiard cues, the clicking of backgammon and the shouts of waiters, in an atmosphere full of the events in Anatolia, we discussed poetry, we organized projects and we would receive the latest war news of Inönü and Sakarya from friends returning late at night from their newly published newspapers.

It was the philosophy students before us who had discovered the first coffee house precisely in the corner of the Sultanahmet courtyard. Hasan Ali Yücel had named it the 'Academy'. It, and others, like the Ikbal, still survive. But the clientèle has changed, the area is impoverished and it is impossible to imagine the former 'Academy' in today's café. On account of the neighbouring public prison and the Courts of

Justice, there was more discussion here than anywhere else of the important lawsuits and trials that took place during the years of the National Struggle for Independence in 1914–1918. I met Elif Naci and the painter Zeki Faik here. One night in Ramazan, Rıza Tevfik[76] danced the zeybek[77] folk dance here before a crowd of students, mostly his own, and mimicked several types of hawkers, particularly the Jewish ones.

Rıza Tevfik was one of those men who would show off all his talents at one sitting to avoid interruption. He was a really wonderful speaker, but the longer his speech, the more its course altered and surprising contradictions would appear. Apropos of that, Yahya Kemal had a very charming story to tell on the subject. One day, the poet who wrote *Ses* ('The Voice') was carrying a fairly large parcel under his arm when he met Rıza Tevfik, returning from his famous London trip. 'What have you got there, Kemal?' asked the latter. Shamefaced, Yahya Kemal replied, 'I took my old clothes to be turned and I'm just bringing them back from the tailor.' 'What a lucky chap you are, Kemal!' sighed Rıza Tevfik. 'You at least have old clothes, I don't even have those!' But after a few minutes of conversation, the Head of the Senators forgot his sighs and began to talk of London and the comfortable clothes he had had made there. 'Monsieur, don't look for any but an English tailor, they are the best.' When I went a few times to hear him lecture, I saw him in his new clothes. They really suited him. In one of his lectures, Rıza Tevfik told us of the comforts in life which, even in those days, were considered unseemly even to think about. His lectures with their personal insights were very interesting. Oriental poetry mingled with philosophy was like a diversion off the main street, with a very luxurious fertile garden at the end, and when he turned in that direction, he would be in total ecstasy.

I liked Rıza Tevfik very much for some of his poems and for his bonhomie. But one day as we crossed the bridge together, we had an argument about the Kemalist movement and my feeling for him cooled. We argued for quite a long time. Stopping right there on the bridge, he suddenly pointed out the battleships of the Allies in the harbour and said, 'As long as they're there, there's not a thing you can do!'

One of my memories connected with this coffee house is a quarrel between Nurullah Ataç and a gigantic medical student who was attacking Yahya Kemal – I don't know why. It happened during the student movement against teachers who betrayed the nationalist cause. Almost dancing with rage, Nurullah stammered at the advancing enemy, 'You can do what you like to me, but I dare you to utter a single word in my presence against the man who is so much loved by the young.'

The late Süleyman Nazif would often come to Yahya Kemal's table in the Yeni Şark café by the mausoleum. There, for the first time, we met Rauf Ahmed Hotinli, who was bringing out his newspaper nearby. More often, that's where we would go with Hilmi Ziya. I had already met Süleyman Nazif at the Pierre Loti conference arranged by the University and also at a discussion with the teachers of the Upper Institution. One evening in Ramazan, I saw him with Yahya Kemal breaking his fast at a kebab stall in Bayezit near Zeynep Hanım's mansion. It was in this kebab shop that Abdülhak Şinasi, famous for his fastidious ways, might have said, 'Garçon, please wash the water too!' At the time, the terraced cafés at Bayezit and *Küllük* in the mosque garden did not appeal to us; moreover, the customers of the latter were a very mixed lot, and it had not yet taken its witty name. We often used to frequent a rather splendid coffee house which was once a grocery shop on the Bayezit–Aksaray road, and which had music on Friday evenings in winter and during Ramazan. It was Yahya Kemal who introduced us to this one. There we met again the nostalgic melodies we had heard on summer days on excursions to Çubuklu and other parts of Istanbul. They reminded us of the smiles and sweet glances of those lovely coquettish women we saw and admired on the street, or on the boat, or behind the screen that separated men and women in the gardens. These performances were conducted by Ismail Hakkı Bey, one of the last great masters. Although his round white beard reminded me of one of our friends in the State Council whose excess gravity annoyed me, I loved the way he sang, as he struck the tambourine and held it up to conduct the other musicians in the old style. His voice was strong and powerful; he was a true Istanbul artist of the old school.

The *Yıldız* coffee house, situated almost below the Oriental Club in Divanyolu, was one of the places we would visit by day, which made it easy for us to move directly to the Şule opposite, where we would spend the night drinking our rakı. But at the time, we preferred a particular drinking booth run by an individual called İsmail Efendi, very near the Sirkeci post office. The whole neighbourhood of Babîâlî came there, with its well-known writers, editors and compositors. Sometimes Yunus Kâzım, Kutsi and I would cross to the European side and eat at the *Liban* restaurant in the park at Taksim, but what attracted us most on our Beyoğlu expeditions were the newly opened Russian restaurants.

For some reason, the influence of those White Russian emigrants on the life of Istanbul has never been discussed. Whatever the influence of the French, and even more of the Italians, at the beginning of the Tanzimat era – the French influence began it with the rush of ideas that followed the French Revolution – the White Russian influence was similar and could be seen particularly in women's clothes; from restaurants and bars, to swimwear on the beach, they introduced many fashions.

After the conquest of Beyoğlu, the Russian emigrants gradually spread to the old Istanbul areas and the coffee houses we liked. A host of princesses and countesses loaded with jewellery, boots and fur coats, their hair smoothly combed, their pale faces and round cheeks heavily made up, brought us our tea and coffee and, in the restaurants, rakı and food which we could hardly pay for, and in the cloakrooms, former colonels and captains and generals bearded to the waist, began to take our torn old overcoats. Aide-de-camps of the tsar, elderly captains or aristocratic youths performed supple Caucasian dances before us. Istanbul had never known so many unfortunates or so much money spent on entertainment, or the balance of the class-system so reversed. The sounds of the balalaika drifted from every corner. The tsar's ballet troupe, which, after 1920, would be responsible for originating so many changes in those French and European theatres and ballet companies, were in Istanbul for a short time, and those citizens of Istanbul who could afford it were able to watch the most modern ballets. Rimsky-Korsakov's *Scheherazade* played for days in Beyoğlu.

After the Kemalist victory, the Ikbal and Sultanahmet cafés were more or less abandoned. We began to foregather in the Bayezit area, but gradually the people of Istanbul were seduced by Beyoğlu and the cinema.

For a long time, Naşit alone protected Şehzadebaşı from this exodus. But when he died, this part of Istanbul life closed down and the spread of radio chased away musicians from the cafés. The *Küllük* and the Bayezit coffee houses, where university students and professors would meet, held out a little longer.

XII

Night life in Beyoğlu in Abdülmecid's time began with a few timid enterprises. Then gradually it expanded from theatres to include café chantants, hotels, European restaurants and pubs. The Beyoğlu night life described by Gérard de Nerval, also by Théophile Gautier and Misemer, was led more by foreigners and local minorities. When Lamartine came to Istanbul for the first time in 1833, like most travellers of note, he became the guest of the European colony when he was in the city and of the Embassy when he was at Tarabya.

While the remnants of Mahmud II's era, the high officials, pursued their customary lives discussing poetry and politics, listening to saz music, drinking coffee and smoking their pipes in their spacious domestic halls reserved for men, among friends, guests, flatterers, intercessors and hangers-on, the new generations educated – more or less successfully – in Europe who had become used to a French way of life, gradually adopted a new lifestyle. And Beyoğlu, Janus-like, entered city life for better or for worse. Thanks to its theatre, the district suddenly blossomed, and in Abdülaziz's era became an attractive corner for the wealthy; there were big hotels, shops, European tailors and dressmakers for the rich, shops of ready-made clothes for the poor, numerous entertainments for all classes introduced from Paris and Europe, and concerts and little-known singers and dancers from the West. A life of entertainments which included various events surrounded the municipality of the newly formed Sixth Department and provided the principal subject for the newspaper gossip columns. Between the Nişantaş quarter, with its few remains from the days of Abdülmecid, and the Kaşımpaşa quarter that was still living in the time of Güzelce Kasım Pasha, a new milieu sprang into life and proceeded to seduce the authentic citizens of Istanbul. But the finest memories of our past are from Abdülmecid's era when the Mevlevi convent was built in Galata and include the Turkish commentator of the Mesnevi, İsmail Efendi, right up to Galip Dede. Certainly the local traditional ways of life, as confirmed by Çaylak Tevfik Bey and other memoir writers, still continued: in the rooms and halls furnished with their low divans and armchairs covered in red velvet and sofas hung with tassels and fringes, where they drank coffee and smoked pipes, and where they passed long evenings exchanging witticisms and reciting lines of poetry or discussing politics. Weddings and circumcisions took place in their wealthy mansions and dwellings, conjurors played their tricks and music played; at Ramazan, communal prayers were held and in dervish convents, ritual ceremonies were observed as in the past. But these nights, closed to the outside world, were disturbed towards morning by the grand sumptuous carriages that rolled past, their rubber wheels colliding noisily with crumbling pavements. Young businessmen, beginning to get used to partners who lived very different lifestyles, wasted their family inheritance on the delights of Beyoğlu and got bored with the narrow restrictions of life in Istanbul. Whatever their social or financial position, the city regarded them with disapproval. Every neighbourhood had several spendthrifts who were censured and taken to task. From their gambling debts to their various mistresses, all were under a spotlight and nothing passed unnoticed. Occasionally, one of them became the hero of the hour and made us forget the others, lavishly distributing handfuls of gold everywhere from wallets crammed with stocks and shares, until one day, suicide or a sudden accident put an end to the story of the man who had disturbed the dreams of schoolgirls. Sometimes, neither of these things happened, and when, with the help of his hangers-on and mistresses, he had devoured his inheritance, he enrolled with the local fire brigade or moved far away from Istanbul, demoted to a minor official appointment. Theirs was an everyday story of old Istanbul. Fearful of imminent bankruptcy, the whole city reflected on such wasteful prodigality, and everyone analysed and interpreted the stories according to their own turn of mind.

From Abdülaziz onwards, there was no longer any stability in Istanbul life. From the palace downwards, every well-known inhabitant of Istanbul, every vizier who owned large mansions on land that could accommodate 40 or 50 homes, all the old family dynasties who, on the nights of Ramazan, received for dinner 100 uninvited guests, were all living in debt, a little ashamed of themselves before the community. It was an Istanbul that had lost its means of production and had cast its future to the winds by imitating Paris, the centre of the world's market. At every turn of the rubber wheels of the fine carriages made at the Bender factories, the age-old empire came a little closer to its predestined fate.

XIII

The Bosphorus for me has always been one of the great crucial knots which ties together all the threads of our tastes and sensibilities. I have always believed that if its significance could be unlocked from deep within us, we would resolve one of our essential truths. It may be only a fantasy. Beautiful things often give us the illusion that they are the equal of all creation. When we come upon them, we feel that we are face to face with a self-evident truth. Isn't that the secret of certain dervish orders who search for God in a beautiful human face or in a fine physique?

Beauty's greatest characteristic is its ability to appear always new and make us aware of it at every moment.

What is more or less true of art and of human beauty, may it not be true also of a landscape which, over centuries, has witnessed so many different lifestyles, tastes, ways of loving and feeling, and which has nourished and even guided and influenced them with its own offerings?

The Bosphorus itself is a work of art, even of music. 'Landscape is a state of the soul,' said Amiel. But there are some landscapes which do not liberate us as much as Amiel claims. They influence our dreams and thoughts. The Bosphorus is a mysterious channel where moments experienced on one side are tasted as memories on the other. The sun neither rises nor sinks in the Bosphorus. Like an opera you listen to it from outside through loudspeakers, every dramatic movement remaining beyond your vision. You hear only the music. Each bank of the Bosphorus holds the mirror of the hours up to the other.

Whether at Beylerbey, Emirgân, Kandilli or İstinye, every hour of the day is different from another. While Beykoz and Çubuklu are still trying to cast off their most recent dreams in the cool shade of their trees, Yeniköy and Büyükdere are awake early with the sun dazzling their eyes. At Kuzguncuk, the waters flow languidly along the shore, and the minarets of Istanbul, like a field of violets scattered with hyacinths, like tall lilies cut off by a fine layer of mist, melt into a light brighter than their own reflections.

Evenings, in particular, are like this. An evening at Rumeli Hisar on the European shore is always felt as remote, an emotional state that penetrates everything. While it sets ablaze the windows of houses opposite with a fiery longing, motes of flame float on the water before you, like a sunken rose garden or a springtime made of pebbles of all colours. I particularly like to watch evening spread to the treetops in a soft golden light, but suddenly along the opposite shore it can appear as a narrow line of silver which is almost pure white. Seen in its white armour, it attracts you like a place you've never known before. Just as you long for the European side in full morning sunlight, you long, too, for the dream world washed in golden-yellow light, even though you know it is only Beykoz or Çubuklu or Paşabahçe that you quit only a few minutes ago. Then all the light and colours fade like the reflections of a fire running out of fuel. Trees and houses enter the dark of night, beings bereft and sad who have been abandoned by a visitor from heaven. They wrap themselvs in night's own garments. Sometimes it is the silver-embroidered kaftan robe of music, sometimes merely the yellow roses of moonlight, sometimes the lingering taste on the tongue and palate of the day just lived, or the successive memories recalled to our imaginations by the names of the neighbourhoods around. But in whatever shape they come, or whatever cup they offer us, they are always accompanied by a feeling of loneliness.

Until the middle of the sixteenth century, the Bosphorus was barely part of Istanbul life. We know that every monarch had a preference for a particular village, and possessed either a garden or a summer house there. Grand viziers and statesmen, sometimes for political reasons and sometimes for pleasure, chose to endow certain villages. On the other hand, the Bosphorus, like every part of Istanbul, is a means of production and, even more than the others, creates its own localities accordingly. Istinye and Bebek were meeting places for sailors from the Black Sea. The Beykoz fishponds had existed since the sixteenth century. But the delights and pleasures of city life were more to be found near the Golden Horn and the Kağıthane districts. Apart from the villages very close to Istanbul like Tophane, Fındıklı and Beşiktaş, the Bosphorus villages were only neighbouring districts for the city, especially with the limited means of transport at the time.

Fatih the Conqueror commissioned the Tokat Garden. And Bayezid II often enjoyed visiting the Bosphorus villages. Yavuz built the summer house at Bebek, Süleyman the Lawgiver loved Istinye, Selim II had a residence built at Beşiktaş and Murad III built the palace at Fındıklı. And he who enlarged the Beşiktaş villa by building up the shore was Ahmed I. Dolmabahçe's name originated in this century. But for a long time, the palace kept its name of 'The Beşiktaş Palace' and was often visited by Ahmed I. From that time, the Bosphorus can be said to have entered Istanbul aesthetic taste, and the voice of the Bosphorus gradually began to be heard in poetry.

It first appeared in Yahya Efendi, Murad IV's *sheikhülislâm*, who loved to listen to the nightingale in İstinye. He wrote the couplet:

Give up the songs of cages and come,
Come listen to the nightingale in İstinye.

The lines are as fine as the two images of Nâilî, famous for his comparison of the nightingale's song with the music of the ney:

The song of the ney comes through the holes in
the reeds
The song of the nightingale comes from branches of
the rosebush.

Yahya Efendi was one of the few who could get on well with Murad IV, distinguished, charming, patient, always in authority when necessary, tolerant and understanding whenever possible and a high-class member of the palace, a favourite as long as he lived. A man who knew his time like the back of his hand. Twice Murad IV's Janissaries tried to force him from his position. But Murad was so fond of his poet Şeyhülislâm that, between the years 1040 and 1043 of the Hejira, he never gave up trying to reinstall him.

It was in Yahya Efendi's time that Istanbul found its own style; in fact, for almost two centuries, our lives in the city had had a certain unity, and since the Conquest, rich merchant families and viziers and ulemas had been installed and a complete line of tradition and education was firmly established. Even the Janissaries had begun to change, acquiring fame by performing the duties of a typical Istanbul *külhanbey*. The city became a crucible for those who came from all over the empire. They passed through it and were transformed; it imposed its language on them. The lines by Yahya Efendi which showed how well *aruz*, or Arabic prosody, could mingle with Turkish, were a favourite of Yahya Kemal:

> If I could tell what this heart suffered
> It would be a tale of bitter complaint.

Nâima[78] had many stories to tell about Yahya Efendi. One of the nicest and most relevant was what he said to his close friends when he was no longer the Şeyhülislâm:

> Now I understand that hypocrites can have good qualities. People love hypocrisy: they have no fear of sincerity, they don't respect it. And so certain dishonesties we didn't originally permit we had to sanction eventually!

The honourable Şeyhülislâm described hypocrisy as '*evil's secret mansion*'.

A very different attitude to behaviour from Molière's! Reading these and similar comments, we might think that Ottoman history had a secret religion and a secret morality. Certainly long before Yahya Efendi, hypocrisy had begun to play a major role in the life of society.

Did Yahya Efendi ever have a summer house in İstinye? I've never given that a thought. The lie of art is always the most truthful of truths. For us, İstinye shone out the first time we heard the couplet above quoted, and my imagination took possession of it then.

Murad IV also loved the Bosphorus; he had the Fındıklı summer house enlarged, and it was he who was really responsible for Beşiktaş Palace. He himself ordered the construction of the big waterfront summer house at Emirgân, which he presented to the son of his companion Mirgûn.

Murad IV was a man of his time, a time made memorable by the Janissaries. For several years, the sultan and the Janissary corps had faced one another eye to eye, exact replicas of each other. But eventually the army, realizing it could not win, sheathed its claws and bowed in submission. The young sultan marched through Istanbul and the whole empire like a predator, taming all before him with a magnetic strength, destroying everything in his path in a furious passion to cleanse and purify. Sad that such strength of will and so much blood was wasted! Neither he nor his courtiers could think of any course of action except intimidation. When you think that it was to him that Koçi Bey's[79] 'Memoirs' and Kâtip Çelebi's 'Book of Reforms' were addressed, you might imagine, even briefly, that he is searching for the part of the outfit that does not work. But although the sultan knew how to keep and hold men and even shape them, he had one great fault. He had no idea of a 'team'. From the time of Gazi Orhan to Murad III, Ottoman history is imbued with the concept of the team. But it disappears after this century. That is why Murad IV, although popular and respected by his people, remained only a faint-hearted apprentice of Murad Pasha the Kuyucu (The Butcher).

In the seventeenth century, when the level of society and its institutions weighed so heavily on the whole empire, what point is there in finding fault with individuals?

There are many similarities between Yahya Efendi and Bahaî Efendi, the Şeyhülislâm of Mehmed IV's reign, both noble, open, big-hearted, intelligent and tolerant men, both addicted to drugs and pleasure. In Abdülhamid's time, a member of a pious foundation remembered that Mehmed IV had given Bahaî Efendi the gift of a residence on the bay of Kanlıca, and the name of this poet and man of religion whose tolerance softened the life of the period was again associated, two centuries later, with the life of the city. Strangely enough, at the other end of Kanlıca lived the fanatical, cruel Beyazi Efendi, who liked to restrict life and was the exact opposite of Bahâi Efendi. Beyazi Efendi is the man who ordered a Moslem woman, accused of lying with a Jew, to be stoned to death in the At Meydan before the whole city. Even the sultan attended the spectacle. But when it was over, a reaction began in the city, and the fanatics could no longer impose their wishes so easily.

Kara Çelebizâde Abdülaziz Efendi, who played a part, sometimes good, sometimes bad, at the beginning of Mehmed IV's reign, also owned a house on the Bosphorus but was, not for long, a neighbour of his rival Bahaî Efendi. He was exiled to Bursa and forbidden to return to Istanbul. But he took his revenge on his contemporaries by writing a history from which Nâimâ borrowed. It is curious that a public man who lived such an unbalanced life and spoke so rashly could give such impartial views on the events and characters of the period.

Vaniköy takes its name from the residence owned by Vanî Mehmed Efendi, whom Fazıl Ahmed Pasha had met in Erzurum and introduced to the palace. Vanî Efendi was described by Asım as without equal in the study of science, a clever, eloquent, fanatical scholar, a brilliant interpreter of the Koran, but so ambitious that when he had the chance he could turn against his protector and complain to the sultan. Of course, he was living in an era of intrigue and treachery.

At the time, the Bosphorus between Rumelihisar and Kanlıca was a very fashionable place. In Naîmâ's 'History' we read of viziers whose adventures in Fındıklı surprise us with their intrigues and ambitions, or whose good nature evokes our sympathy, of treasurers always at pains to find money for the state of courteous and gentlemanly diplomats and a number of Moslem theologians who hardly ever went far from the palace; most of these had summer residences on the Bosphorus to which they moved as soon as the Istanbul spring arrived. Here they smoked their pipes and drank their coffees or chewed their opium, as they watched from their windows the misty south-west mornings, or the orgy of blood-red light in the evenings, or the silvery solitudes of a group of trees or a rocky headland on the opposite shore. At night, they would leap from their beds to see once again the swollen water by moonlight, or the lightning on stormy nights or the colourful rushing currents of the Bosphorus like the fearful Chinese dragons they saw in old miniature paintings. In short, the beautiful moments of today when we see a Monet or a Bonnard, a Marquet, a Turner or a Canaletto are for them daily events and they take great pleasure in the experiences.

It is sad that nowhere else except in Venice and Naples do we find life lived so close to the sea – but in our literature, the influence of the Bosphorus is hardly to be seen. The absence of prose and painting, and the fact that our poetry is only an aesthetic game, throws real life into the shade. If we look for the influence of the Bosphorus on our artists, we'll find it only by chance, like daytime memories that arise among the many events of a random world.

Mehmed IV also loved the Bosphorus and undoubtedly his is the playful couplet:

My heart inclines neither to Göksu nor Sarıyer,
To escape an army of suffering, it shelters in
    Rumelihisar.

Perhaps it was written in one of the uprisings that made his childhood so stormy, or from a memory of them. Very often, the sultan's caique glided smoothly through the waters of the Bosphorus like an extra page added to 'A Thousand and One Nights'. This sultan was keener on hunting and magnificent processions. He went on his first hunt when he was nine, two years after he succeeded to the throne. Till just before Köprülü Mehmed Pasha became vizier, he liked to spend his summers in the palace at Üsküdar, occasionally hunting near Çatalca. After a period of relative peace brought about by Köprülü, although important matters were not tackled from the root, the situation stabilized and the state seemed to have regained its former strength, specially in the time of Fazıl Ahmed Pasha and Kara Mustafa Pasha when it became very active. Even if the sultan did not participate fully in military expeditions, he preferred to remain in the palace at Edirne which was certainly his own choice and that of his ministers. There were more intrigues in the Istanbul palace. In this strange seventeenth century, the sultans had no freedom, either in the city or in their own palaces.

There are few fates as strange and sad as the fate of this man who came to head one of the greatest empires of the world at the age of seven. He spent his youth with disasters and tragedies, one after the other. Only a few days after he came to the throne, his father was murdered before his very eyes. How often did he hear from his courtiers the story of how Sultan İbrahim, the Koran in his hand, was strangled as he pleaded for his life with the foolish, hypocritical Sofu Mehmed Pasha and the Şeyhülislâm Abdürrahim Efendi? The death of Sultan Osman had been the result of a kind of crazy hysteria among the Janissaries, but Sultan İbrahim was strangled with the consent of ministers responsible to the state and of the sultan's mother whose role was more or less that of a regent. The event was so sad, cruel and scandalous that Kara Çelebizade Aziz Efendi, who was present, could not bear it and felt that he must plead with the great mother of the sultan and her ministers: '*At least you could have chosen to poison him.*'

This grandmother, who should have been tenderness itself, tried to poison him when he was 11 or 12 years old. Eventually, she herself would be strangled one midnight by Sultana Turhan's faction, in a room where she slept separated from the sultan by only two corridors or a hall. Perhaps this murder was committed with his agreement in return for the attempted assassination.

It was from then that the Janissaries and others began to suspect him of wishing to murder his brothers and threatened to depose him. Never before had the Ottoman Empire been governed as it was during this sultan's childhood, both by everyone and no one. It often happened that the appointment of the grand vizier was left to the State Council, the ulema or even to the Janissaries. The two revolts which occurred at the beginning and end of the period, one in 1650, the other in 1688, at the worst moment of the war with Austria, were directly crushed by the people. If public opinion had been in the least prepared, or if there had been a single spark to promote an idea, the situation would have resulted in constitutional government. But at the time, the idea of a communal city did not yet exist. There were only the ulema, the Imperial Council, the army and the market, and all their entourage.

However, the people's participation in crushing two revolts, the preference of their ruler for the Edirne Palace rather than Istanbul, the nervousness of the citizens which lasted until the Feyzullah Efendi affair in 1703, all account for the birth of an urban psychology.

Mehmed IV was not raised like any normal child, nor was he treated and approved as a ruler. The poor child, weighed down by his crown, was both scolded and spoiled by viziers, scholars and his entourage. In the absence of a really competent regent, the fact that the business of an empire fell on the shoulders of a child hardly old enough to understand it was the worst feature of his fate.

Mehmed IV, praised by his favourite Afife Kadın, '*My royal sovereign, you are like the ocean*,' grew up under this burden. He never learned anything from events. His reign as sultan is like a magnificent flight full of great unhappy awakenings.

However, he kept his promise to the Köprülü family. But they too did not believe in teamwork, preferring to remove their rivals rather than educate them. Nevertheless, until the Siege of Vienna, the Ottoman Empire was perceived from abroad as unarguably at the height of its power and splendour.

When Galland observed in Edirne the departure of the army for the expedition initiated by Fazil Mustafa Pasha in 1673, he described for us the pomp by which Mehmed IV lived:

I saw examples of the magnificence of the Ottoman Empire in the Sultan's journeys to and from the mosque

during the Kurban and Şeker bayrams, in the audi-
ence he gave to His Excellency the ambassador, and in
the victorious return of the fleet after the conquest of
Kandiye. The splendour and beauty of that day when
I saw the sultan leaving Edirne to go on his campaign
was unequalled and immeasurable. I do not remember
reading in any romance anything to compare with its
magnificence, or any descriptions of triumphant returns
from war, victory celebrations, javelin competitions,
carousels, masquerades.

After commenting that the magnificence could only be
shown by means of a picture, he goes on to describe the
sultan's hunting cortège:

Thirty horsemen, each carrying a falcon on his wrist,
rode in front. Behind them seven riders, each carrying a
new breed of tiger on his horse (or it might be a leopard
or some such animal) that the sultan sometimes used for
chasing hares. Every tiger had a richly-brocaded shawl on
his back, and their calm postures, in contrast with their
wild, ferocious looks, aroused in onlookers a mixture of
fear and wonder. Behind these came janissaries leading
about fifty greyhounds, undoubtedly the most beautiful greyhounds in the world. Their beauty was even
more enhanced by the rich coverings of gold and silver
on their backs, and their decorated collars. They were
followed by five or six large guinea-pigs whose pendu-
lous lips reached their chins, and who were uncovered
to show off the mottled spots that beautified the skin of
their massive bodies. Then came twelve tigerish hounds,
each led by a halter, with white backs, spotted and
striped in red and black, and I thought these dogs must
be of the finest breed in the world, and to leave them to
the last was certainly so that their beauty could best be
appreciated. After this hunting cortège came a single file
of twenty riders in uniform, each leading a horse. Shall

I speak of the magnificence of these richly-caparisoned horses, special favourites of the sultan, or of the silver and gold enamel on their bridles, their coats splendidly adorned with pearls and a wealth of precious stones, or of the excellent quality of the swords, quivers, bows and shields that they bore? To do this well, every detail would need to be examined separately at close quarters.

In the middle of this glorious display sits Mehmed IV like a veritable idol, the jewels on his mount worth a complete treasury, his armour studded with pearls and precious stones, his bejewelled jacket thrown over his left shoulder. Truly, it was all the Orient, nurtured for centuries on a literature of tales and legends, that we recognized in this magnificence.

Thus, with pomp and circumstance, Mehmed IV set out on his expedition to Vienna, which turned out to be the gateway to a terrible disaster. Readers of the day-to-day account of the defeat in Fındıklı's 'History' cannot help comparing the splendour of the expedition with the declining light of an evening sun.

Nothing was as damaging to the Ottoman Empire as the pride and ambition of Kara Mustafa Pasha of Merzifon. He preceded the sultan as far as Belgrade, with the same pomp and splendour, but never uttered a word of his intention to conquer Vienna himself. It was only on the march that he revealed his real decision, in spite of the objections of all the experienced generals and men of war. At a time when lack of work and economic crises had reached their limit, when every year revolts in Anatolia endangered the state, when insecurity and fear of treachery caused men of the state to behave like wolves, Mustafa Pasha wanted to surpass Süleyman the Lawgiver and succeed where he had failed.

The defeat at Vienna was only the first of many battles lost by the state. If Mehmed IV had not lost his nerve, a disastrous situation could have been quickly mended and a little rectification of frontiers could have righted the matter. But the sultan was not the man to deal with the situation, and Kara Mustafa had got rid of most of the great military commanders.

After the defeat, Mehmed IV lingered for a while in Belgrade and then came to Edirne. But he could not face returning to Istanbul from which he had once fled and where he had been so depressed. His comment reported by Fındıklı, *'I haven't the heart to face Istanbul!'* indicates the awakening of a whole psychological condition in this shadowy sultan.

Strange that he took to hunting again in the midst of the fire and bloodshed on the frontiers. After his inevitable return to Istanbul, he preferred to remain in the palace at Üsküdar for hunting, and according to Fındıklı, he began to go hunting at night. At the time, Istanbul was living under daily measures against the serious threat of famine. Understandably, the people had begun to complain. Sermons were preached against him, even in mosques where he was present, and his way of life was criticized. Under such bitter reproaches, the sultan promised to forego the chase, and he even sold off some of his birds of prey and his hounds. But in the end, Mehmed IV's obsession with hunting took a morbid turn. In the days before his removal from the throne, he said he could not sleep at night or survive without hunting; eventually, he was given permission to hunt on the condition that he should not go beyond Davutpaşa. And so the beginning and end of the life of a sultan came together. The pages of Fındıklı that describe his dethronement give quite the other side of the pomp and splendour of the reign which had dazzled the eyes of Galland and other foreigners. The same historian recounts that he found Süleyman II before he came to the throne, 'prostrate and destitute' in a corner of his prison cell, wearing only a satin robe, and for his enthronement a fur cloak was lent by one of his attendants.

What are the significant works of the period? Is it the sad folk song sung in Rumeli for Budapest after the destruction in blood and fire to as far as Skopje?

Austria has taken our lovely Budapest
Twelve thousand young girls are lined up
Alas, my Sultan, we who are Moslems

Or is it the poetry of Neşat and Naîlî, or the sea symphony of Yeni Cami or the music composed by Seyyid Nuh, Itrî and Hâfiz Post?

When the well-intentioned but unsuccessful Süleyman II returned to Istanbul at the insistence of his ministers, everywhere he went there were days when the Rumeli people hung on his horse's neck and asked him, 'Where are you going, my Sultan, why are you leaving us?'; in besieged cities where Anatolian soldiers and Janissaries, a mere handful of men, had been salvaged from massacres and fought on without hope, in the melancholy evenings this folk song could always be heard.

XIV

It was in this seventeenth century that ended so disastrously that our entertainments were established.

After two centuries of reflection and indecision, our civil architecture had found a style that would suit the Bosphorus. Besides, our lives had come to a point where we could admit its subtle beauty and the expenses we must incur. At the time, both shores of the Bosphorus were covered with the summer residences of ministers, the cultured élite, important officials and rich citizens. After the eighteenth century, when the Şeyhülislâm were no longer dismissed and exiled to the provinces, but were permitted to stay in their estates at a short distance from the city, the Bosphorus became a little more attractive.

By the end of the seventeenth century, Bahaî Efendi's summer house (mentioned above) and Amcazade Hüseyin Pasha's were the finest of all. In one or other, dinner parties were given for the Austrian ambassadors. At the party in Hüseyin Pasha's residence in 1700, 400 guests were rowed in a great galley to Anadolu Hisar. The vast reception hall and the *selamlık* of the residence, which we now know as *Meşruta Yalı*, are the subject of a good book prefaced by Pierre Loti.

This is where, in the reign of Ahmed III, the grand vizier Teberdar Mehmed Pasha gave a banquet for the Persian ambassador and boasted proudly in the course of conversation, 'You have your Çarbağ, but we have our Anadolu Hisar'. At the beginning of the eighteenth century, the Bosphorus was one of the great prides of the Ottoman Empire. Teberder Mehmed Pasha's successor, Ali Pasha of Çorlu, had a summer villa at Ortaköy. One night, he invited Sultan Ahmed and arranged an evening by candlelight which lasted, Ottoman style, until five hours after sunset.

At the beginning of his reign, Ahmed III took a liking to the Karaağaç Palace on the Golden Horn. Then, in 1717, he had Aynalıkavak Palace (The Palace of Mirrors) built at Hasköy. The mirrors that gave this residence its name were sent from Venice. But as the sultan was ill with smallpox, he spent only one summer on the Golden Horn, later preferring the palace at Beşiktaş. Although Sâdâbâd[80] on the Golden Horn was a major theme in the literature of the period, the Bosphorus also held its own. But there were far more entertainments held at Sâdâbâd. To appreciate the attraction of Sâdâbâd, we must remember that in those days, the Golden Horn had not yet been abandoned to industry as it is today and was not divided from the city's panorama by two bridges. İbrahim Pasha loved to build. Sculpted marble, gilded inscriptions, carved wood-work, beautiful manuscripts – he loved them all. Then he loved Istanbul. He took pleasure in a life surrounded by beautiful things and was the patron of creative artists. He was not only the sultan's vizier but also the minister who oversaw his entertainments, and everyday he invented something new to amuse Mehmed IV's son.

This was the period of Nedim's genius, and we all know that Nedim's genius partly belongs to Istanbul, partly to the Turkish language. The Tulip Period would be nothing but waterfalls, fountains and other charming trivia imitated from the French, nothing but wasteful amusements if Nedim had not been there to make it great.

The line where he remarks

the bubbling waters are like the sound of applause

shows us the years 1720–1730 in a very different light from
their reality.

How much Nedim loved Istanbul and the times he lived
in, how close he felt to all its manners and fashions! How he
enjoyed and described all its pleasures! This poet, whose family
we can trace right back to Fatih the Conqueror, was a true son
of the city. He carried Istanbul within him like a taste on his
tongue and a light in his eyes.

In a poem he wrote to wish Ahmed III a good recovery
from an illness, he suggests he should drink

marmalades, perfumed coffee, pure sherbets

instead of medicines; he is almost like a young Istanbul
roughneck who brings the coffee, cheekily swinging his tray
from side to side, then suddenly takes wing and becomes a star-
studded entertainment; the couplet from one of his quatrains
reflects the enjoyments of the Bosphorus at the time:

It is not thunder and lightning that roars, o cupbearer,
It's splendid gunfire from the castle.

But the Tulip Period is not only Nedim. There is also the
music that developed from Itrî. Our music was as creative
as the poetry which nurtured Nedim, and our architecture,
which, a little later, would produce the Hekimoğlu Ali Pasha
Mosque. Perhaps the torch passed on to music. Hâfiz Post died
in 1689 and İtrî in 1712. In Ibrahim Pasha's time, the work of
both composers slowly spread to the middle classes. A little
later, the Eastern mode of the *nüfüht* began with Seyyid Nuh.
And along with them appeared Kara İsmail Ağa, Tab'î Mustafa
Efendi and Ebubekir Ağa, whose genius followed so naturally
the passage of music from İtrî to İsmail Dede – a whole firma-
ment of stars. It is sad that a complete recording of Turkish
music has not yet been made.

İbrahim Pasha repaired and enlarged his Emnâbâd residence for his wife. He also had the palace of Süreyya built

at Kuruçeşme, and at Bebek Humayunâbâd, which foreigners nicknamed 'The Conference Pavilion', because of the endless discussions that went on in Abdülhamid's reign between the Minister of Ottoman Affairs and the representatives of European countries. He was also responsible for the Neşâtâbâd Palace at Ortaköy which was soon to be replaced by Hatice Sultan's summer residence. Almost all the officials and statesmen had summer homes and entertainment kiosks along the Bosphorus shores, on its high hills and in its valleys. The Bosphorus had recovered its pre-1683 appearance.

Among the summer houses restored, though most were rebuilt from scratch, was the old Palace at Kandilli. Like others of the time, nothing of this palace remains today, and little is left of the building that replaced it, or of the various dwellings close to it in time and space. But occasionally, a single line from Vecdi's poem written to describe the restoration of this building shoots like a star from the page of some book, fills us with its light and disappears.

Old Kandilli's shores of a thousand flames are come again

Look at the magic of words: a single line is enough to revive in us all the splendour of the past. One night at Kuzguncuk, during one of the blackouts of World War II, a line came to me like magic out of the blue. As I repeated it at the dinner table and again in bed, I'm sure I wasn't particularly thinking of our neighbour Kandilli which I knew to be deeply asleep under the dark blue silk of a Bosphorus night in its flower gardens, those delights of Istanbul summer noons. But what came to mind was an old-time vessel, all its masts and bulwarks lit by coloured lanterns, overwhelming its surroundings with the brilliance of uncut jewels.

The next morning, I could not help going to Kandilli with friends. There was no sign of any of the dreams that had oppressed my imagination the night before and stifled my thoughts with a crystal jingle I could not silence. A few gardens, a handful of boatmen and, along the bank, a crumbling quayside like a broken organ. On our return, there was an animal lying in the sun on one of the wharves, which we guessed was a sick baby otter. No, the Kandilli of the past was to be found only in Vecdi's lines and in a few scattered memories.

Everything begun by İbrahim Pasha was continued by Mahmud I in his reign, but with a certain reserve. The music and architecture that the sultan personally liked so much gathered their own momentum without stirring up the bigotry of the Janissaries, those angry monsters grumbling in the background who knew only too well how to use it to their own advantage. Palaces by the shore were restored, charitable foundations renewed and gardens tended again. But the view of the era seen from abroad was of the unheard-of splendours of the religious rites that celebrated the birth of Mohammed and the pilgrimages to visit the Prophet's Mantle.

Mahmud I was like the Italian cardinal described by Barrès: when he liked to walk in the garden with his beloved, he was followed closely by a gardener erasing their footsteps with a rake. Mahmud I's gardener was Beşir Ağa, the first of that name.

In his memoirs, Baron de Tott, who was in Istanbul during Mustafa III's reign, describes a musical evening in the French Embassy at Büyükdere, and he writes how that night, the Greeks of the area, incited by jealousy, leapt into their boats with their own musical instruments and planted themselves before the Embassy building. This rivalry may have been the beginning of those moonlight entertainments on the Bosphorus which became a well-known feature of the Tanzimat period. The spirit of the age was not very favourable to public musical events organized by Moslem people and particularly by high officials. Such events took place in the palaces, the pavilions, in private houses or in the dervish convents. It seems more likely, therefore, that any references to musical boat trips before the Tanzimat era are probably the results of fantasy.

Foreigners began to live on the Bosphorus in the eighteenth century, but a little more freely, just as they did in Beyoğlu. From

Mehmed IV's reign, embassy staff took to making trips to the seven reservoirs and to the Belgrade forest. In İbrahim Pasha's time and immediately after, the foreigners' summer residence was Büyükdere, but when Selim III donated a summer house to the French Embassy, Tarabya became the summer quarters for the foreign colony. Here, they organized entertainments which included some of the wealthy minority families, and they even gave huge night parties at the reservoirs.

In Istanbul in the Tulip Period and in the years following, guests of the embassies or members of staff included a number of painters. It is strange that we do not possess a single painting by these Istanbul artists, who owe their reputation to works they achieved among us and with decor that belongs to us. The most impressive is Van Mour. Most of his paintings are in the 'Turkish' style which was just beginning to spread through France and Europe.

The European taste for the Bosphorus and the reservoirs developed even more in the reigns of Mustafa III and Abdülhamid I. And now there was also an influx of archaeologists and architects attached to the embassies and scholars interested in antiquity. From among these, Selim III had chosen Melling to demonstrate the delights of gardens and the century's new architecture. Most of Melling's works, with the exception of his album, have not survived, but alongside Şeyh Galip's 'Divan', the album is the most eloquent commentator on the period. An important part of the album was prepared with the encouragement of Selim III and his sister Hatice Sultan. As with everything that came from Europe, the sultan loved painting and design.

Melling was not the only European painter who lived in Istanbul, and several other books and albums were published at the same time as his. Before him and after, there were many illustrations that depicted typical scenes from our lives. It was a century of large folios, of carefully prepared publications with wide-set print, recalling the paved courtyards of mansions of another age. There were writers like d'Ohsson who tried to understand us, living among us with respect and even love.

But there were others who were openly hostile, like Choiseul Gouffier, who betrayed his office by bringing wounded prisoners of war to his embassy and on their recovery sent them back to the enemy to fight against us.

What distinguishes Melling from the latter is the fact that he lived among us, researching neither ancient Greece nor the Eastern Roman Empire. The architect of Hatice Sultan's palace and garden loved Istanbul for its own sake, like a true native of the city. He had savoured the great white domes of lead, the harsh summer light melting away into an evanescent mist and had known the beauty of cypresses and plane trees rising from the shores of the Golden Horn and from the gardens by the Bosphorus. In his pictures, it is possible to catch, as in an old song, the feeling of Üsküdar and of Istanbul, Kandilli, Ortaköy and the reservoirs.

Our taste in architecture and gardens was formed long before Selim III came to the throne. In spite of certain backward glances at a classical past, Turkish rococo had arrived, and Melling was to promote this new style. It appeared in little pavilions with the domestic style that began in Nuruosmaniye and even in the decorative wall tiles of Aynalıkavak – compare that, for example, with the Emirgân pavilion. Our old architects were not afraid to borrow European motifs; they knew that when a fine piece of calligraphy set its stamp on anything from abroad, all problems would be solved. When Yeşârizâde's Arabic script united with Galip's poetry, the two-storeyed windows and the debased rococo style of the eighteenth-century French designs in Aynalıkavak became invisible. In creating this hybrid style, Melling was of the greatest assistance to the sultan.

The principal works in Istanbul entrusted to Melling were Hatice Sultan's residence on the Defterdar Point (the old Neşât-âbâd), the reception hall of the old Beşiktaş Palace and the apartments of Valide Sultan, the sultan's mother. Melling treats these three buildings in a Western style but without offending local taste. So we have no problem at all today when we look at the row of Ionian pillars he put in the reception hall of Beşiktaş Palace. There are no gardens or pavilions there today. Selim III had wished to build a new palace within Topkapı Palace, but Melling had not the courage for the project, which was then given to an architect from the retinue of the Danish ambassador, Baron de Hubsch, but abandoned after the occupation of Egypt by the French. All that remained of the project were the military storehouses at Paşalimanı, the Selimiye Mosque in Üsküdar and a few army bases here and there.

We have already commented on how the English traveller Dallaway grieved for the palace in Üsküdar, destroyed to make way for Hatice Sultan's residence, and also for the palace project outlined in Melling's album. In truth, our taste in gardens was to allow nature a certain freedom, planting fruit trees and decorative trees together, rather like an English garden, but very different from the style of Versailles which was organized according to a definite labyrinthine design.

It is a curious fact that despite the destruction of the Üsküdar palace, the surroundings still seem to breathe its presence, due no doubt to the Selimiye barracks and to the mosque which is still there and to the wide, peaceful streets about them. In today's landscape, the streets and environment hardly give us a feeling of the time in which they were built. But the scene has a peculiar characteristic; once a place and a name are associated in our imagination, they are always felt as one.

Selim III[81] loved the Bosphorus and frequently sailed on its waters in his caique which, as we learn again from Melling's album, was named *The Swallow* and had the figure of a sea swallow in gold on its long bowsprit. He held moonlight parties at his Bosphorus mansions. The moonlight and bejewelled brilliance that fill Galip's poems tell us that not only the sultan but his courtiers too enjoyed them. Galip is the first to write a moonlight eulogy. In his divan poems for Hatice Sultan, there is a well-known historical ode praising the gardens of her residence by moonlight, the fountain and her rose garden in particular.

Many buildings of the period carry lines of Sheikh Galip inscribed above their gates and on the smooth stones round their fountains. This unfortunate ruler seemed to divide his reign between poetry and the music in which he himself excelled; architecture had not yet fully found its feet. Our image of the period comes from the superior rank occupied by the arts. But just beyond the arts, the horizon is unbearably suffocating. When we come across memories of the period we can't help thinking of Sheikh Galip's line,

Am I just the signature to your sad and pitiful edict?

Gold shines through the ruins. In my view, Sheikh Galip's only prediction is the verse from which the above line is taken.

There is no captain to take us over the
sea of disaster
let loose like a whirlpool of grief
a cry no one hears reaches the shores of nothing.

Certainly, the greatest responsibility for this situation lay with the sultan who was not strong enough to carry through the enterprises he undertook, nor did he have the wisdom and personality to shoulder great changes. His era required a ruthless man. And this Selim III was not. That's the reason the tree of novelty he planted could only take root and produce a flower after it was watered with his blood.

What made Selim III's musical pieces and songs so profound and full of meaning for us? Was it the good intentions they revealed, the love of novelty, the dreams of world conquest, the doubts and despair and despondencies, the bloody and tragic adventure our nation had lived through on account of a whole complex psychology? We who know his life and half-finished projects, the disastrous adventure of the empire which resembled a ship sunk to its gunwales, can we approach his works with our modern thoughts and feelings? Or do they, in fact, come to us now, full of a fear of decline, a morbid taste for degeneration laden with torments, dangerous instincts, accusations and flights from reality?

These are questions which can only be answered by experts who know our music and its entire history and can see it objectively. The past only comes into existence through its echo in ourselves. Just as we create our world from our own associations, we recreate the past according to our thoughts and feelings and our value judgements. But it happened that this sultan, a genuine Istanbulian composer unlike other men, was separated from his contemporaries by his birth and by an empire whose destiny lay in his hands. Inevitably, whether we wish to or not, we interpret his every action differently from that of another. Perhaps that is why we want to imagine that there are traces, in his compositions and hymns, of the hours he spent contemplating the many painful events that were taking place on distant frontiers, not knowing whom to trust or whom to fear, relying on the merest hopes and misinterpreting rumours and whispers, driven to distraction by the thought of Istanbul threatened by the English fleet and of Emperor Napoleon whom he had believed to be his friend; we imagine him in the two-roomed pavilion in his Topkapı palace or in the palace of Aynalıkavak, among the tiles and verses of the Koran and the mirrors now tarnished, inscribed with Galib's couplets, or in his Beşiktaş palace and Bosphorus villas, in his sister's mansions, or on the Levent roads where he went with his entourage to inspect his newly organized army or, finally, on his naval expeditions when he would be greeted with a salvo of cannon fire.

As well as knowledge of the period, I believe we learned much of its intimate and significant details through the work of Selim III. The isolation of art, and music in particular, brings with it far more understanding than we could possibly imagine.

The texture of Selim III's music was always elegant, distinguished, moving in a strange way and light; traditional arrangements often refined into new forms. His works composed in the Suzidilâra mode are one of the most refined pieces of our classical music and in some aspects prefigure the art of Dede.

The uprising of 1807 did not extinguish the life of pleasure on the Bosphorus; perhaps it only altered the participants. The new officials were not as refined and distinguished as those in Selim III's reign. Two successive rebellions in one year had altered the *crème de la crème* of Istanbul, and some time had to pass before good taste could flower again. But Mahmud II also loved music and the Bosphorus, and often organized pleasure outings. The interior of his palace almost became an academy of music. Despite several wars, rebellions and national disasters, Istanbul enjoyed itself. It was the period when the writer Vasıf wrote, '*Before one party was over, we had booked the next.*'

But although life was relatively free, it was dull and restricted. Poetry had nothing to say. Architectural style had deteriorated. Palaces and mansions were all furnished like the houses of the European bourgeoisie, and when von Moltke was received into the presence of Mahmud II in Beylerbey Palace, he was astonished at the poverty it had been allowed to fall into. Only a lonely man can fill the emptiness.

Dede had a characteristic melancholy, not entirely explicable by his era or by life's difficulties, not even by his connections with the Mevlevi order. Our souls stir as soon as we come into contact with his music. Perhaps his melancholy resulted from his overwhelming sense of fate, and perhaps that intuition was the only point where his music was in tune with his time. For the unique phenomenon of the period was the hurricane of Dede's golden music. It is quite hard to find a connection between the spirit that breathed through him and the disturbances around him. Although they gave him facilities for work and a great traditional musical background, neither the palace, the city, the Mevlevi convent nor the other arts were enough to explain the heights of his own musical genius. As for the personalities of the period, we find them in the stories of the palace, in the divan poems of Vâsıf and Keçecizâde, in the collections of Şanizade and Esad Efendi and in collections of chronicles of events. No other period of our history has left us such lively eloquent accounts of the time. Even Mahmud II was a stranger to Dede's life, though he loved Dede Efendi and his music so much that he got up from his deathbed to attend the Mevlevi convent at Topkapı to hear the Ferâhfezâ hymn which he himself had commissioned. Undoubtedly, Dede was not so close to Mehmed II as he had been to his first patron. Dede and Selim III were kneaded from the same dough. The Şakir Ağas, the Mehmed Ağas and other promising talents, who developed daily in his warmth as in a fertile autumn, only carried away the merest echoes of his style and technique: none had the teeth and claws to bite deep. They were not even aware of the spiritual pursuit involved. They were men of great ability who had learned a skill and simply repeated it.

Dede does not repeat – he remembers. His cosmos is one of memory and longing and must have come from the Mevlevi culture. But on this dervish of the tender soul, life weighs heavily. İsmail Dede is like the Italian painters of the fifteenth century who combined a taste for pagan pleasures with Christian faith.

All the Orient is there, like an elixir extracted from the purest metals, precious stones present in the darkness of this work, which at every moment is illuminated by amazing modulations of sound, every aspect of it touched as by cosmic rays by the ecstasy of Union, the yearning for the Sacred, the sadness of exile, and the inexorable emotion of love and pain. To love Dede – as in all works of art – means to get to know him well. But for his music to open all its doors to us and for its secret to pierce our flesh like fire, for it to stay with us like a fixed idea or an intimate agony, we must come to it unexpectedly, be caught by it unawares and be awakened by it at least once. Then we will understand what it means to contemplate the world from the heavens and the stars, with the music of the Ferâhfezâ and the Acemaşiran modes all about us.

With Dede we emerge from a country of mystical longings where death is seen as an eternal union of lovers. His tree of death grows up in the real world like the ancient trees that appear lofty and solitary here and there in Istanbul, in gardens by the Bosphorus, on the hills of Üsküdar!

In Dede's music, there's always a feeling of the Bosphorus and the Istanbul landscapes. We might even say that our music, which had already appeared in the outside world in the previous era, wins its real victory over nature, thanks to him. But don't be deceived. Dede, unlike his contemporaries in the West, could not express that landscape as he desired, nor say everything he wished to say. Our old classical music speaks with the natural sounds of the human voice. It has no dictionary and no syntax. That is its power and also its weakness. It was never able to become a world of symbols on its own. Without ever exceeding their boundaries, its emotions of ecstatic joy, and sometimes the heartbreaking power of its sadness, lie in their closeness to a scream. He expresses what he wants to say by passing it through the crystal medium of the human voice. Thus, Dede, with the inexplicable melancholy I described above, gives us the landscape as something accumulated within us from a distant other world.

We cannot recognize anything in him of the concrete world. But as we listen to his Mâhurs, his Acemaşirans, his Rasts, his Sultanî Yegâhs and his Ferâhfezas (oriental modes in which he excelled), we find ourselves suddenly airborne, for the eagle wings of his melody always transport us elsewhere to a world enriched. Listen to İtrî's *Na'tı Mevlânâ* ('Praise of the Mevlânâ') together with any of Dede's hymns, and you will feel you have moved from Arabic calligraphy to a great landscape painting.

In some of Dede's compositions, the Istanbul and Bosphorus landscapes gleam like the filigree on big precious stones, fossils from hundreds and thousands of years ago.

Without wishing to, Dede became the fairy-story hero. When a new European lifestyle began in Abdülmecid's reign, he fled from Istanbul to die in Hicaz. If you think of the world he represented, the story of his death can be read as highly symbolic.

Nevertheless, the Istanbul of the era of his finest work is no less European than the Istanbul that succeeded the Tanzimat era. We had become so accustomed to the West through the many experiences of 150 years and more, that when the Janissary corps was abolished, a number of modern new fashions were ready to spring into life in the city.

The development of Turkish music after İsmail Dede is to be found in the rich, sensitive, hard-to-describe modulations he brought to the human voice, which made it the most meaningful, most expressive medium of the inner world. It can be said that from this time our music perfected the instrument of the human voice. Never did the reciters and singers of the Koran and its music reign over Istanbul so completely as they did in the Tanzimat years and after. The larynx won complete freedom, encompassing horizons and landscapes. The voice rose from every hill, from every open window, summer residence and kiosk, from every garden.

When Vasıf says in one of his poems,

I no longer remember what you promised me!
Was it a kiss or union with the beloved?

he was no doubt addressing Christian women – for at this time Moslem women could not take a pleasure trip by boat unaccompanied – or perhaps he was drawn to Armenian women, whom Lamartine liked so much and always compared with beauties from elsewhere. In fact, when Lamartine was in Istanbul in the spring of 1833, he describes the Christian women returning from their country homes, their boats laden with baskets of flowers, just as we can see today on the Bosphorus and Island ferryboats.

Many pages of Lamartine overflow with praise for the beautiful Bosphorus; he especially admired Beylerbey Palace, and this famous romantic poet must certainly be placed in the first rank of lovers of Istanbul. Later, he would say, '*I love the light of this country*,' and even thought of ending his days in the country estate near Izmir which Sultan Abdülmecid had bestowed on him as a gift.

It seems that Lamartine's boat was passing one of the royal pavilions of Beylerbey Palace when Mahmud II along with Ahmed Pasha – possibly Ahmet Pasha 'The Deserter' – signalled from an open window, curious to know the stranger's identity. Lamartine, who had greatly admired the sultan's courage but wondered if he could successfully conclude his enterprise of abolishing the Janissaries, responded to the sultan's interest with a respectful salute and even received one in return.

Lamartine also saw the royal caiques gathered in front of the palace. The first vessel carried on its 25-foot-long prow a golden swan with open wings; Lamartine compared the second to a golden arrow let loose from the bow. He saw these caiques again at Emirgân when he was present there for the *selâmlık*, the Friday ceremony, and he wrote that nothing in the West, neither horses nor carriages, equalled the splendour and grandeur of the scene. The portrait Lamartine drew of Mahmud II on that occasion is a very good likeness. When the sultan leapt from his caique, he was talking to Ahmed Pasha and Namık and entered the mosque between them. According to Lamartine, when the sultan arrived, he looked very troubled. But emerging 20 minutes later he seemed calmer. During the whole ceremony and at the time of prayer, military pieces from Mozart and Rossini were being played.

But Lamartine's favourite was Sultan Abdülmecid. At the beginning of his *Histoire de la Turquie*, possibly a commissioned work, he describes a conversation he had with the sultan and draws a very detailed picture, commenting on the freedom and personal security he had given his people.

There are two more portraits of Abdülmecid: one by Nerval, the other by Gautier. The two poets, not experienced like Lamartine even after several years, were not men to reach the forefront of political life. They lived by journalism. Behind them was a mass of readers to be entertained, whose curiosity and preconceived ideas they must satisfy. They were both impressed by Mahmud II's son.

In Istanbul, Nerval met with Sultan Abülmecid's imperial carriage and, along with a friend, followed it on foot to the Unkapanı Bridge and from there to the Mevlevi Convent in Galata. The imperial carriage with two wheels, drawn by two horses one behind the other, described by the poet of *El Desdichaido* bore no resemblance to the royal carriages we know. The sultan was dressed very simply. He wore an overcoat buttoned to the neck – Istanbul style – and his fez was crested with diamonds. At the time, a carriage could not enter the bridge, so he descended from his carriage at what is now called Unkapanı, mounted his horse and entered the Beyoğlu precincts by the paths that bordered the Galata walls. Nerval very much liked Abdülmecid's looks and his calm face.

Gautier saw the sultan of the Tanzimat at the Friday religious ceremony at the Ortaköy Mosque, which the sultan had built. Gautier was envious when he thought about the women of the royal harem and boasted of an Italian woman who accompanied him, to whom the sultan had paid particular attention.

We shouldn't be annoyed with Théophile Gautier for his frivolity. The existence of the harem was a fact and Europe almost always imagined the East as living its life behind bars. But it is worth observing that Gautier was the first poet among us and from the West to shed a tear for the Janissaries who were abolished in such a bloody manner. When he tells us how he wandered through the Museum of Ancient Ottoman Costume at Sultanahmet (now the military museum), he really seems like one of us in his empathy and grief for the past. On the same page is his fine portrait of Sultan Abdülmecid on horseback, resembling the great paintings we can see today in the Topkapı Palace.

Nearly everyone who spoke about this ruler agreed in noting his facial immobility and sad expression. Abdülmecid came to the throne at 19 in very difficult conditions; he had to surmount many dangerous situations and managed to subdue Mehmed Ali Pasha, who had seized half of Anatolia. Sultan Mecid's most important quality was to be the right man at the right time, and although he was determined to hold on to power, he gave Reşid Pasha's team the opportunity to act. With him everything began again.

The Bosphorus and the Çamlica hills that still represent for us the true landscape of the past, so many traces have they left in our everyday lives of memories, splendours and artistic pleasures of that era. But, in fact, they were greatly transformed as a result of Abdülmecid's enlightened ideas of personal security and equality, and the freer lifestyle of the sultan's women and ministers, particularly also by the summer visits to Istanbul enjoyed by members of the Egyptian dynasty after the Crimean War, and by their construction of summer houses and pavilions and the planting of groups of trees.

A chain of ferryboats on the Bosphorus led to an increase in the population of the Bosphorus villages and encouraged people to enjoy pleasure trips. In country houses where the wealthy met, women's clothes were no longer considered a major topic for discussion. And a tolerance for love stories began. Cevdet Pasha tells us in his 'Observations', some parts of which are a kind of memoir, that for well-known people and high officials of the era, it was almost compulsory to spend the summer on the Bosphorus, and that the public were beginning to appreciate the beauty of nature.

Half of the city used to go to admire the 'Silver Cypress' reflected in the waters on moonlit nights. And in the evenings, women were gradually included in the cooling walks by the sea – of course, accompanied by their eunuchs, for men were forbidden to accompany them. At this period, music very naturally accompanied the landscape, and with it began the taste for the echoing hills of Çamlica and the Bosphorus, bays like Kanlıca, Bebek and Mihrâbâd. It is from this period that the real success of urban music belongs.

At no other period was there such a special enthusiasm for the caique as in Abdülaziz's reign. In slender barques, shaped like the birds' wings of fairy tales and rowed by beautiful youths in sumptuous garments, the city could savour so-called 'feminine beauty' in the glitter of parasols, yashmaks and precious stones. Later, in some of Hamdi Bey's pictures and in some pages of 'Forbidden Love', we can see traces in our painting and literature of a very refined style of life and sensibility.

As nature and lifestyles opened up, eventually one of the most remarkable events of the history of our tastes was born – the fashion for moonlight parties. All these festive moonlight occasions were organized with ceremony and propriety by a different villa, like a grand opera or a kind of moonlight worship. In this way, the city, like the Venetian doges who married the sea, honoured its own beauty, its own lifestyle, its wealth of artworks and all the special characteristics which it owed to the sea. The Bosphorus, which fills such an important and inspiring place in our lives, was here united with the most exalted of our arts, music.

The boat of singers and musicians led the way, followed by boats of special guests; then a number of caiques, and even barges, moved from bay to bay along a moonlit path, and later that night they would disperse before the house that had organized the outing. Like Venice and Naples, Istanbul had its own way of achieving genius.

What began with Süleyman the Lawgiver's royal caique, which we could not find described anywhere, was followed by Mahmud IV's wrecked vessel, now gleaming like a broken oyster shell in the darkness of the Maritime Museum, its bed full of the whisper of waves and the smell of seaweed; Selim III's royal boat, the *Swallow*, and Mahmud II's *Boat-hook*, then the little gold and silver caiques, adopted by Abdülaziz and his mother to demonstrate their closeness to the people of the city, all became an art form that included the whole of life. Often when I contemplate the fall of the Ottoman Empire, I remember a story I heard of the last moonlight party in the summer of 1914. And I compared the crumbling empire to a legendary vessel sinking, accompanied by saz music, into waters limned by moonlight to a golden precipice.

XV

So many memories, so many people. In discussing Istanbul and the Bosphorus, why have I evoked everything so impossible to resurrect? Why are we drawn to time past as to an empty well? I realize it is not the people themselves I look for, nor am I nostalgic for the era in which they lived. What satisfaction would it give me to see Mehmed IV in his royal vessel gleaming with gold and precious stones like a bird in a fairy story, cleaving the dark blue waters to approach Kandilli? Or to stroll through a

Ramazan fair in the Istanbul of my early years – wearing an overcoat and a fez, fingering wooden prayerbeads with one hand and holding a gold-headed walking-stick in the other, with a carefully trimmed beard as in one of the descriptions of Ahmed Riza Bey – inhaling odours of rose oils, cinnamon oil and every kind of spice? I couldn't live for more than 10 minutes even in the Istanbul of Süleyman the Lawgiver, or of Sokullu. To do so would mean to ignore so much I had gained, to cut off and throw away vital parts of my being. To see Sülemaniye as a newly built mosque is to deprive the Süleymaniye we know and love of an imperial history that stretches as far as our own time, like those golden palaces created at night by the long lights in the waters of the Bosphorus bays. We savour its beauty with the experience of four centuries behind us, and two different world views between us, our inner wealth keener every day. Without Yahya Kemal or Mallarmé or Proust or Debussy, the Süleymaniye or the elegy for Süleyman the Lawgiver would be more impoverished than we could ever imagine; Sinan and Bâkî cannot be understood without Neşâtî and Nedim, Hâfiz Post and Dede.

No, my search is not for past time nor for those who lived in it.

Perhaps the past of the Bosphorus attracts us more than anything because what we would like to find in it is no longer there. All the Neşâtâbâds, Humayunâbâds, Ferahâbâds, Kandilli palaces and summer pavilions which, since the seventeenth century, have appeared to our imaginations like gleaming jewelled boxes along both banks, we now see only as the last rays of a setting sun. If they existed today, we would feel ourselves richer in a different way but we would never know the emotion that their absence stirs in us. We would be happy to see them from time to time like old relations we visit only on special occasions, for their generations and ways of thinking are so very different from ours. We tire very quickly, alas, of memories of the past and gilded ceilings and silver ornaments. We certainly don't love these old things for themselves; we are attracted by the feeling of emptiness they leave. Whether any traces remain or not, what we struggle to find in them is a part of ourselves we thought lost. If I had lived in Merkez Efendi's lifetime, I might have been one of his dervishes. Or else I might have followed another path from theirs, or fought against them, or simply remained indifferent. But now I see him and his like with a different eye. In the divine wisdom of those men who followed their ideals in silence, I am searching for a lost world. I yearn to reach their heights, but failing, I turn to poetry and literature. I want to drink from the cup of music; the cup empties, my thirst remains, for art, like love, is thirst-making, and can never be assuaged,. I run from mirage to mirage. Whatever spring I run to, enigmatic faces appear before me and beckon; lips I don't recognize talk to me with voices I don't recognize, in endless signs, but I understand nothing they say; as soon as my soul turns aside from their lips I see nothing has changed. Perhaps they talk to me of their own experiences or of harsh obstacles that face them at every step. 'We are like you,' they say. 'Your questions will never be answered. The only reality is the desire within you. Try not to let the fire go out.' And to keep it alive for ever, they sometimes raise before me a Ferâlfezâ, or the melody of an Acemaşiran Yürük Semâi, or the white dawn ship of Süleymâniye, or the cypress groves of Karacaahmet; they offer me a multitude of names like the broken marble basins of Şerefâbâd, that I may fill these ready vessels with my longings.

The most pressing problem for all of us is, where and how shall we relate to the past? We are all children of consciousness and the identity crisis. We all live even more keenly than Hamlet with the problem, 'to be or not to be'. The more we acknowledge this, the better we can control our lives and our work. Perhaps it is just enough to search and knock on every door.

Perhaps nostalgia is a realm of its own and we can best explain the past with its help. To the silent melody of the ney our dead come to life again with their well-loved faces, and because this is the way it is, by its light we can live more deeply, more genuinely in the present.

Nature is like a stage. Our nostalgic longing makes it possible for us to people it with our own actors and atmosphere. But however delicious the drink, however powerful its effects, we must not forget that Turkish society stands on the threshold of a new age. Istanbul itself waits eagerly for a new age that will create new values.

It is best to leave memories to decide for themselves when they want to talk to us. Only in such moments of awareness does the voice of the past become a moment of enlightenment, a discovery – in short, something that enriches our day. What we must do is surrender to the winds of the present, to the lively fertilizing winds of the new. They will carry us off to a world of energy and happiness where beauty and goodness, understanding and dreams, will go hand in hand.

Translated from the Turkish by Ruth Christie © 2018

Notes

1   Üsküdar – An Istanbul district, often named 'Scutari' in old texts, on the Asiatic shore of the Bosphorus. With its extensive cemetery and many mosques, it is one of the most typically Turkish areas.

2   Çamlica – A hill on the Asiatic shore of the Bosphorus with a marvellous view of the city, once covered by pinewoods and Turkish summer houses.

3   Beyoğlu – The district below Galata on the left bank of the Golden Horn, and the heart of the European sector of Istanbul, as opposed to the old Turkish city on the right bank.

4   Erenköy – In Tanpınar's era, a village on the Asiatic coast of the Sea of Marmara.

5   Çekmece – Two villages near Istanbul on the European bank of the Sea of Marmara, noted for their lakes or lagoons.

6   Bendler – The seven artificial reservoirs near the village of Belgrade, 25 km north of Istanbul, first established by the Byzantines, and surrounded by a forest of oak and chestnut trees.

7   The Princes' Islands – These islands (called by the Turks 'Kızıl Adalar') form a small archipelago 20 km from Istanbul, in the Sea of Marmara, used by Istanbul citizens as summer homes. The four biggest islands are

Büyükada, Heybeli, Burgaz and Kınalı. In the nineteenth century, these islands were largely populated by Greeks and Armenians but today have a mixed population.

8 Göztepe – A little town on the Asiatic shore of Marmara.

9 Nişantaş – A smart area of Istanbul.

10 Sarıyer – A village on the hills above the Bosphorus near the meeting place of the straits and the Black Sea.

11 Büyükdere – On the European bank of the Bosphorus, about 20 km from the city.

12 Vaniköy – On the Asiatic bank of the Bosphorus.

13 Beykoz – A village on the Asiatic shore which has a fine forest.

14 Bebek – On the European shore of the Bosphorus, a charming summer playground for Europeans and Turkish alike.

15 Beylerbey – A village on the Asiatic shore at the end of the eighteenth century. Abdülhamid I built a little mosque there.

16 Tarabya – (Greek, 'therapy') On the European shore of the Bosphorus, where the nineteenth-century embassies of France, Italy and England had their summer palaces.

17 Mahmud II (1784–1839) – A great Ottoman sultan who reigned for 30 years, initiating several reforms that opened the way to the westernization of the Ottoman Empire.

18 The 'Capitulations' – Privileges accorded by the Ottoman sultan to Western powers in matters of commerce and taxation, first documented in the sixteenth century.

19 Bedesten – The inner covered market where the most valuable goods were kept.

20 Antoine Galland (1646–1715) – French orientalist and archaeologist, and the first European translator of 'The Arabian Nights'. He learned Arabic, Turkish and Persian. His writings include a translation of the Koran, a history of the Turkish emperors and a journal of his year in Constantinople, between 1672 and 1673.

21 Ayvansaray – Originally a Byzantine quarter of the city which had deteriorated by the beginning of the twentieth century to a rundown, impoverished environment.

22 Dallaway (James) – Author of 'Constantinople Ancient and Modern: With Excursions to the Shores and Islands of the Archipelago and to the Troad' (1797).

23 Hadiths –The traditions of the deeds and sayings of Prophet Muhammed.

24 simit – A sesame-covered ring-shaped bread roll.

25 macun – A fruit paste like toffee.

26 Tanbûri Cemil (1871–1916) – A composer for the long-necked eight-stringed instrument, the tanbur. He was influenced by Western music and some popular genres.

27 Hüseyin Rahmi Gürpinar (1864–1944) – A prolific Turkish writer who produced about 40 novels of a realist-naturalist tone, describing the Turkish society of his time.

28 Ahmed Rasim (1864–1932) – A Turkish writer who specialized in short, anecdotal passages for the daily newspapers and popularized scientific and historical subjects.

29 Valens Aqueduct – Built by Emperor Valens in AD 375. Water brought underground from outside the city near the Edirne gate needed to cross the valley to reach the storage cistern. Most of the aqueduct still stands.

30 Topkapı – The area between Santa Sophia and the complex known as Topkapı Saray, dating from 1460 but with additions built by every sultan: kiosks, mosques, libraries, fountains and gardens.

31 Yedikule (The Castle of the Seven Towers) – Fortifications first built by the Byzantines, then the Ottomans, to surround and defend the city.

32 Eyüp – An area at the head of the Golden Horn which became a major cemetery famous for its old tombs and monuments among cypress trees.

33 Edirne (Adrianople) – In Thrace, it was founded to defend Byzantium against barbarian attacks. It was taken by the Turks in 1363 to become the Ottoman capital till just after the Conquest of Constantinople. For a few centuries, the court was often to be found at Edirne.

34 Kastamono – Anatolian village on the Black Sea at the foot of a mountain covered with giant pine trees.

35 Sokullu Mehmed Pasha – An able statesman and military commander who became grand vizier for 14 years under three sultans. He came from a Serbian family and was a product of the youth levy. He virtually ran the empire and married Selim II's daughter.

36 Piyale Pasha – Admiral of the Ottoman fleet. A mosque was dedicated to him in 1593.

37 Hüsrev Pasha (1480–1541) – A great Ottoman military commander who played a major part in the conquest of Serbia, Bosnia, Croatia and Hungary.

38 Sultan Ahmed Mosque – Constructed between 1606 and 1616 near the Byzantine Hippodrome and called 'The Blue Mosque' from its interior decoration.

39 Yeni Cami Mosque – The mosque of the Sultan's mother, built at the end of the sixteenth century for Murad II's wife, the mother of Mehmed III, by one of Sinan's successors.

40 Hafiz Post (1630–1693) – A very prolific artist (poetry, calligraphy, music). Considered to be one of the greatest Ottoman composers of the seventeenth century.

41 Seyyid Nuh (??–1714) – A great Ottoman composer. Much of his work has disappeared.

42 Neşati (??–1674) – A member of the religious order of the Mevlevi and a great poet.

43 Naîllî (??–1666) – A humble Ottoman administrator but a poet renowned for his ghazels.

44 Tâib (1660–1724) – Poet of the Tulip Period and a rival to Nedim.

45 Tab'î Mustafa Efendi (??–1770) – One of the great composers of his time. Also a poet and calligrapher.

46 Ebubekir Ağa (1685–1759) – Poet and composer. His works are thought to be entirely expressive of the spirit of the Tulip Period.

47 Aziz Mahmud Hüdâî (1541–1628) – Mystic poet and founder of the religious order of the Celveti. Ahmed I belonged to his order. He was buried at Üsküdar and his mausoleum is still a place of pilgrimage.

48 Yahıya Efendi (??–1570) – A great mystic in the reign of Süleyman the Lawgiver.

49 Sümbül Sinan (1480–1529) – Founder of a branch of the religious order of the Halveti. He preached in most of the city's imperial mosques. He was also known for his exegesis of the Koran.

50 Merkez Efendi (1460–1552) – A Halveti sheikh who lived in Anatolia but came to Istanbul after the death of Sünbül Efendi to become head of the order. Poet and interpreter of the Koran.

51 Koca Mustafa Pasha (??–1512) – A Great Ottoman vizier in the reigns of Bayezid II and Selim I. He was sent to negotiate with Pope Alexander VI to detain Cem Sultan. He was executed in 1512 by Selim I on suspicion of treason. An area of Istanbul is named after him.

52 Gedik Ahmed Pasha (??–1482) – Grand vizier to Mehmed III and a brave military leader, fighting in campaigns in Anatolia and the Balkans. But he was accused of taking Prince Cem's part and was executed by order of Bayezid II.

53 Üftade of Bursa (??–1580) – Sheikh and poet of Bursa. One of Haci Bayram's successors.

54 Melâmî order – A religious order founded in 1475 by a spiritual follower of Haci Bayram.

55 Sunullah Gaybi (1615–1663) – A mystic poet from Kütahya in Western Anatolia.

56 Idris-i Muhtefi (??–1615) – A Sufi sheikh who was both a mystic poet and philosopher.

57 Mehmed the Hunter – This name in Turkish was given to Mehmed IV because of his obsession with hunting.

58 Tepebaşı and Ayazpaşa – Christian cemeteries which once covered the hills of Beyoğlu, overlooking the Bosphorus. In the nineteenth century, they were built over.

59 Ibrahim Peçevi (1574–1649) – Ottoman chronicler originally from Hungary. His work covers the period from Süleyman (1520) to the death of Murad IV (1640).

60 Osman II (1604–1622) – Came to the throne at the age of 12 but was assassinated by the Janissaries who feared his projected reforms, which included replacing the Janissaries with a new army.

61 Abaza Mehmed Pasha (??–1634) – With the Janissaries, he headed a revolt after the death of Osman II, and for two years, he ravaged Anatolia and seized several strongholds. But the sultan feared his intrigues and ordered his execution.

62 Mehmed Raşid Efendi – Official chronicler of the Ottoman court and writer of a history of the Ottoman Empire from 1660 to 1722.

63 Nefî (1572–1635) – Very talented poet of satires and kasides (a poem of 15 couplets either of praise or an elegy). His satires were so strong that the grand vizier ordered him to be strangled.

64 Tevfik Ebüzziya (1848–1913) – A well-known Turkish journalist and publisher of his time.

65 Nâbizâde Nazim (1862–1893) – An early Turkish realist writer who wrote about the life of an Anatolian peasant and of the poorer quarters in Istanbul.

66 Tevfik Fikret (1867–1915) – A great nineteenth-century poet who wanted Turkish poetry to follow Western poetic forms.

67 Namik Kemal (1840–1888) – Poet, journalist, novelist, dramatist and a leader of the 'Young Ottomans', a movement (including Halide Edip) that opposed Atatürk.

68 Karagöz – Shadow puppets, a theatrical entertainment very popular in the early twentieth century, named after the principal character, 'Black Eye'.

69 Seyranî (1807–1866) – A popular poet of satirical works.

70 Kadir Gecesi – The 'Night of Power' – 27th night of Ramazan, when the Koran was revealed by the angel Gabriel. On that night, every mosque is illuminated.

71 Fazlı Necip (1863–1932) – One of the great Turkish journalists and a prolific writer, though his novels are now forgotten.

72 Ramazan – The ninth Moslem month, the month of fasting.

73 Lütfi Efendi (1815–1907) – One of the last official chroniclers of the Ottoman state.

74 Ahmed Haşım (1885–1933) – Poet, essayist. One of the great masters of symbolism in Turkish poetry.

75 Abdülhak Şinasi Hisar (1883–1963) – One of the principal novelists of his time.

76 Riza Tevfik (1869–1949) – Poet, philosopher, politician. Accused of betraying the national cause, he was exiled.

77 Zeybek – A local folk dance from the Aegean coast.

78 Nâima (1655–1716) – A famous Ottoman chronicler, particularly of the years 1591–1659.

79 Koçi Bey – A seventeenth-century statesman, writer of two memoirs, analysing the causes of the empire's decline and offering suggestions for reform.

80 Sâdâbâd (The Place of Happiness) – A luxurious palace built in Ahmed III's reign, now no longer in existence, but a favourite image in poetry of the period.

81 Selim III (1761–1808) – His accession coincided with the beginning of the French Revolution and began an era of reforms. Deposed in 1807 after a revolt by the janissaries, he was assassinated by orders of his successor.